Pastoral Misconduct

Pastoral Misconduct

The American Black Church Examined

Anson Shupe and
Janelle M. Eliasson-Nannini

Transaction Publishers
New Brunswick (U.S.A.) and London (U.K.)

Copyright © 2012 by Transaction Publishers, New Brunswick, New Jersey.

All rights reserved under International and Pan-American Copyright Conventions. No part of this book may be reproduced or transmitted in any form or by any means, electronic or mechanical, including photocopy, recording, or any information storage and retrieval system, without prior permission in writing from the publisher. All inquiries should be addressed to Transaction Publishers, Rutgers—The State University of New Jersey, 35 Berrue Circle, Piscataway, New Jersey 08854-8042. www.transactionpub.com

This book is printed on acid-free paper that meets the American National Standard for Permanence of Paper for Printed Library Materials.

Library of Congress Catalog Number: 2012007441
ISBN: 978-1-4128-4778-0
Printed in the United States of America

Library of Congress Cataloging-in-Publication Data

Shupe, Anson D.
   Pastoral misconduct : the American black church examined / Anson Shupe and Janelle M. Eliasson-Nannini.
     p. cm.
   Includes bibliographical references (p.   ) and index.
   ISBN 978-1-4128-4778-0
   1. African Americans—Religion. 2. African American clergy. 3. Clergy—Conduct of life. 4. Pastoral theology. I. Eliasson-Nannini, Janelle M. II. Title.
   BR563.N4S525 2012
   253.089'96073—dc23

2012007441

Toby and Molly. We've scouted, suffered the elements, and fought together
　　　　　　　　　　　　　　　AS

To my daughter, Madi, with optimism
　　　　　　　　　　　　　　J E-N

Contents

Preface		ix
Acknowledgments		xiii
1.	Minority Religions in the American Context—An Introduction	1
2.	Black History, Black Religion, and the Salient Identity of Pastor and Congregation in the Minority Church	31
3.	The Abuses of Black Pastoral Power	49
4.	Authority and Aggrandizement within the American Black Church	79
5.	Black Pastoral Misdeeds, Charisma, and Identity Salience	131
6.	Understanding Black Pastoral Malfeasance and Laity	155
References		177
Index		191

Preface

Curtis White II, aged 59, was pastor of the Divine Faith Baptist Church in Fort Wayne, Indiana. He also hosted the "Gospel Train Unity Inspirational Hour" radio program on a local FM station. But in 2009, based on tips from several persons that the Reverend White was selling crack cocaine to persons in his congregation, police met up with him and a female accomplice (who had been instrumental in previously purchasing the drugs) with a search warrant at a local motel. They found 6.6 grams of crack cocaine in the motel room, $124 cash lying on a bed, and "instruments for the distribution" of the illegal drug. Moreover, when White was arrested and taken to an undisclosed location for an interview, it was discovered during a body cavity search that White had hid another 6.5 grams in a suspected rectal cavity. Further investigation of White revealed that he had spent time in prison during the late 1990s for three prior convictions for dealing illegal narcotic drugs in Indiana. A judge in 2010 added a fourth conviction: fifteen years and eight months in a federal prison plus four years of supervised release. Meanwhile, White's church was likely in trouble; during a brief period of media coverage reporters found that the phone number for the church was no longer in service. (Green 2010)

This local, small-time example of clergy malfeasance, a seeming anomaly in the otherwise wholesome life of the American black church, is part of a pattern as viewed by us, for we are sociologists trained in the sociological imagination to "see the general" (patterns and systemic issues) "in the specific." This book is an outcome of that imagination. Here we examine the phenomenon of malfeasance, or misconduct—*immoral*, by the standards of the very congregations to which these clergy minister, *and/or illegal*, according to local, state, and federal penal codes—in the North American black church institution. Such behavior is, admittedly, an unsavory topic of religion, in general, and about any local church or denomination, in particular. That this type of behavior is a historically and culturally important part of American religion has been so long ignored except in journalistic anecdotes and rare scholarship represents a major lacuna both in the sociologies of religion and deviant behavior.

At the outset we want to be clear about aspects of this study.

We do *not* claim that black pastors—Protestant, Catholic, or otherwise—have inherent predispositions toward betrayals of their congregations, their callings, or their faiths, or to violate the law.

We do *not* claim that American black churches or black religion itself is rife with fraud, hypocrisy, or pastoral misconduct.

We do *not* claim that the American black church as an institution displays proportionately more such untoward behavior by clergy than any other sectarian, denominational, racial, or ethnic category of churches. Certainly one of us (Shupe), as will be documented through this book, has examined clergy abuse of congregations within a host of white congregations and religious traditions in North America: Protestant (Baptist, Methodist, Pentecostal, Episcopalian, Presbyterian, and so forth), Mormon, Roman Catholic, and Jewish (Reform, Conservative, and Orthodox). Indeed, as one anonymous colleague suggested to us, at least larger Protestant black denominational affiliations in many ways are historically "connected at the hipbone" to their white counterparts. The point is that in all these churches and synagogues, white or black, can be found the same or similar levels of misconduct, or worse. Clergy malfeasance, as we formally term it, is neither limited to any creed nor to any category of congregants and their leaders.

We *do* claim that the history and traditions of black pastoral leadership, coupled with the close identity of many black congregants with their pastor, congregation, and racial subculture creates *affinity opportunity structures* that are a major contextual factor facilitating (*not* causing) predatory behavior on occasion. Thus, these conditions are influenced by black American religious concerns with a return to, or rediscovery of, such larger issues as black identity, black nationalism, and the feeling of belongingness within a particular minority church whose membership is embedded in its round of church attendance, participation, and subculture.

Let us be clear on these terms. *Opportunity structures* are those group situations and arrangements involving persons in social roles that present them with unique advantages for personal gain and of which they may or may not take advantage. *Affinity* (from the Latin *affinis*, meaning neighbor or neighboring) is a condition of mutual membership or resemblance that involves both perpetrators and victims in the same subculture (racial, ethnic, and sectarian). In the phenomenon of affinity crimes, such familiarity and mutual identity more than rarely lead victims to drop their normal levels of wariness, i.e., to become more trusting and consequently rendering them particularly vulnerable to exploitation. This trust, of course, is generally true of all church traditions. But black pastoral or clergy malfeasance in the United States offers the phenomenon of *racial affinity leadership deviance*, often involving crimes, and putting at jeopardy a particular type of religiously based victim.

The eventual purpose in our focus on black churches, which we will develop in the final chapter, is to develop a general theory of clergy misconduct in minority religious bodies. To that extent, the black church is simply our vehicle.

We offer no opinion as to why the subject has so often been neglected except by certain journalists or historians nor why it has been virtually ignored by social scientists. This lack of attention to minority clergy misconduct mirrors the general neglect of clergy malfeasance before the mid-1980s (Shupe 1995: 8–11). At one time the very topic of clergy malfeasance was mentioned only *in* sotto voce by group adherents and seemingly anathema or mysteriously invisible to social scientists of any subdiscipline. Moreover, to study it was to be stigmatized as ipso facto hostile to religion itself. The mists of denial and avoidance were dispersed, however, starting in the late 1980s, and now clergy misconduct is an acknowledged social problem with growing conceptual and theoretical exploration. Major denominations and minor sects, Western and Eastern, have been previously examined by us and others. Now in this study we extend our project of pursuing the nuances of pastoral bad behavior into a new context. That it is no less sensitive or, to many types of adherents, offensive, we have no doubt. That was the angry judgment against the initial clergy malfeasance studies twenty-five years ago. Ironically, a quarter of a century from now observers will probably wonder why this phase took so long to happen.

Acknowledgments

We have a limited but important number of persons to thank. Both of us owe a debt of gratitude to Christopher S. Bradley for coaching us on the issues of social identity and identity salience with regard to black church participation. And yet again, we thank a patient but instructive Irving Louis Horowitz for his wisdom and seeing the bigger picture of our task here. Eliasson-Nannini also wishes to thank her professors at the joint campus of Indiana University Purdue University Fort Wayne for her undergraduate instruction as well as her parents and her patient understanding daughter for all the times E-N took the latter to the park, but had to read rather than play. Shupe regards this volume as his capstone work on clergy malfeasance and wishes his parents were alive to see it.

1

Minority Religions in the American Context—An Introduction

The Reverend Wilbert Thomas proclaimed himself a "bishop" though he was unaffiliated with any denomination. He pastored an independent black congregation, the Christian Alliance Holiness church, with approximately three thousand members. The Mercer, New Jersey prosecutor's office conducted a seven-month investigation after word began to leak out of some of the Reverend Mr. Thomas' ministerial actions. Thomas and two other men in the Church were eventually indicted on aggravated assault and criminal coercion. . . . Thomas could be provoked easily and unpredictably. One woman told a journalist that Thomas had once whipped her when she cut her hair without asking his permission, this after having had to provide him with sex on demand. Another member, Franklin Delano Adams, went to Thomas two weeks before Thanksgiving and asked him whether Adams should consider a career change to become a dental technician (in the context of asking Thomas' permission). Thomas became enraged at Adams "wasting Thomas' time" and had Adams beaten by a group of elders and senior members. They bent Adams naked over a table and each man whipped him at least five times until his thighs, hips, and back were severely lacerated. (*Rogue Clerics* 2008, 23–24)

[The Reverend Henry Lyons, 1994–99, President of the black National Baptist Church USA and pastor of a St. Petersburg, Florida congregation] pled guilty to five fraud charges; another forty-nine charges were dropped by plea bargain. Among the charges he admitted to were failure to pay back taxes on $1.3 million on income, defrauding a bank, and cheating other financial and federal housing officials. On February 23, 1998, Lyons was convicted in a Florida court of racketeering and grand theft of at least $4 million from companies to which he had sold fraudulent membership lists of his denomination for commercial purposes. Until the end Lyons denied any wrongdoing, at the same time he was purchasing several homes, expensive cars (such as a Mercedes Benz), and, as it was learned, supporting several mistresses in royal style. He was sentenced to five and a half years in prison and ordered to pay $2.5 million in restitution. (*Spoils of the Kingdom* 2007, 69)

Let the preceding vignettes—examples of physical, economic, and authoritative abuse—introduce our subject matter. This is a study of a particular type of elite deviant behavior: pastoral misconduct, or malfeasance committed by those in the clerical role. Moreover, our analysis reviews such deviance within a particular category of clerics: *black* clergypersons. Further, we examine the phenomenon of malfeasant black religious leaders within one specific cultural context: that of the United States of America.

To be sure, during the past two decades the social problem of clergy malfeasance in its sexual, economic, and authoritative forms has been noted and examined for a variety of religious groups. For example, social science studies exist for clergy scandals in Roman Catholicism (see, for example, Berry 1992; Berry and Renner 2004; Sipe 1990, 2003), Protestant denominations and para-churches (e.g., Fortune 1989; Hadden and Shupe 1988; Stockton 2000a), and Judaism (Schwab 2002). There have also been broader conceptual surveys of elite deviance in such groups as well as in others (Shupe 1995, 1998, 2007, 2008; Shupe et al. 2000) and numerous case studies of ministerial misdeeds across an array of Eastern and Western controversial religious movements, including the Peoples Temple, the AUM Shinrikyo, the Heaven's Gate UFO cult, and the Branch Davidian millennial sect (Bromley and Melton 2002; Hall 1989; Hall et al. 2000; Shupe and Darnell 2006), to cite only a few. At the same time, other than historical treatments of such controversial pre–World War II figures as the flamboyant clergymen Father Divine or Bishop "Daddy" Grace (both to be discussed later), and exposes of a few "celebrity" pastors in the modern era, there has been a relative paucity of analyses of clergy malfeasance within one particular minority's religious subculture, that of Afro-Americans. Indeed, even in the latest edition of one recently promoted textbook entitled *Race and Crime* (Gabbidon and Greene 2008), not a single instance of clergy malfeasance is mentioned. In the broader academic areas of criminology and the sociology of deviance, the situation is virtually the same. Such a lacuna persists because the very subject of clergy misconduct, which Shupe (1995, 8–11) suggested is dealt with *at best* by both criminologists and scholars of religion in sotto voce (because the former are often uninformed concerning religion and the latter are just too embarrassed by scandal), when coupled with the "politically" sensitive issue of race and deviance culpability, is somehow doubly taboo.

We propose in this volume to challenge this conventional reluctance. However, let us be clear at the outset as to the domain of our analysis. By "minority religion," we mean *an organized church or organizational enterprise which shares in the religious heritage of an ethnic/racial minority group* and not simply a culturally marginal or small religious group per se, such as "Jesus-freak" communitarians, flying saucer cults, or Wiccans. When we employ the term "clergy," we refer to *functionaries/fiduciaries in a religious group who are ordained, delegated, or self-appointed to positions of church leadership/stewardship*, or elites, from pastors to church treasurers to youth leaders and mentors. The term "malfeasance" embraces *actions that injure (psychologically, physically, or economically)*. Thus the synonyms "clergy malfeasance" or "clergy misconduct" are intended to mean *actions of a person in the clergy role that are deviant and/or harmful, i.e., that violate either norms of the group itself and/or legal standards of the larger society*. (See Shupe 2008, 4–8 for an elaboration of the implications and nuances of such a definition.)

Now we turn to the political–legal and historical context within which such a minority form of religion and its clergy abuse operate.

The U.S. Constitutional Basis for Religious Pluralism

The First Amendment of the Bill of Rights to the United States Constitution, ratified by the Constitutional Congress on December 15, 1791, unequivocally states:

> CONGRESS SHALL MAKE NO LAW RESPECTING AN ESTABLISHMENT OF RELIGION, OR PROHIBITING THE FREE EXERCISE THEREOF; OR ABRIDGING THE FREEDOM OF SPEECH, OR OF THE PRESS; OR THE RIGHT OF THE PEOPLE PEACEABLY TO ASSEMBLE, AND TO PETITION THE GOVERNMENT FOR A REDRESS OF GRIEVANCES.

Obviously our concern here lies with the initial, religious portion of the amendment, traditionally referred to as a pair of concerns: (1) the "establishment" clause and (2) the "free exercise" clause. While elegant in the simplicity of its wording respecting the government's constitutional lack of authority either to create any state-supported or preferred religion or religious body or likewise to interfere with citizens' freedom *to practice* their beliefs, the history of attempts by federal and state courts to implement this part of the First Amendment in ways that are faithful both to the apparent sentiments of the amendment's authors and current social exigencies is a complicated and sometimes seemingly contradictory one. Many numbers of volumes have been published just on separate issues and aspects of that history, and we do not attempt to rehash them here. However, a few general words on each of the two seminal clauses are in order to set the context for our later analysis.

Establishment Clause Issues

This first clause did not at first sit well with a number of leaders in former colonies that possessed in fact enfranchised church bodies. Proponents of a central national church argued that such an entity would promote (indeed, was necessary for) social stability, moral certainty, and sheer political expediency to help unite sometimes fractious, geographically disparate states. Writes Edwin Scott Gaustad (1985, 25):

> All for the force of history and tradition pressed upon a new nation to recognize its own national church, if not in 1776, then surely in 1787. Church-state alliance had been the pattern in the Western world for over fourteen hundred years, in England (even without the Vatican) for over three hundred years, and in colonies such as Virginia and Massachusetts for a century or more. The precedent was powerful.

Moreover, Gaustad adds: "One could, of course, find large numbers of church leaders who strongly favored a national church, with the single proviso that the church in question be their own."

But there was simply too much diversity in colonial and regional areas by the late eighteenth century, no possible "gentlemen's agreement" on a common denomination or compromise group. Observes political scientist Richard E. Morgan (1968, 20–1):

> No one should suppose that because so many different Protestant bodies took root in America, they were tolerant of each other. Indeed, the evidence from the colonial and revolutionary period suggests the reverse. . . . There was little real tolerance; much of the "religious freedom" which is supposed to have characterized early America resulted from the openness and sparsely settled nature of the country. Unorthodox belief or behavior was not tolerated, but the nonconformist could always turn his deviance into orthodoxy by walking out into the woods and setting up on his own.

Meanwhile, the more nationalistically (and perhaps less majoritarian-minded) Enlightenment thinkers on the problems facing a new national society were certainly aware of the bitterly violent past internecine struggles within European Christianity. A fragile democracy did not need that perennial source of contention.

A major factor spearheading the establishment (or really, the "disestablishment") clause were a group often termed by historians as "the dissidents." These were, for example, in Virginia the well-known figures of Patrick Henry, Thomas Jefferson, and James Madison, the latter two statesmen undoubtedly most responsible for the most notable adumbration of the First Amendment's initial two clauses. This was the "Bill for Establishing Religious Freedom," with both its own establishment and free exercise clauses. The legislation was passed, after six years of debate and discussion and despite considerable opposition by a variety of denominational religionists, by the Virginia Assembly on December 17, 1785. It became law on January 19, 1786, as the Statute of Virginia for Religious Freedom. (Along with his writing of the Declaration of Independence and the founding of the University of Virginia, Jefferson displayed his pride in playing a major role in promoting the Statute by having these three accomplishments inscribed on his grave's headstone.) Writes William W. Sweet (1950, 192): "Religious freedom had triumphed in Virginia and was soon to spread throughout the nation, and a few years later in the form of the first amendment to the Federal Constitution." Another historian (Sperry 1946, 45) has effusively claimed that this statute was said to be "The first law ever passed by a popular Assembly giving perfect freedom of conscience."

Some years later, U.S. Supreme Court Justice Hugo Black, writing for the majority in 1947's *Everson v. Board of Education* (see Black 1947), laid out the clear implications of the establishment clause, to paraphrase:

- Neither federal nor state governments may create an officially recognized or preferred church group;
- nor can these governments pass laws to provide any religious groups special treatment;
- nor can they force any person to attend church nor can they make any person refrain from attending;
- nor can they force a person to profess or support any particular belief or unbelief regarding any religion, nor punish any person for beliefs or unbeliefs.

There is one further dealing with religion in the Constitution beyond the Bill of Rights: Article 6, clause 3, which states that "No religious test shall ever be required as a qualification to any office or public trust under the United States." But the important point is that both the Constitution, as a whole, and the First Amendment, in particular, provide for impartial and equitable treatment of all religions. Interestingly, nowhere in this document is there a mention of God, much less even a definition of religion per se (Konvitz 1985), a fact to prove contentious for the courts in implementing the second clause (and for later purposes when trying to determine if certain clerical practices are legitimately spiritual or abusive).

Free Exercise Clause Issues

In principle, the Free Exercise clause proposes a straightforward "hands off" position or total tolerance of all religions, but in practical matters of public morality and social order that stance is unrealistic. No one is free to do anything without restrictions in the name of religion. As the late Richard Delgado (1980, 25), an attorney who argued over the years for containment of various controversial new religious movements that he summarily criticized as "cults," pointed out:

> A person may believe in a system which society labels bizarre or ridiculous but the state has no power whatsoever to interfere. It is when religious belief spills over into action that the degree of protection afforded to an individual or group is no longer absolute . . .

Likewise, the redoubtable constitutional scholar Leo Pfeffer (1974, 15–16), some years earlier, drew a similar line between belief and behavior:

> With the theology of a religious group the government may have no legal concern; but where its practices trench upon or threaten such important secular interests as the integrity of the monogamous family or of human life, it may and indeed must intervene for the protection of these interests.

As we shall show in cases discovered in later chapters, the devil is therein the details, for the following reasons. Assuming that the religious institution is not immune to the propensity of some persons to exploit what sociologists of deviance term "opportunity structures" in any human organization (and there is no reason to think so), religion can be a haven for those who are unscrupulous, hypocritical, and/or predatory or who confuse their immediate self-interests with higher sacred purposes. Furthermore, it is a safe generalization that government at all levels in the United States has no clear "acid test" nor certain guidelines for separating voluntary congregant sacrifice from leadership exploitation when the latter is cloaked in the majesty and awe of religious rhetoric. Nor, to be sure, can many followers of a faith, particularly of charismatic pastors, easily make the distinction on many occasions.

A major consequence of the Free Exercise clause is that governments are usually loath to step in and prosecute clergy malfeasance or clergy abuse at its various levels (just as government does not want to have to distinguish "true" religions or "authentic" pastors from "false" ones), which is how a ministry such as that involving the Jim and Tammy Faye Bakker PTL scandal could have lasted as long as it did and the more spectacular Peoples Temple and Branch Davidian disasters could have evolved into such destructive church–state confrontations. "Abuse" is, after all, a politically "loaded," subjective concept in the absence of clear legal evidence of harm, including witnesses/victims acknowledging that harm and willing to testify against it. Frequently the latter are not as forthcoming as one might suppose. For example, as sociologist Anson Shupe reported in the book *Rogue Clerics* (2008, 87–90), victims of economic "affinity crimes" (con-games such as fraudulent investment scams, pyramid schemes, and so forth) are often either unaware of their victimization (chalking up their losses to bad luck) and/or unwilling to blow the whistle on otherwise prestigious, respected religious leaders who might have endorsed the frauds but who also possess that daunting factor that Wach (1967, 337) termed the "charisma of office."

Thus, in our study of pastoral misbehavior there is a tension between free exercise of beliefs, which means putting the latter into practice, and having to observe for the public good some limitations on religious actions without violating the clause's spirit. In effect, this is not much different from the tension implicit in the Establishment Clause, i.e., when government is forbidden to designate any "official church" yet at the same time there are groups and denominations in the United States that persistently seek to receive some recognition of their majoritarian status, whether they call themselves, the Moral Majority or the Christian Right or repeatedly refer to the United States as a Christian nation.

This tension in American religion is perennial and can be clearly seen, as we briefly present in the following sections of this chapter, in controversies over sects and cults in North America. It seems inevitable in a culture where free exercise of religion is so touted. As one U.S. Supreme Court justice stated in a 1944 trial of a "fringe" religious leader as a charlatan (cited in Pfeffer 1974, 22):

> There are those who hunger and thirst after high values which they feel wanting in their humdrum lives. They live in mental confusion or moral anarchy and seek vaguely for truth and beauty and moral support. When they are deluded and disillusioned, cynicism and confusion follow. The wrong of these things, as I see it, is not in the money victims' part with half so much as in the mental and spiritual poison they get. But that is precisely the thing the Constitution put beyond the reach of the prosecutor, for the price of freedom of religion or of speech or of the press is that we must put up with, and even pay for, a good deal of rubbish.

Pluralist Controversies in the American Religious Marketplace

Seymour Martin Lipset (1967, 180–81) in *The First New Nation*, a title he provided the young republic of the United States, argues that equality and opportunity are not merely characteristic values of Americans but also of their institutions, including religion. Unlike the European situation with its myriad of established church–state regulative entanglements (Richardson 2004), American religion can be further viewed through the primary lens of *voluntarism* and therefore group competition, an observation famously made by Tocqueville (1954), among others during the nineteenth century: "In seeking to explain the special character of American religion many of the foreign visitors singled out the effect of the separation of church and state, which resulted in American churches being voluntary organizations in which congregational self-government was the predominant form of church government..."

Indeed, the voluntary nature of churches and the ensuing competition for adherents and parishioners created a new set of circumstances for religious survival:

> To exist, American churches had to compete in the marketplace for support. And conversely, membership in a given religious denomination was a voluntary act. (Lipset 1967, 182)

Lipset presaged the now influential view held by many sociologists of religion toward pluralistic American religion, i.e., that it can be understood by the market or economic metaphor, with beliefs and even salvation envisioned as commodities, with sacraments seen as services rendered, with religious groups considered akin to firms and their variations as brands, and with brand loyalties maintained by consumers or congregants. (See, e.g., Finke 1990; Finke and Iannaccone 1993.) Stark and Bainbridge (1980, 1985) have pushed the metaphor so as to regard all of religion in social exchange terms in which religion offers IOU's or symbolic promissory notes to be redeemed later for intangible but desired spiritual benefits in exchange for compliance to its norms here and now. Shupe (2008, 49–51) goes still further in posturing pastors and clerics as "brokers" in this marketplace of social exchange, "the middle men" as it were, between the sacred and the profane, with all the leverage and influence over rank-and-file believers that such a role would entail. (More on that later.)

The further relevance of this metaphor to American religion's relative freedom from government control can be seen in the analogy to supply-side economics. Stark (1987, 19) writes of a favorable ecology (or socio-political environment) for any religion's success, particularly struggling new ones, and suggests that it is ideally a marketplace unfettered by government interference or monopolistic church–state relationship:

> When a single religious organization has been granted monopoly rights in a religious economy backed by coercive power of the state, it will be more difficult for new faiths to flourish. . . . Still other things being equal, it will be much easier to build a new faith where such activity is legal, and even easier when all religions have equal standing vis-à-vis the state and the legal system. [and] . . . new religious movements will *not* succeed so long as conventional religious organizations are effectively serving market demand. [Emphasis in the original.]

Thus, the American religious context since the inception of the Republic in the late eighteenth century and continuing to the present is one that closely approximates laissez-faire economics: choice and options in an atmosphere of voluntary belief or unbelief, mandating (in the absence of more than minimal state regulating) competition among religious bodies for survival wherein consumer-believers can vote for support or nonsupport with their presence and presents.

This has been a significant factor for the emergence of many alternative religious developments in America, not least of all (we shall argue) in American black churches.

Evidence for the Fertile Marketplace

The history of American religion is hardly one of statically entrenched mainline denominations. Rather, religion in the United States has been a constantly evolving progression of growth and popular involvement in formal organizational religion since Colonial times (Finke and Stark 1992). Moreover, the nation has experienced episodic upheavals of Awakenings (defined as broad cultural shifts or transformation in religious belief/alignment that affect adherents and nonadherents alike) as well as regional/local revivals, rural and urban, in the Protestant groups alone (McLoughlin 1978). The religious landscape of the period of a single decade, for example, might yield a misleading perspective of stability, like the effect of a still photograph, but its artificiality would become apparent when compared to the fluidity of a motion picture. This reality of constant religious evolution and flux can be seen in two examples in American culture.

One case in point has been the emergence of the electric, or electronic, church, now commonly termed "televangelism" (from Hadden and Swann 1981), that literally accompanied the invention and expansion of the broadcast medium. This religious phenomenon became a classic case of theology evolving to become symbiotic with the medium within which it is preached. Religious spokespersons of various Judeo-Christian persuasions, Catholic and Protestant, took aggressive advantage of radio during the 1920s and 1930s to actualize Jesus Christ's Great Commission (Matthew 28:19–20) to take the gospel message out to all lands and peoples of the world. Most of the free or "sustaining" airtime that networks and local stations provided churches and community groups as part of their licensing agreement to use of the public airwave was an obligation mandated by the Communications Act of 1934. And most of that time (hence exposure) went to mainline denominational groups. By the era of television in the 1950s, the arrangement remained the same. But in 1960, the Federal Communications Commission issued a new policy with radical effects on both American religion and television broadcasting. Instead of simply giving away (often otherwise undesirable) time slots in order to receive community service credit, the local stations and networks could *sell* the time slots (and at better times), particularly to religious groups that could afford it, and still receive the same credit.

The impact of that new policy took about a decade to be felt, but it was powerful. A number of religious groups, many representing traditions previously feeling "shut out" of prime time exposure, began buying airtime. Many became termed "para-churches" because while they had the trappings of churches they were not under the control of regular denominational groups. Rather, they operated as independent fiefdoms, often run by virtually autonomous evangelists. In fairly short order, such groups that could raise the money for purchasing airtime and managing production costs thrived. Born was the phenomenon of television ministries, thoroughly embedded in the broadcast technology with their colorful studio sets, spectacular music and production values, and charismatic (if not always esthetically photogenic) "televangelist" superstars like Oral Roberts, Pat Robertson, Jimmy Swaggart, Jim and Tammy Faye Bakker, and a legion of regional and local evangelists who aspired (once given the added opportunity of cable access) to reach national and international audiences.

Born also were new forms of fundraising, including nonstop telethons *a la* Jerry Lewis' Labor Day format, tearful and biblically flavored pleas for money to stay on the air and continue their "soul-winning" activities, and, perhaps inevitably, the promotion of feel-good "prosperity" theology in which sending or pledging money to the Lord (via the particular pastor asking for it, of course) would bring viewer-donors in investment-fashion multiple material rewards, health-happiness, and a variety of spiritual blessings. (See Hadden and Shupe 1988, 38–54 for a history and the dynamics of this gospel construction.)

More to the point for our purposes here, what also occurred was that such a theology of financial giving promulgated opportunity structures for greed and outright fraud, matched both by enormous egos of the televangelists and an almost total lack of accountability for the money (with the ministries' invisible processing and monitoring agents). So much has been written about the specific scandals of the late 1980s, such as the Jim and Tammy Faye Bakker PTL Network debacle, with its impassioned fundraising for nonexistent overseas ministries/income tax evasion/personal greed/sexual hijinks/pilfering of cash flows, along with the similar actions of such lesser luminaries as Dallas' Reverends Robert Tilton and Larry Lea (and subsequent prison sentences for some, such as PTL's Jim Bakker and Dallas' W. V. Grant, Jr.) that we refer readers elsewhere for the many more criminological details available (see, e.g., Shupe 1995, 69–77; Shupe 2008, 154–58). Meanwhile, government, it could and has been argued, was reluctant to step in to monitor the enormous amounts of money flowing into the coffers and how it was being spent and still more reluctant to take action against all but the most egregious televangelist offenders on account of First Amendment, particularly Free Exercise, considerations.

A second source of religious development, reflecting the ongoing ferment and constant competitive multiplicity of constitutionally guaranteed freedom of religion, can be seen in the post–World War II cult-sect phenomenon which only several decades ago provoked a major hysteria among some Americans. (A cult, for present and later definitions in this volume, is sociologically defined as a relatively small group, with minimal division of labor and culturally unique beliefs deviating noticeably from majority religion(s) in a society, led most often by a charismatic leader. A sect, alternately, represents usually a larger group, breaking away organizationally from a mainstream religious church-tradition, often making purity-claims and intending to return to the latter tradition's founder's original message. Sects obviously are less deviant than cults, hence less rejected by society and tending to survive longer.)

During the 1960s until the mid-to-late 1990s, various unconventional religious groups in the United States began to receive attention by the mass media as well as some state governments. Some were of Christian origin (for example, the Reverend Sun Myung Moon's Unification Church, David "Moses" Berg's Children of God—later The Family, the Peoples Temple, and Jews for Jesus); others were of foreign "import" with various gurus, swamis, and adepts (such as the Hare Krishnas, the Divine Light Mission, or Transcendental Meditation); and some were entirely new with no ties to established religions but with quasi-spiritual-therapeutic aims (among these, the Church of Scientology, est, or Order of the Solar Temple). To many persons, particularly friends and families of those who joined such groups, the appearance of such phenomena on the American spiritual scene seemed strange and unprecedented. Their critics, fed by a sensationalist media, xenophobia, and most persons' sheer unfamiliarity with religious innovation, cultivated counter-movements to "expose" such groups and lobby for government investigations of them if not actual laws to restrict operations of such groups (Shupe and Bromley 1980).

To be sure, the "sudden" awareness (not necessarily "overnight," in any event) of many such groups did indeed have precedence in

American history, as did the concerns that they were not only different and offensive to some but also possibly subversive. The nineteenth century, after all, had the Millerites, the Cambellites, the Church of Jesus Christ of Latter-day Saints (Mormons), the Jehovah's Witnesses, the Christian Scientists, the Theosophists, the Spiritualists and Transcendentalists, and many more. All raised a lot of fears in their times and were denounced by more than rival group's pastors from their pulpits. In fact, four Quakers were hanged on Boston Common between 1659 and 1661 as strange and antisocial by the law-abiding folks of that eastern city (Bromley and Shupe 1981, xi). Mormons were tarred and feathered, shot at, and their founder murdered by an Illinois mob. (On Mormonism and their deviant standing in America at one time, see, e.g., Brodie 1995.)

This time-honored concern regarding unconventional religious groups, along with a persistent historical amnesia and Free Exercise clause myopia, has been standard fare in North American popular culture. Public alarms over "cults" or "sects," as Jenkins (2000, 5) reminds us,

> imply that the contemporary American situation is a frightening novelty, with few or no historical parallels. . . . but far from being a novelty, cults and cult-like movements have a very long history on American soil. Extreme and bizarre religious ideas are so commonplace in American history that it is difficult to speak of them as fringe as all.

Jenkins, in fact, concludes that departures from whatever beliefs happen to be considered mainstream in America at any given time are so common that they constitute "a separate tradition running parallel to better known and much larger schools like liberal Protestantism, evangelical enthusiasm, or the Catholic heritage" (7).

We do not have the inclination or the space here to deflate or debunk all the stereotypes about the so-called "cult controversy" starting in the 1960s and winding down by the end of the century. (Sociologists of religion prefer the more neutral, if not always accurate, phrase "new religious movements" to the much-abused, over-used term "cult.") Among the "howlers" that competent field researchers have destroyed are that these groups employ sinister, little understood recruitment tactics of mind control; that they all gather financial resources by panhandling; that their members all live communally in poverty and either in strict celibacy or rampant promiscuity; that their leaders are all maniacal money-loving hypocrites; that these groups are individually parts of a grand satanic plot against American society; that the only way to rescue a son, daughter, or loved one from such a nefarious groups is to abduct and coercively deprogram him or her; and so forth. There exists a wealth of established, objective social science data published in professional journals, and literal libraries of case study reports on separate groups as well as reliable analyses on all these issues, readily available and requiring little additional comment by us. (For just a few of the many overviews, see Bromley and Shupe 1981; Cowan and Bromley 2008; Lewis 2004; Shupe and Darnell 2006.)

But at the same time, we do not wish to maintain here or later in this volume a purely civil libertarian position that all such innovative religious developments are merely benign extensions of the First Amendment's logic. Indeed, in clergy malfeasance generally, and in the cases we will incorporate into our analysis, there is not generally a lot of benignity.

Yet while religious ferment has been a "constant" in both the Colonial era and later in the maturing Republic, awareness and concern over it in recent history, for whatever (though understandable) reasons, has been more episodic. Certainly the existence of, and fascination with, uniquely *black* cults and sects fits such a sporadic pattern. Though the focus of this volume largely concerns modern instances of social movement groups and congregations, it is worth a brief digression for background purposes to examine several controversial black groups and their leaders of the first half of the twentieth century.

Black Cults, Sects, and Religious Movements

Focusing just on the first half of the twentieth century, it is indisputable that unconventional or "fringe" religious groups have been a vibrant and visible element in American black religion. But it is misleading to stereotype or lump them all within the same category simply because they may have seemed bizarre. Washington (1973, 9) distinguishes between black cults and sects by attributing to cults a foremost affirmation of blackness for the group, seeking a secular (albeit couched in religious rhetoric) *black* social power, while in sects (most often descendants of Holiness/Pentecostals, Baptists, and Methodists) the blackness issue is not explicitly elevated above the authority of orthodox-evangelical Christian beliefs. (There is a bias in his cult–sect distinction against the Nation of Islam, clearly a non-Judeo-Christian group with its own lineage.)

However, in practice, authors and researchers of unconventional black religious groups have not employed either term consistently. "Cult" seems the preferred dismissive label for the more extreme groups. Thus, Dallam (2007, 23), in her study of Bishop "Daddy" Grace's House of Prayer, prefers to move toward the more sociologically current "new religious movement" designation. Dallam points out in a thorough review of research literature on such religious groups that "cult" and "sect" are often used pejoratively. Such terms tend to be thrown out along with implicit but noticeable assumptions that many of the leaders of these unconventional churches and movements are ersatz clergy, hypocrites, and, at times, outright flim-flam artists. For example, Washington (1973, 116), in his otherwise authoritative *Black Cults and Sects*, matter-of-factly generalizes about "fly-by-night cult leaders" and almost casually states that "Individual shysters have been frequent leaders of cults . . ." While in this section we cannot nuance the complex personalities or motives of black "cult" and "sect" leaders, suffice it to say that many popular as well as academic views of these persons stem largely from such one-dimensional features as their flamboyant dress, checkered dealings in money and property, and subsequent adversarial encounters with the United States. Internal Revenue Service (not to mention the criminal justice system), alleged and observed sexual relationships (marital and otherwise), and their unquestionably immodest if not outrageous proclamations and self-claims.

Below we present only a brief sampler, based on first-hand observations ranging from (black) anthropologist Arthur H. Fauset (1970) in his classic *Black Gods of the Metropolis*, first published in 1944, to religion scholar Marie W. Dallam's 2007 *Daddy Grace*. Our intention here is not to present anything resembling a thorough analysis but only to set the later context for inspection of clergy behavior in later chapters. We agree with Washington (1973, xi) in that "there is a fundamental and common ethnic ethic shared by black people which gives continuity to their discontinuous religious experience," that is, a common thread transcending particular religious expressions. That ethic is the this-worldly realization of power. Writes Washington (1973, 1):

> The intention of black church, sect, and cult types is to be power communities. . . . In the absence of relative black economic, social, ecclesiastical, and political power, sectarians have led their people to the ultimate power of the spirit as the way to the secular power

rather than as a substitute for it.... Any sectarian movement which focuses on a priority other than gaining real power in this real world runs counter to the central black religious intention.

Though it was fashionable among social science researchers to depict the followers of the "black gods of the metropolis" as financially destitute and underclass, hope-starved, and relatively uneducated, despite a lack of reliable data demonstrating such demographics (in keeping with an older "deprivational" approach to the motives of social movement converts generally), there unquestionably was a level of poverty among many Depression-era black cult and sect members. ("Deprivation" as a motive to inscribe oneself in any movement is always nebulous, of course, for among most persons some level of discontent over, and deprivation of, *something* is a constant in life.) Certainly an observable trait which still continues in some black groups, was the vicarious identification with an affluent successful leader, even if those qualities were ostentatiously displayed. For example, writing of Bishop "Daddy" grace's considerable property acquisition and membership pride thereof, Dallam (2007, 86) notes:

> In fact, this kind of close identification with Grace's wealth seems to have been fostered by church leadership; numerous writers observed the curious tradition of photos of church real estate framed and hung on sanctuary walls. This was especially true of the El Dorado, a building that received so much attention that it was nearly fetishized.... As Norman Eddy told a reporter upon Grace's death, "They might live in slums, but Daddy was rich, and they could feel like big shots."

At any rate, consider several of the more notable black cult and sect leaders in the United States during the first half of the twentieth century.

Several fringe groups which closely match Washington's cult definition conform to the general category of Black Jews, i.e., claiming that blacks are really Jewish and real Jews are all black. Two such examples were The Church of God and Saints of Christ, founded by Prophet William S. Crowdy, and the Church of God (or "Black Jews"), founded by Prophet F. S. Cherry. There were, to be sure, many fine differences in theologies and practices between them (for example, Crowdy forbade wine in church, Cherry actually encouraged moderate social drinking of alcohol), but the two groups nevertheless had close parallels. Both subscribed to the belief that black Americans had a long forgotten history in which they were the authentic Israelites of the Old Testament (according to Crowdy, blacks were the "lost tribe of Israel"; for Cherry, blacks were the first created human beings on earth); both despised and rejected the historic legitimacy of white Jews; both mixed the Christian scriptures with the Talmud and Torah; both claimed Jesus of Nazareth was black (Cherry also added God, Jacob, and Essau); both celebrated Passover and emphasized the Ten Commandments, and both observed ceremonial washing (Crowdy's group of feet, Cherry's of faces with perfumed water). Both held contempt for more sect-like black Christians as well as for many whites (Washington 1973, 132–33; see also Mathison 1960).

Neither group should be confused with the more visible Black Jews of Harlem (also called The Commandment Keepers of the Living God, or alternately, Royal Order of Ethiopian Hebrews) of the 1930s. Their founder, West Indian Rabbi Wentworth A. Matthew, claimed that the biblical Jacob was black and modern blacks were descendants of the romantic liaison between ancient Israel's King Solomon and the Queen of Sheba. These Black Jews observed strict Kosher food laws along with other conservative Jewish norms (including holidays), yet were cordial with (and reasonably accepted by) many white Jews (Bortz 1970, 30–34). Of these Harlem Black Jews, as of the Crowdy and Cherry cults, Washington (1973, 134) observes that they all rejected the more mainstream black sectarian practices of emotional, Holiness-Pentecostal-style praise worship and music or in Rabbi Matthew's contemptuous term, "niggeritions." In doing so, "They invented culture, a history, and a religion to compensate for their hatred of their black past and rejection of whites."

Considerably less cultural isolationism and world-rejection can be found in the two best publicized and largest black movements which saw their peaks in membership and finances during the 1930s and 1940s: the Peace Movement of Father Divine and the House of Prayer for All People of Bishop "Daddy" Grace.

Both Divine and Grace (originally George Baker and Marcelino Manuel de Garca, respectively) were born in the late nineteenth century, spent much of their lives in the South, and carried the emotional praise-style of worship out of that region's Holiness/Pentecostal tradition (Burgess et al. 1988, 82) into the cities of (primarily) the Eastern seaboard. (Interestingly, Grace technically came from a Roman Catholic background.) Moreover, they became rivals and grew to be major figures in pre–World War II Harlem in New York City.

The controversies surrounding these two leaders and their followers can be reduced to five parallel dimensions: leadership claims, personal and movement wealth, flamboyant lifestyles, style of worship (particularly involving women), and eventual entanglements with the courts.

Leadership Claims

Their self-proclaimed identities were outrageous by standards of the Depression era as well as any other time in American history. Father Divine pronounced himself to be God, the Judeo-Christian deity incarnated and everlasting. Those who believed in him, he assured followers, would also experience immortality in the Kingdom of God on Earth. Death, Divine preached, came only to those of little faith (in him) or to the wicked. As one participant observer, anthropologist Arthur H. Fauset (1970, 62), wrote during the 1940s:

> What is to occur should anything happen to Father Divine is an unintelligible question to any follower in the movement. Nothing can happen to Father Divine. He will never die; he is God.

Nor, Divine claimed, should true followers ever become ill with disease. One Peace Mission publication also stated that Divine "fulfills the Scriptural Prophecy of the Second Coming of Christ for the Christian world . . ." (Burnham 1979, 126), but in most ordinarily discourse among members, Divine was directly referred to as God. All such beliefs were to prove devastating for the Peace Mission movement, which Divine founded in 1919, when he did indeed eventually expire in the mid-1960s.

Bishop "Daddy" Grace only somewhat less audaciously asserted that his followers could dispense with God, that Grace, "had given God a vacation," and that "If you sin against God, Grace can save you, but if you sin against Grace, God cannot save you" (Fauset 1970, 267). Dallam (2007, 86–7), who raises the possibility that Grace never actually said these exact words, suggests a better understanding of Grace (both from his own perspective and in the eyes of his followers) as an intermediary or intercessory between God and human beings, at the same time serving as a superior role model, particularly for impecunious inner-city blacks. (Unlike the effects of Divine's death, Grace's final exit in 1960 did not end his movement but rather prompted a legal struggle among lieutenants over assets and control of the corporate House of Prayer for All People, with its numerous satellite churches. Grace's promotion of a constitution and other bureaucratic entities meant that his organization has survived to date.)

Personal and Movement Wealth

Divine and Grace both promoted entrepreneurship among black Americans and lived their entrepreneurial sermons. Divine required all members to contribute their incomes and wealth—indeed, to sell and donate the proceeds of all their possessions to his Peace Mission, and he used much of the movement's subsequent funds to underwrite a far-flung series of cooperative businesses staffed by committed members, the profits from which were never officially made public or tabulated by more than a few in the movement (i.e., Divine and his hand-picked board of trustees). Members lived communally and worked for pittance wages, reducing overhead and allowing the movement to invest its profits in its Peace Mission initiatives of racial harmony and equality as well as to spend inordinate amounts of money on luxuries enjoyed (but never legally owned) by Divine.

Burnham (1979, 137–40) examined the Peace Mission's newsletter *New Day* from 1938 to 1978 to gauge numbers and types of businesses of the group. His results reveal a broad array of enterprises: from men's and women's clothing stores and manufacturing, jewelry, and shoe repairing/shining to barbershops, restaurants, grocery stores and markets, tailors, paper-hanging, auto-repair, and landscape services. Using the same sources for more sacred uses he catalogued for 1958 alone seventeen mansions (where services were often held), training schools, and churches.

Burnham's partial findings are undoubtedly gross underestimates of scope and diversity in businesses and property-holding. Harris (1970, 2330) notes that the Peace Mission movement (in which Father Divine was officially only an advisor, never an owner) Divine's followers owned thirteen incorporated homes and training schools, fourteen residence clubs for Mission's women and men, eighteen "tremendous and expensive country mansions," twenty-nine apartment homes, eight small hotels and four larger ones, and eleven properties in countries as diverse as Austria, Canada, Panama, England, Australia, West Germany, and Switzerland. None were in Divine's name: the deed to the Newark, New Jersey Forest Hill mansion, for example, listed twenty-five different members as co-owners. (For more complete tallies, see Harris 1970, 45–58, 227–46.) After his death in 1965, individual residential properties exclusively for Divine's use were valued at and sold for hundreds of thousands of dollars each.

Bishop "Daddy" Grace's personal wealth and that of his House of Prayer movement never approached that of Father Divine's Peace mission. Divine claimed millions of members, but its size in fact could realistically be estimated at only about a half million souls. Grace's various House of Prayer congregations ranged from small store-fronts to impressive edifices, and the number of his followers might never have exceeded a few hundred thousand. But Grace oversaw members' tithes, gifts, and continually solicited offerings with a complicated but efficient top-down directed system. (See Robinson 1974, 216–17 for reprinted sections of the "General Council Laws of the United House of Prayer for All People" for the mandated meticulous process of collection and accountability for fundraising down to the smallest congregation.)

Grace initially received financial gifts from grateful members in his role as a healer, but as the membership and congregations grew he moved to selling various items useful for vicarious healing or as souvenirs, many promoting (or said to promote) health, beauty, and spiritual merit. For example, he prayed over and/or blessed special handkerchiefs to cure diseases and drive away evil spirits. From the success of that "premium," Grace began selling what Dallam (2007, 70–72) calls a "Grace product line" of items which all carried his picture. Such merchandise included facial creams and lotions, cookies, shoe polish and toothpaste, coffee beans, and stationary, many of which were touted as having curative powers. Daddy Grace soap, for example, was not just for cleansing but also for preventing or curing disease and for weight loss. Robinson (1974, 221) records that, in addition to the above items, there was hair pomade for men and women, transcontinental tea, and talcum powder. Also, "There were numerous emblems, buttons, badges, banners, and finally, elaborate uniforms with accessories of swords, batons, and walking sticks whose sale swelled the total of funds garnered by the bishop in his United House of Prayer." It was even claimed that if an issue of *Grace Magazine* was placed on the chest, it would cure colds as well as tuberculosis.

Unlike Divine, Grace was an open owner and investor in personal property and amassed a good deal of real estate. Though he was continually at odds with the Internal Revenue Service in disputes over back taxes, at the time of his death in 1960, Grace and the House of Prayer were ascertained to be worth $4.5 million (Robinson 1974, 228), with Grace keeping at least ninety known bank accounts simultaneously. Unlike Divine, who was foremost a champion of racial equality and nonviolence, Grace unabashedly sought to be the model of personal prosperity for his followers.

Yet both men also steered considerable funds toward civil improvements, constructed orphanages and homes for the aged, and taught self-reliance as well as charity within their movements. Of just Divine, Weisbrot (1983, 142) could say: "His programs extended employment, training, and business opportunities to ghetto residents within the framework of a highly successful and rapidly expanding cooperative association."

Flamboyant Lifestyles

The movements overseen by Father Divine and Bishop "Daddy" Grace, respectively, with their highly centralized fiscal controls, made millions of dollars. Whether one served merely as an "advisor" and nonowner in his movement, as Divine claimed, or as the CEO and self-made entrepreneurial millionaire, as Grace boasted, both men lived materially very well. They wore expensive clothing, resided in sumptuous accommodations, and had chauffeurs to drive them in fleets of the most luxurious automobiles of the era.

As religious leaders pretending to greater-than-average spiritual status, therefore, they both received an enormous amount of media criticism and outright scorn. Their popular images were ones of hucksters and insincere con-men; the best that often could be said by critics of their followers was that the latter were impressionable dupes. Neither leader attempted to disguise or even moderate the wealth accumulating in their groups. This also brought the predictable accusation that as spiritual leaders they lived a double-standard, flaunting the possessions they either owned or had exclusive access to while their generous believers lived in far more modest, if not far leaner, circumstances. (This is an issue that returns for some contemporary malfeasant black pastors, as will be seen in later chapters.) There was also a streak of eccentricity in each man, perhaps more immediately visible in Grace than Divine. Rather than belabor readers with lists of possessions and public actions that were quite curious, following are two short vignettes that provide some flavor of the flamboyance both men displayed in their lifestyles and public comportment.

First, Washington (1973, 117–18) recounts a meeting between Father Divine and a lesser black luminary, Prophet Jones:

> When Prophet Jones journeyed to meet Father Divine, he wore an eight-hundred-and-twelve diamond bracelet and a fifty-one karat topaz. He had come to see Father Divine's newly acquired seventy-three-acre, thirty-two-room gothic chateau in Montgomery County, Pennsylvania, the latest of his seventy-five heavens. Father Divine met him at the railroad station in New York with fifteen limousines, greeting his guest with these opening words: "I'm happy to meet you, your holiness." Prophet Jones replied: "God bless you, your godliness." They did not exchange many words throughout that visit. It may be that Prophet Jones was stunned by the real estate holdings of Father Divine, who made him look like a piker.

For Grace's part, Marie W. Dallam (2007, 6), in her balanced appraisal of his ministry, provides a succinct portrait of the man's bodacious style in just his personal appearance:

> Although Grace was only five feet eight inches tall, he made certain he stood apart from other men by adorning himself with nothing less than flamboyance. His clothes were unpredictable, but usually flashy. He often wore tailor-made suits of lush fabrics, sometimes in vibrant colors and decorated with gold piping or shiny buttons. He paired the suits with brightly striped vests and hand-painted neckties. For less formal occasions, Grace might wear a kimono or his red and silver cowboy shirt or his long, northern fur seal coat. His fingers and wrists invariably clanged with gold bracelets and rings containing precious stones. The fingernails of his left hand, which he allowed to grow several inches, were often painted in red, white, and blue. Grace kept his hair at shoulder length, and in early years he had a mustache and goatee, while later on he often simply drew his mustache on with an eye pencil.

Those are merely two tips of gigantically eccentric icebergs.

Styles of Worship (Involving Women)

This dimension is mentioned for the notoriety it caused by both these black clerics. The worship-styles of both Divine and Grace were clearly within the black Holiness and Pentecostal traditions: loud ecstatic singing, Holy Spirit prayer/praise/dancing, prophecy, glossolalia (tongue-speaking), swaying, weeping exhortations to the preachers, and so forth. Such exuberant sanctuary demeanor, of course, would have been anathema if not totally foreign to most white, staid, mainstream Christians (who were typical of the critics). But it was the behavior of women during the services who caused such a furor for many outsiders.

Divine preached that there was no need for further reproduction in his kingdom on Earth, certainly not for his faithful immortal believers. Therefore, celibacy to eliminate the evil of lust was mandatory. Members were segregated into communal living quarters by sex, including husbands and wives (no longer to enjoy conjugal relations) who also surrendered their children to a kindergarten arrangement.

As a result, in the emotional worship services of Father Divine, which often lasted hours, some (primarily women) began to act in ways that suggest these events would at times serve as outlets for repressed sexuality. In essence, verbal exclamations and body movements, including auto-caressing and fondling, appear to have led to orgasmic fulfillment, all with Father Divine as a symbolic focus for sexual energy. This observation has been made in detail by Harris (1970, 97–118). The following description of "vibrating" (the Peace Mission term) certainly lends itself to this interpretation. In this excerpt, a young woman named Holy Light has tried to overcome her libidinal feelings for men generally. She is not alone in the effort and believes she has succeeded. Says Harris (1970, 117): "They have learned, however, to direct those lustful feelings into channels that are socially approved in the Peace Mission movement." Harris (1970, 117–18) continues:

> There is a physical outlet in the Peace Mission movement, and it is known as "vibrating." It is highly regarded, not merely as a vent for repressed sexual feeling, but rather as a tremendous way in which followers, men as well as women, can display their love for God.

Holy Light, Harris tells us, has earned a reputation as one of the group's most effective vibrators. She can apparently, by suggestive contagion, stimulate the begging' of arousal over Divine in other women, and others regard her as a "vibrating" leader:

> Holy's vibration follow this pattern: She looks at Father and jerks her hips. She looks for a long moment with the love shining out of her eyes. . . . She says [in low voice], "From the very first moment I saw that precious holy body of your'n I fell in love head over heels. Oh, I loved you. Gee, I love you!"
>
> [These endearments are repeated. She calls Father Divine pretty, cute, and his mate. Divine regards her solemnly, with no expression.

She tells him he is her one and only repeatedly calling him "God."
Other women started chanting "God!"]

Tears come to her eyes. She screams, "You is my lover. You is my everything." She reaches Father's seat. She falls on the floor in front of him. She falls hard but does not hurt herself. She bangs her head against the floor with utmost deliberation. She lifts one leg into the air and beats the floor with her other one.

[She tells Divine he is all she needs and gives him an amorous expression.] Then she closes her eyes and dances away. She jerks her hips again, and her breasts. She takes her head in her hands.... "Halleliujah!" she screams out. "I love you—love, love, love you." She releases her head and drops her right hand onto her bosom. She holds it there caressingly. "Love, love you." She stops moving and sits down with a happy look on her face. Her vibration is finished. It is apparent that, in her testimony to Father Divine, she has reached a sublime climax of fulfillment. [Harris mentions how her eyes were shut tight, her fists clenched, and her breathing harsh up until the denouement of this "testimony."]

Harris (1970, 78) says that Father Divine's allegedly orgiastic and lurid sex life was undoubtedly the most publicized accusation against him. Divine also surrounded himself with an elite corps of young females (both black and white) whom he termed "Heaven's secretaries," usually over two dozen of them, selected for having found his particular favor at one time or another. (Harris refers to them as "Father's harem.") Like Holy Light, they, too, could at times drift into orgasmic paroxysms as they shrieked and put their arms and hands over their bodies (Harris 1970, 257).

Thus, it is not difficult to understand why, as stories leaked outside the movement, Father Divine became regarded popularly as a satyr figure.

Bishop "Daddy" Grace, unlike Divine, had no theology of celibacy nor had he any reason to promote one. Like Divine, however, he did practice serial monogamy (Grace, perhaps even bigamy once), and past wives were to cause problems later in their movements. Grace, however, did preach against adultery and fornication, and Dallam (2007, 92) observes that women were encouraged to cultivate chaste or conservative virtues and look for commitment and marriage in men. Yet, in worship services, which featured the enthusiastic, ecstatic, spirit-filled Holiness/Pentecostal mode, there were suggestions of strong sexual expression thinly veiled. Consider this brief description of a religious service by anthropologist Fauset (1970, 28):

> The bass drummer beats his drum and begins to sing, aided by tambourines struck by women in various parts of the room—one woman dressed in red and making grimaces and queer gesticulations beats very weird rhythms. Other men and women clap their hands, while still others clap two pieces of wood together. There are cries of "Daddy! You feel so good!" "Sweet Daddy!" "Come to Daddy!" "Oh, Daddy!" . . . More singing and dancing follows. Women become convulsed, contort themselves, cavort through the house of prayer, finally falling in a heap on the sawdust. They lie outstretched, inert . . .

The sexual atmosphere of such services may have been exaggerated by the observers or nonexistent, in Grace's case, and certainly more explicitly circumstantial with Divine. But sex, money, and flashing spending, combined with a style of worship totally unfamiliar to many Americans, and seemingly outrageous pretensions to spiritual authority by both Divine and Grace, were bound to locate these men within the popular and academic category of "black cult" with all the negative associations thereof.

Legal Entanglements

Essentially there was a duality of reasons that both Father Divine and Bishop "Daddy" Grace became embroiled with the courts.

One reason had to do directly with all the money they raised and spent. It should not be surprising that two outspoken, highly visible minority men, neither with much formal education or previous experience in handling money, yet each with a largely centralized (and in Grace's instance, authoritarian) system of fundraising and minimal accountability, would encounter legal entanglements.

In the case of Divine, according to Weisbrot (1983, 74–5):

> Father Divine took a keener interest in this realm of Caesar than he cared publicly to admit. . . . Whether or not administrators turned over money directly to Father Divine or simply accounted for its whereabouts, there is little question that he ultimately controlled the uses to which it was put. [And later] This rapidly expanding bureaucracy enabled a successful transition from a modest commune to a corporate network spanning the globe and managing millions of dollars in personal and real property.

As merely an official "advisor" to the dispersal of funds in the Peace Mission, even when things like automobiles, expensive clothes, and impressive homes were clearly purchased for his exclusive use, Divine would be coy when denying he owned any of it. But biographers of

Divine and the Peace Mission, while alluding to repeated attempts by the Internal Revenue Service to uncover any evidence that Divine was avoiding payment of income taxes do not indicate that he encountered significant legal trouble there (e.g., Harris 1970, 55).

In Grace's case, just the sheer number of banks in which he kept accounts and his constant personal investments *and* his micromanagement of funds accrued by the House of Prayer movement made his tax situation unavoidably problematic. His estate, according to Robinson (1974, 218), included 111 House of Prayer churches and missions in about ninety cities and towns. Most were small, but Grace owned properties (such as stores and apartment buildings) as well as co-owned other properties; he had a lot of money involved with his homes (if not always mansions) in at least nine cities, one of which on a twenty-one-acre estate near Havana. The Internal Revenue Service had been on Grace's trail repeatedly for back income tax payments. He either won their lawsuits or escaped penalties during most of his active ministry. Robinson (1974, 217–18) reports that at his death the IRS assessed the net worth of Grace's estate (as of 1956) as $4,081,511.62. Dallam (2007, 164–65) acknowledges that shortly after Grace's death in 1960 that

> the most daunting of all the suits came from the government. Claiming that Grace had failed to pay enough income tax for several years, the IRS froze all of Grace's personal and corporate assets until it could determine what was owed. The initial estimates of taxes owed was $5.9 million; the IRS eventually settled for $1.9 million in June 1961.

She adds: "It is hard to know whether Grace's poor record keeping made lawsuits truly inevitable, or if it was just that people viewed his death as an opportunity to skim wealth from the estate."

A second reason for legal entanglements would be subsumed under "sexual and family matters." Flamboyant personalities making (what seemed to outsiders) outlandish spiritual claims and raking in large amounts of cash were suspect enough in matters of worldly power. Both men were plagued by former wives (or women claiming to be so), other relatives, and assorted persons who claimed victimization suing them (Dallam 2007, 152–53; Harris 1970, 85–96; Robinson 1974, 223).

For example, there were disillusioned followers who had donated lifesavings and assets to Father Divine as God but reached the conclusion that he was much less than a deity. The case of Verinda

Brown and her husband Thomas is illustrative. They had surrendered to Divine all their worldly possessions, cashing in life insurance policies and emptying out bank accounts. Later, a bitter Verinda hired a white lawyer to sue for return of the money (an estimated total of $4,476). Divine, despite the bad publicity that followed, adamantly refused to acknowledge her claim. After courtroom proceedings the first judge entered a judgment against Divine. (During the trial, 600 of Divine's "angels" or followers in robes picketed the courtroom.) Divine refused to pay, appealed, and lost again. The case was reopened yet again, and this third time Divine lost yet still refused to pay a dime. Bucking the courts' decisions, Divine's ultimate response was to leave New York's jurisdiction (never able to return) and move to Philadelphia.

Divine was involved in a host of other legal battles, a most famous one involving his trial as a public nuisance; after his conviction (with a jury suggesting leniency) and the bigoted judge (continually contemptuous of Divine) dropping dead three days later, Divine immediately (if not immodestly) told his visitors in jail: "I hated to do it." (Weisbrot 1983, 51–3).

Grace, for his part, was put on trial in March 1934 and indicted for violating the Mann Act, i.e., transporting a person across state lines for illicit or immoral purposes (in this case a young white female follower who claimed he raped her in the backseat of a limousine, ultimately causing her to give birth to an illegitimate son). It made for a sensational courtroom situation, with conflicting witnesses, Grace himself cross-examined, and an attendant media circus. Dallam (2007, 102) reports that "newspapers continued to paint a guilty picture of Grace, even referring to him as a 'convicted white slaver.'" In the end Grace was both convicted and exonerated, but it greatly wounded the public image of his ministry. (See Dallam 2007, 96–106 for the complicated scenario.)

Such trials and lawsuits were embarrassing to both men and their followers. All were grist for critical media observers (largely white) who mistrusted the leaders' motives and misunderstood sectarian black religion as cultic. Such observations illustrate the fact that levels of possible criminality differ, and some accusations eventuate in trials, civil or criminal, while others remain at the focus of merely media innuendos and assaults. Pre–World War II North American newspapers, in particular, always considered the eccentricities of these two black leaders, their legal problems, and their religious deviance good for a laugh.

**

A penultimate word: The above-described media motif is not the spirit in which we conduct the following analysis. We deliberately avoid the casual label of "cult" that early researchers of some unconventional black groups almost casually used. And we do not consider pastoral malfeasance in black congregations either a laughing matter or a strange anomaly. Pastoral misconduct is a stain, not merely a blemish, on any religious tradition. It is more than discomforting. It is hurtful to faith and trust; sociologically destructive of individuals, families, and communities; and subtly corrosive of hope even for nonmembers.

At the same time, the bureaucracies of Divine and Grace, operating as they did in Harlem and other inner-city areas during the 1930s, performed the magic trick of turning pennies into dimes and then into dollars. Now such manufacturing schemes by pastors have turned dollars into megadollars and millions. Similarly, whereas numbers running in Depression-era New York may have been winked at or pragmatically ignored by more mainline black clergymen, as suggested by Horowtiz (2012) in his autobiographical account of such illegal activities, today with cable networks and wider audiences, similar activities are sometimes countenanced or explained way by fellow minority televangelists, or professionally speaking, colleagues.

The Final Context: Power, Exchange, and Pastors

Religious power in a Durkheimian sense is a collectively constructed social fact. As Borg (2009, 195) eloquently states it, power and religion are the very cornerstones of human life, and therefore religious power can be dangerous. Therefore, the final or ultimate context for observing black religion in the United States, or with any religion in any culture, is one of religious power: the power to define reality, the discerning power to distinguish between sacred and profane aspects of life, and the unique fiduciary power to link the affairs of human beings to both these realms. This, then, is the micro or social psychological context of social exchange within which clergy work.

Employing the exchange model, Borg (2009, 201) isolates the need many persons have for individuals in the pastoral role and which entail the former ceding their power to the latter:

> What people are actually doing when they submit their dilemmas and doubts to religious authority is to delegate their own religious power to somebody else, hoping for a higher return. In their quest

for a superhuman guarantee for their worldview, they realize that the efficacy of their own self-empowerment or mutual exchange is insufficient. The task of religious empowerment is now transferred to somebody who is seen to wield sufficient religious power to be able to fulfill the desire for a guarantee.

Borg continues with his description of this religious specialist:

> The functionary is invested with a special dignity, and his position is marked with special attributes, which place him somewhere in between the believer and the divinity. He will wear special clothing, and display special behavior, and even his lifestyle may be distinctive and special . . . all of this to underline his special status.

As a consequence, the social capital of the religious leader emerges with his or her ability to exchange spiritual capital as if it was an available resource, a transferal process at times frequently requiring an expert to smooth its acquisition or even create it. Put another way, the pastor, minister, cleric, priest, or shaman becomes a *broker* in the spiritual marketplace of human beings, goods, and spiritual energy. Following this analogy, Shupe (2008, 49) maintains:

> A dictionary definition of a fiduciary broker is "an agent who negotiates contracts, purchases, or sales in return for a fee." They are the "middlepersons" between the promised spiritual benefits, or IOUs, from supernatural sources (such as deities) and the buyers (such as supplicants and laity). The brokers negotiate between supplies of intangibles and demand by presenting/interpreting commandments, prescriptions and proscriptions, and scriptures/sacred writings with the help of prayer and rituals. The latter include confessions, marriage and burial rites, and communions and baptisms. Clergy are the agents of faith traditions. Thus, religious elites are special trusted fiduciaries in the go-between brokerage role.

Therefore, the misconduct of the black pastor has to be located within black religion, which here has been cursorily fixed within the United States religio-political pluralistic system. The black pastor's role in that minority subculture, in history as well as modernity, must be considered. The accompanying issues of opportunity structures for deviance, victim response ("victim" written larger to mean not just primary recipients of exploitation but also the larger community of faith), and victimization processes, leadership neutralization, and normalization of deviance must all be understood within the framework of that subculture and its members' aspirations. That is our first task in this volume. The second task will be to building a bridge from the specific black experience of clergy misconduct to a larger theory of clergy malfeasance in minority religions.

2

Black History, Black Religion, and the Salient Identity of Pastor and Congregation in the Minority Church

It is a sociological truism in the study of religion that the latter phenomenon can either serve as a conservative force preserving the status quo or become a radical force for its change. But an even more primary truth in the analysis of religion, social structure, and ideology is that religious groups' theologies predictably adjust to, and are periodically recast to accommodate, the social circumstances of those groups. Thus, privileged groups tend to cultivate theological apologies to justify their wealth just as poorer groups spiritually rationalize their unfortunate situations with hopes and eventual soteriological promises of vindication. So agree classic conflict theorists like Marx (Saul 1974) and the logic of the anthropology of religion perspective (Swanson 1960).

Along the same lines, German sociologist Max Weber (1964a, 107–8) observed the relation between theology and social structure:

> When a man who is happy compares his position with that of one who is unhappy he is not content with the fact of his happiness, but desires something more, namely the right to this happiness, the consciousness that he has earned his good fortune, in contrast to the unfortunate one who must equally have earned his misfortune.

Privileged classes, in other words, seem to demand the "psychological assurance of legitimacy" to assuage their privilege in a system of inequality. Likewise, Weber (1964a, 108) adds, "Correspondingly different is the situation of the disprivileged. Their particular need is for release from suffering." Thus, there is on the part of the latter an expectation and hope for salvation, liberation, freedom, and ultimate compensation.

This second accommodation of religious beliefs to disprivileged reality results in what Lanternari (1963) half a century ago generally referred to as "religions of the oppressed." This necessary, even desperate accommodation to cope with oppression is the primary thrust, motif, and context of American black Christianity. Some would call it the genius of black religion in North America, i.e., to identify with the archetypal and mythological themes of the Bible, particularly the Jewish parts emphasizing the bondage/slavery of ancient Hebrews and their divine promise of liberation, and then utilize these for psychological survival and succor during the two and one-half centuries of legalized slavery *and then* ultimately use them to legitimate the civil rights movement of the twentieth century.

So much has been written of the origins and conditions of black chattel existence in early American history that we need only sketch here an outline of the background of the origins of black Christianity and its emerging pastoral leadership. Our purpose in this chapter is to pair this religious history with the social psychology of social group identity for black parishioners. Only then can the phenomenon of black pastoral malfeasance and the black community's reaction to it be understood. This black reaction, we maintain, is grounded in a praxis resembling, but not identical to, the reactions of white parishioners and believers to the same violations of norms and expectations when revealed or exposed. At no time do we intend to suggest that either because of the history of the black church and the development of its black pastors that the latter are more prone in some straight-line way to excesses or crimogenic motives than their white counterparts. Indeed, being more numerous in congregations and denominational size, the plates of white pastors, in particular flamboyant ones, are more replete with abuses and exploitations than those of black pastors in sheer quantity (Shupe 1995, 2007, 2008; Shupe et al. 2000). A less than thorough glance at just white televangelism and its excesses (Hadden and Shupe 1988), decades ago or today, should satisfy that point.

Emergence of the Black Christian Church

Wrote two North American economic historians (Fogel and Engerman 1974, 3) of slavery's impact on North American culture:

The years of black enslavement and the Civil War in which they terminated were our nation's time on the cross. The desire of historians to lay bare the economic, political, and social forces which produced the tensions of the antebellum era and exploded into the worst holocaust of our history is not difficult to appreciate.

The black church has unquestionably been the most important macro and micro institution in historical African-American subculture, at times more persistent in its influence than even the family, and certainly more central to maintaining the values of the black community than any other ethnic or racial legacy (Lincoln and Mamiya 1990). This faith community irrevocably conditioned by the "peculiar institution" of slavery (Stampp 1956) is unique in the American Christian heritage.

White evangelizing efforts directed at black slaves during the seventeenth and eighteenth centuries, particularly supported by the Anglican Church but also encouraged by other Protestant "sects," such as the Methodists and Baptists, began for three basic reasons: (1) to "deculturate" blacks of their indigenous African religious beliefs (a strategy employed alongside the breakup of preexisting families and deliberate segregation of slaves coming from the same original tribes or communities); (2) to pacify and subdue the slaves' ambitions for freedom, escape, or revenge; and (3) to impress on slaves the "naturalness" of their submission and obedience to white authority (Johnstone 2004, 289). Obedience to white masters, as impressed on the slaves, was made equivalent to obedience to God (Stampp 1956, 158).

Missionizing efforts were not initially successful (Wood 1990). Jones (1974, 9) points out that the obvious message black slave received, however implicitly, was that "the central reason for the failure of the mission to the slaves lies mainly in the inability of the Blacks to reconcile the faith of the evangelists with their conduct." Moreover, despite the message of the St. Paul in First Corinthians that in Christ there is no Greek, freeman, slave, and so forth, the reality was far different. For example, there was the hypocritically segregated joint attendance at New England church services, whites in the main floor pews and slaves in the balcony or back by the doors. Eventually it dawned on white owners in the South that both audiences were being exposed to the same messages, whether about captive/liberated Hebrews in Egypt/Palestine or Christian liberation from Roman oppression, but both might not be taking away the same lesson.

Whites focused on Mosaic law to justify slavery by biblical precedent, i.e., social control; blacks understood the broader experience of Moses and the Israelites in and out of Egypt as a mirror image of their own plight, i.e., liberation from bondage. Moreover, some white Christians were concerned that slave conversions would elevate the latter group to equal status, here or hereafter. (Would slaves confront their masters and mistresses in heaven? Obviously an embarrassment for some. Would such conversions ultimately confer on blacks' enfranchisement and other secular political rights? In other words, would current social stratification dimensions continued in the afterlife? (See Butler 1984.)

Thus, by the late eighteenth century specially "approved" or appointed and/or "trusted" preachers and biblical interpreters were thrust on slaves, meeting separately from whites. *That was the beginning of the black church.* Whether later revisionist historians/activists would call these pastors "Uncle Toms" or tools of white owners, the segregation of whites and blacks at distinct altars created opportunities for the seeds of the black Christian Church and black leadership to flourish in a quasi-independent (however fragile) soil.

The major historical impetus for the growth of both white and black Christianity in North America was the seismic spiritual epoch recognized by most historians as The Second Great Awakening. An *awakening* is not merely a localized religious revival or a temporary craze or even an event per se. Awakenings, according to renowned American historian William G. McLoughlin, can be known for their larger results, often shattering older, staid spiritual understandings and forging new examinations and visions of the present and future. And their effects are not limited to just the believers or the faithful. They realign whole cultures. Revivals come and go; awakenings last decades or longer. Writes McLoughlin (1978, 2):

> They are not brief outbursts of mass emotionalism by one group or another but profound cultural transformations affecting all Americans and extending over a generation or more. . . . They eventuate in basic restructurings of our institutions and redefinitions of our social goals.
>
> . . . They restore our cultural verve and our self-confidence, helping us to maintain faith in ourselves, our ideals, and our "covenant with God" even while they compel us to reinterpret that covenant in the light of new experience.

The Second Great Awakening (as opposed to the eighteenth century's First Great Awakening, a largely white Protestant urban New England phenomenon) began in rural Appalachia in the early nineteenth century and stamped on this religious transformation its low-brow style and direct level of emotional appeal. The Awakening—actually a series of appearances, services, revivals, and visits by various Protestant evangelists—quickly spread and continued for decades across the western frontier in previously "un-churched" regions. It offered a practical "low-church" democratized form of Christianity more attuned and accessible to minimally educated persons in which salvation (eternal life and forgiveness of sins) was not some rationed gift to Calvinist Puritans or other "elect" bodies but rather was freely available through Christ for the asking by *All* if they wanted it. The preaching, by the standards of older churches, was rustic, sometimes even crude. It was populist and entertaining, suitable to the rough conditions of frontier life. Its message was also one of stability: "A central function of the Great Revival between 1800 and 1815 was to substitute the order and discipline of Christian society for the disordered frontier world of violence and irresponsibility" (Flynt 1981, 31).

The fruits of the Second Great Awakening have also been calculated. In 1800, it is estimated, only one in fifteen Americans was a church member or had a denominational affiliation; by 1850, as the Awakening cooled with the advent of slave-free state issues and the impending Civil War, one in seven American belonged to a church (Flynt 1981, 24).

Along with whites, slaves were taken to the open-air camp meetings, often held in fields or under tents, in the hope they would capture the moral messages of obedience and responsibility. But in these out-door free-wheeling services there was none of the hierarchical segregated partitioning as had been seen in staid in-door Protestant services. Moreover, the encouragement of emotional responses from the crowd, the foot-stomping, the hand clapping, the exhortations by the audience to preachers at dramatic points in the oratories, the lack of hymnals, and yes, the sweat, all resonated well with the slaves because of their previous unforgotten African heritage. This was a participatory style of religion from which they were in many cases only a generation or two removed.

Much has been made of the debate over whether the slaves' African cultural heritage was wiped out or retained during efforts at their

Christianization. The older view, championed by E. Franklin Frazier (1974), was that most "Africanisms" in black religion were successfully expunged by white owners and missionaries, that white Christianity filled the vacuum left by the loss of African religious beliefs and worship styles. In more recent years that view has been in serious retreat, if not now totally discredited. Wrote Henry Mitchell (1974, 70):

> Black Preaching and Black Religion generally are inescapably the product of the confluence of two streams of culture, one West African and the other Euro-American. The error of E. Franklin Frazier, and many other scholars of all races, has been to assume that the former was all but wiped out, and that the latter was the basic culture and religion which took their place in America.

Indeed, over a half century ago anthropologist Melville J. Herskovitz (1941), by tracing records of the actual geographic regions of slave raids and the similarities of slave languages and cultures, had definitively shown that there was surprising homogeneity in the African religious backgrounds of North American slaves. Their exhortations to preachers during sermons, their use of sounds and physicality in worship services, their identity as believers with a community (not as individual monads or souls apart from others): all survived, Herskovitz maintained, but they were overlain with the doctrinal veneer of Christianity. Thus, Herskovitz (1941, 7) offered the African link to even popular African-American culture through black religion:

> Denied the use of drums and other hand instruments by masters who feared slaves communicating, the irrepressible bondsman substituted hand-clapping and foot-stomping in plantation dances that ultimately worked their way into the popular dances of the early twentieth century.

The influence of "Africanisms" in black hymns (and their coded messages of outrage and anger) or in preacher's messages of hope all had African ancestral precedents which were never really erased and could resurface in Christianity's adaptation to the black community (Holloway 1990; Wilmore 1973, 15–17, 101; Work 1974).

Thus, by the end of the Second Great Awakening in the first half of the nineteenth century, black slave culture was permitted its full indulgence in Christian traditions and mythology, the consequences of which white owners never seemed to fully appreciate. In doing so, black slaves from Africa cultivated an appreciation of the potential of this

Middle Eastern-turned-Hellenistic faith for their own hopes of justice and liberation, though it is undoubtedly true that blacks, probably more than most whites, possessed a greater sense of the contractions within a two-caste Christianity. Raboteau (1984, 182) has described the contradiction between the realities of racial inequality confronting blacks and the historical "curiosity" of slave Christianity. Indeed, the entire *theodicy* of it all—that posed issues for these minority believers during the nineteenth century:

> The existence of chattel slavery in a nation that claimed to be Christian and the use of Christianity to justify enslavement, confronted evangelicals with a basic dilemma, which may be most clearly formulated in the question: what meaning did Christianity, if it were a white man's religion, as it seemed, have for blacks, and why did the Christian God, if he were just as claimed, permit blacks to suffer so?

The answer is that blacks developed, in Raboteau's words, a "distinctive evangelical tradition" of a special identity with the suffering of God's Special Children or Chosen People, as with the ancient Israelites. To put it in the words of religious historian Martin E. Marty (1970, 24), black slaves and later freed minority people came to feel that

> they were in America, but not yet fully of it. They had not been rescued or liberated. And when these black Americans would evoke the symbols of exodus they looked subversive to those around them.

Thus, while white owners may have hoped Christianity's nostrums might pacify slave resentment, they seemed also to hold a liminal awareness that there was nevertheless something subversive to the institution of slavery in allowing slaves to worship on the basis of a common religion. The logic of racial segregation in secular society, therefore, had to be carried forth in religious services. This in turn presented the opportunity for a separate black religious institution, with different worship styles and foci, to develop. The larger cultural themes and styles of the Second Great Awakening's spirituality made a good fit with the African-American religious experience up to that point: communal, emotional, heavily mythological, and largely presupposing illiteracy. Mostly left to themselves, blacks had the right ingredients to reshape Christianity to fit their own needs. As Gayrand S. Wilmore (1973, 18–19) concluded: "What both the slave churches of the South—'the invisible institution'—and the free churches of the

North developed was a religion suffused with a sublimated outrage that was balanced with a potent cheerfulness and boundless confidence in the ultimate justice of God."

Emergence of the Black Pastor

The charismatic black preacher and pastor, like many aspects of the black religious community given some reign of autonomy by slave masters and then more so after the Civil War, emerged during the formative years of the Second Great Awakening. The relatively learned but illiterate folk storyteller of indigenous African-American culture found a good fit with frontier Christianity. Writes Mitchell (1974, 66), "In the informal, folk-oriented atmosphere of the Awakening, even a black preacher could exhort and be heard and appreciated."

As the black church before and after Emancipation in white majority segregated society became a major hub for religious inspiration, moral instruction, social activities and family involvement, entertainment, charity, educational opportunities, and social control in the black community (Du Bois 1899; Myrdal 1944), so the black pastor came to fill a number of roles often simultaneously: charismatic preacher, biblical expert, at times political adviser/lobbyist in local elections and even labor broker in urban disputes, congregants' counselor, fiscal manager and fund-raiser for churches and related charitable causes, educational role model, and symbol of a congregation's material aspirations. Particularly in a minority subculture where formal education was long denied and then when eventually provided often was inferior to that of whites (either by overt or de facto segregation), "The church was the main area of social life in which Negroes could aspire to become the leaders of men" (Frazier 1974, 50). In a society of continuing discrimination and inequality, the black preacher emerged as the unique spokesperson for his (or sometimes her) constituency, an advocate, a role model, importantly a symbol of status and success, and someone more akin to the metaphor of a shepherd of a flock than was the white pastor. And while mainline denomination-switching has long been an option for many dissatisfied white Protestant congregants, such realignments had more serious implications for a black parishioner. The potential loss of an identity community was involved. The black church has been a stable safe point in a changing, sometimes hostile, world and the black pastor has been the ship's captain whose perceived strength and leadership wisdom provides real help and succor for church members.

In later chapters we develop with specific examples these themes and details concerning the black pastor in the black sacred community. What we can point to here overall is that what has impressed on the black Christian faith community the importance of the pastor is that as an institution it is a potential source of upward mobility potentially for all (Jones 1974). Moreover, the black pastor in the African-American community has assumed both prophetic and administratively priestly positions in serving the role of gatekeeper to larger majority society. (More on this Weberian point later.) The black preacher, summarized C. Eric Lincoln (1974b, 65), has always been

> The central figure in the Black Church. He has no exact counterpart in the White Church and to attempt to see the white minister or pastor on the same plane is to risk confusion, for the black preacher includes a dimension peculiar to the black experience.

This black preacher thus was both the temporal leader and symbolic spiritual figurehead for black persons' aspirations. Lincoln (1974b, 67) continued his description:

> His credentials were most often his "gifts" as they had been observed to develop from childhood. When he made good as a preacher, the community shared in his accomplishment, and when they rewarded him for his faithfulness, it was a vicarious expression of the satisfaction the people felt with their own attainments. He was more than leader and pastor, he was the projection of the people themselves, copying with adversity. Symbolizing their success, denouncing their oppressors in clever metaphor and scriptural selection, and moving them on toward that day of Jubilee which would be their liberation.

This tripartite role played by the black pastor—prophet, priest, and proxy of world social attainment—has had significant implications for the modern black congregant's experience of and reaction to clergy malfeasance. The key to understanding both of these rests in the identity which black congregants share with their religious tradition and community as embodied in the physical person they call religious guide and mentor.

Social Identities, Hierarchies of Identity Salience, and Emotion

In the remainder of this chapter we wade into the dominant social psychological perspective of sociology: symbolic interactionism.

Sometimes called more formally Symbolic Interaction Theory (though it is not really an elegant deductive theoretical paradigm in the strictest scientific sense), "SI" offers a set (and descending subsets) of related concepts that seek to explain several significant questions:

1. How do human beings as symbol-creating/symbol-manipulating creatures create social realities (as opposed to purely physical realities) made up of symbols and attached meanings within which they exchange and interact?
2. What is the impact of such learned social realities on persons' understandings of themselves simultaneously as individuals and group members, and how do these understandings in turn influence their behavior?
3. What is the individual–group intersect within these social realities?

It is not our intention to survey the voluminous research and theoretical SI literature in order to answer these three orienting questions, nor do we expect to offer anything like a primer that would adequately address the premises of the SI approach. Our interests here are too narrow and our space too restricted. However, we do need, for pragmatic reasons, to delimit the subset of SI terms and concepts that we will use to interpret the domain of black pastoral malfeasance in the black socio-spiritual context. Below we present a framework of definitions, clarifications, and conceptual demarcations to that end. Readers should consider it a progressive syllogism of relevant SI concepts, mindful that there is often overlap and not a small amount of redundancy among concepts.

The Self-Concept, Roles, and Identities

While sociologists generally define the "self" as the ongoing accumulation of social experiences and social interactions that an individual has over time, their real practical, "middle range" interest has been in the more specific *self-concept*, i.e., that an individual possesses a multifaceted sense or image of his or her own person. A person can reflect on, and have an opinion and reaction, about himself or herself just as he/she can toward another person. No one is born possessing a self-concept. Who one feels one *is*, not just in the eyes of others but also in one's own eyes with all his/her accompanying attributes, is incrementally learned through the positive–negative reinforcements of interaction with real persons according to psychological learning theory. (For a detailed discussion of the origins of the notion of the self and self-concept in both psychology and sociology, see Shupe and Bradley 2010, 39–57.) It is one of the most potent concepts in sociological social psychology.

In sum, a person's self-concept is the personally learned result of others' reactions to his or her behavior. Are you a good boy or girl? Good looking or homely? A good pianist or a clunker on the keys? You know through the eyes of others, which eventually become your own eyes of evaluation (Stryker 2002).

But as a social psychological construct, the concept of self-concept over the years has been nuanced theoretically and "broken down" into component parts or dimensions. It is not the simple qualitative concept of William James or Charles Horton Cooley of the early twentieth century. The modern understanding of self is multifaceted: among many things, it has the *self-concept*, or one's attitudes and opinions towards one's own person; it has a dimension called the *generalized other*, a supposed distillation of normative lessons learned in prior life from significant others that becomes analogous to one's internal gyroscope or conscience as a source of conformity; and it has *identities*, which are the meanings attributed to the self by the person as well as by others.

Identities, in particular, are action oriented. They are not merely our ideas about ourselves formed by experiences and others' definitions of us, but also deal with how we should consistently behave in situations (Emmons et al. 1986). The concept of identity then brings us to the notion of *role*. A role is the expected behavior of someone in a specific group position. And, importantly for the analysis to follow in later chapters, social roles and the identities formed therein, or *social identities*, are the connections between individual identity and group allegiances. One's identity with whatever group and the role that person plays form the link between the individual's concept of self and larger society. Role identity ultimately mirrors the structure of society, group demands on the individual, and the individual's sense of self, who she or he is, and needs to be done on that basis.

Thus emerges the syllogistic flow from the individual's sense of who he or she is, to psychological identification with given groups of like-minded or like-characteristic persons to which the individual is attached (emotionally or as an actual statistic), to group influence through demands of the roles that an individual fills, to the notion of social identity. True, it is an individual who has personal identity, but that identity is grounded in group attachment, involvement, identification, resemblance, membership, and even dependence. Social identities can be based on any social category: race/ethnicity, gender and/or sexual preference, religious affiliation, political allegiances, mental/physical disabilities, geographic origins, and so forth. Any role identity entails becoming initiated (socialized) and made to feel a member of a group or organization in which that role plays a part, or at the very least made conscious of one's resemblance to others who do hold a consciousness of kind. A social identity in the sense we use the term here involves the individual quite consciously feeling the identity and association with the group or category (see, e.g., Burke 1991; Gecas and Burke 1995; Hogg et al. 1995; Stryker 2002; Stryker and Burke 2000; Stryker and Statham 1985).

In their definitive statement of social identity, Stets and Burke (2000, 225, 226) maintain that one's sense of "belongingness" to a group is paramount:

> A social group is a set of individuals who hold a common social identification or view themselves as members of the same social category.... Having a particular social identity means being at one with a certain group, being like others in the group, and seeing things from the group's perspective.

Hierarchies of Identity Salience

It is truism of role theory that any person fills or acts within many roles (for example, a man is someone's father, son, employee, military officer, husband, and so forth), though usually only one role's expectations are called upon to be fulfilled at any given time. (In the event two or more roles' expectations are simultaneously demanded, then indeed there is an obvious problem—*role conflict*.) It is also true that to an individual all his or her social roles are not equally important or simultaneously demanding, just as all the groups of which he or she is a member are not self-perceived as having the same significance. Consequently, the social identities for the individual, each embedded in these multiple group memberships, are rarely equivalent. Individuals make decisions, conscious or otherwise, as to the dominance of their various group allegiances and obligations. Membership on a church-sponsored women's softball team, for example, would not ordinarily be regarded as highly salient compared to being an employee in a business or as a wife or daughter.

In sum, not all social identities are equally important, or have the same salience, to a person's self-concept. This notion of identity salience, that *social groups and therefore their accompanying social identities for individual members can be ranked or prioritized into hierarchies of perceived importance*, is a major consideration in symbolic interaction theory (see, e.g., Brewer 2001; Callero 1985; Stryker and Serpe 1994). Some attachments, loyalties, and obligations are more dominant than others. And this fact is a key factor in our analysis of black congregant response to, and experience of, revelations of pastoral misconduct.[1]

Thus, a major part of our thesis to be inductively pursued in later chapters is that the American black church's unique creation and evolution during slavery and later in a (legal or de facto) segregated society has created a special social identity for black parishioners. This social identity can result in an insular, even "garrison" mentality if members perceive their sacred community or its representatives are under attack or siege. In the case of the black church, it is racially and ethnically grounded. In other words, this identity carries over not only to their personal statuses as specific church members but goes beyond to their membership in their particular church *as membership in a minority church* in a (sometimes hostile, often culturally distinct) majority society. It then encompasses identification with the pastor as not only the members' leader but also as their spiritual representative to the supernatural and as symbolic spokesperson to the secular world.

Therefore, the effect of the black church member's social identity may ripple beyond personal membership and intersect between the individual, the church community, and into wider minority society. It is an accompanying factor of the minority community, historically and sociologically, and mediates interpretation of scandals involving church leaders, i.e., how members respond to leaders' shortcoming and misdeeds. Shortly, we will consider some axiomatic consequences of these micro–macro relationships. However, first we need to consider one final factor in the black religious social identity mix: the role of emotions within any dominance hierarchy of identities.

Identity Salience and Emotions

In the ABC model of attitudes (where A = Affect, B = Behavior, C = Cognition) maintained by most social psychologists, the emotional dimension until fairly recently has been downplayed if not neglected. Emotion can be a nebulous and "slippery" dimension after call, compared to, say, cognition. This was certainly a trend in the early symbolic interactionist thinking of SI pioneers such as George Herbert Mead (Stryker 2004, 4). This neglect of the emotional dimension in attitude study is curious since early social psychologists posited that the affective was a significant component of attitudes. As late nineteenth–early twentieth-century psychologist William James (1985, 240, 241) put the matter:

> As inner mental conditions, emotions are quite indescribable. Description, moreover, would be superfluous, for the reader knows already how they feel. Their relations to the objects which prompt them and to the reactions which they provoke are all that one can put down in a book. . . . Their internal shadings merge endlessly into one another . . .

Indeed, the early twentieth-century "James-Lange Hypothesis" of psychologists William James and C. G. Lange was the independently arrived-at proposition that immediate experience in the social environment can stimulate a visceral or somatic reaction in the person which then is cognitively processed and interpreted as this or that emotion based on cues in his or her immediate environment and/or memory. Later, more sophisticated analyses of attitude as multivariate constructs, with the aid of computers have only been able to parse out the emotion constructs from other aspects of the concept (Shupe and Bradley 2010, 71–82). That an emotional attachment to a social identity and the community, symbols and personages incorporated therein would naturally occur requires little speculation. Recent symbolic interactionist writings on group/individual identities and emotions buttress this assumption concerning the reciprocal relationship between emotional attachment to a group identity and the self-concept. As Stryker (2004, 2, 16) observes:

> In contemporary society people do not live their lives in society as a whole but in multiple smaller or small networks. I suggested [earlier] that the salience of any identity depends on commitment, the strength of persons' ties to networks in which they have roles and related identities. . . . emotional outbursts can be expected to intensify that impact of such outbursts on commitment. [Insert ours.]

And given a negative event involving a black pastor, particularly if close identification with the former by a parishioner exists, an affectively defensive response complete with denial or rationalization would be anticipated (Stets and Burke 2000). Concludes Stryker

(2004, 16), "should the expression of a highly salient identity be blocked structurally or interactionally a highly charged negative emotional response can be expected."

Thus our brief theoretical syllogism is presented. To summarize:

1. the plural roles that persons fill regularly in groups lead them to cultivate group identities, or identifications with and attachments to groups;
2. persons prioritize these social identities into hierarchies of salience, since not all identities are equally important (or dominant) within the individual's self-concept or to their self-interests; and
3. these hierarchies of identity salience have emotional dimensions, which is to say, they are also hierarchies of emotional attachment; identity salience is therefore also in some ways a hierarchy of emotional salience. Emotions, sense of group identity, and reactions to pastoral misconduct cannot be realistically separated.

With this conceptual background, we are now ready to move into the final stage of preparing an inductive examination of pastoral malfeasance in the American black (Christian) church. Given the facts of the historical evolution of that church from a religion of oppressed slaves to a free persons' (but minority) faith and its constant presence in a larger majority society, there are certain reasonable assumptions and predictions that can be made about pastors in such churches who abuse their fiduciary responsibilities and charges. To these we now turn to establish the thrust of the following chapters.

Axiomatic Principles and Expectations about Identity Salience and Race

We offer four preliminary statements about minority churches, their leadership, and the fundamental exchange relationship between both. These are literally axiomatic assumptions, not intended either as hypotheses or propositions, which underlay our interpretations of the cases presented in this volume.

1. Minority status calls forth marginalization of the group, if not discrimination and even persecution, and consequently develops a sense of solidarity and shared identity among group members.
2. Pastors of minority churches serve both *internally* as clerical fiduciaries/brokers between parishioners and the supernatural and *externally* as representatives and "frontline" responders to outside majority social institutions.

3. Congregants of minority churches lend their material and social capital, including obedience and reverence, to pastors in exchange for intangible spiritual benefits not available elsewhere.
4. As a consequence, congregants of minority churches will only reluctantly abandon that social exchange, tending to defend a pastor against critics and revealers of scandal precisely because he or she is a minority pastor.

To use a religious term regarding the fourth point, there ought to be more *forgiveness*, if not deliberately "looking the other way," to avoid confronting unpleasant realities of clergy misconduct or chalking the behavior up to idiosyncrasy credits for an otherwise revered minister, among members of a minority church. Even in the cases to be considered here, which include rape, adultery, larceny, fraud, misrepresentation and outright deception, child abuse and adult assault, not to mention verbal abuse and excessive control of persons' intimate lives, this pattern should hold true.

In a minority church, members' social identity should tend to make them more likely, at least for a time, to "circle the wagons" against nonchurch critics and adopt a defensive posture protecting the image of the pastor than would members in a nonminority church. While ours is not a comparative analysis of white–black or minority–majority churches and their responses to pastoral scandal, we believe the above assumptions help make better sense of the frequently encountered tolerance among minority church members for their leaders' deviance. We reject the conclusion that minority church members who assail the critics and whistle-blowers of their pastors' misdeeds are somehow "brainwashed" or are naïve dupes or are simplistic lockstep apologists or are intimidated into obedience or ultimately delusional. There is, as we noted above, a complex social and spiritual exchange underlining congregants' responses to scandal, or as any basic social psychology text would term it, a *transactional* base of minority church leadership (e.g., DeLamater and Myers 2011, 302).

There is little question that social identity, in this case grounded in racial and spiritual affinities, shapes allegiances and loyalties (Stetz 2004). For example, racial identity has been well researched among white and black students and athletes (Emmons et al. 1986; Sanders 1999; Sellers et al. 1998; Shelton et al. 2000; Steck et al. 2003; Thompson 2003), among other types of persons (Larkey and Hecht 1995). Social identity, we maintain, also affects perceptions of clerical scandal and betrayal of fiduciary oversight of a congregation or spiritually based group. This is an aspect of identity theory in social psychology overlapping with the sociology of religion, deviance, criminology, and victimization that has never to our knowledge been explored.

In the following chapters we turn to a variety of religious leaders within the black (Christian) church community, some minor local luminaries unfamiliar to most readers and others nationally prominent personages. We will examine sexual, economic, and power abuses, reflecting periodically on the roles of the black pastor in the black church as well as the congregants' roles. We will reflect on how those roles affect the reactions to pastoral abuse recidivism, or secondary deviance, and the part played in all this by the black and white media. Our goal in the final chapter is to present a set of inductively constructed propositions about minority church pastoral misconduct that will hopefully serve as a springboard for future research and analysis.

Note

1. The authors are indebted to Christopher S. Bradley for helping clarify identity salience as a useful dimension of self in conceptualizing the black religious response to pastoral malfeasance.

3

The Abuses of Black Pastoral Power

The "black sacred cosmos," as C. Eric Lincoln and Lawrence E. Mamiya (1990, 2) rightly state, "is the religious worldview of African Americans . . . their own unique and distinctive form of culture . . ." that authentically represents a parallel, not merely a duplicative or fine-tuned version, of white religion (albeit often Christian). The modern black church emerged out of the specific needs, hopes, frustrations, and oppressive circumstances of the black community during its pre-captivity, enslavement, and postchattel eras. According to Charles V. Hamilton, in his classic *The Black Preacher in America*, this church "was pretty much unrivaled in the black community as the major institution of black folk" (1972, 15). Long before black Americans could meaningfully belong to labor unions or join major political parties, their church was unique as an institution with "a black head and a black body." Moreover, in Hamilton's words, the black church

> was an adaptive institution. It was not wholly African, and it by no means was entirely Anglican or Western. (35)

Likewise, as we and many others have reviewed, the black preacher emerged as the first recognized, legitimate beacon of stable leadership for African-Americans as well as their link to the wider white community and *its* institutions. Congruent with similar assertions that when one speaks of the black pastor one in the same breath also refers to the black church, these black clergy have served as the gatekeepers of their sacred institutions, hence fiduciaries of their congregations. Thus, since the days of legal and later de facto segregation, they have been intercessories (or brokers) for their congregants as well as often for American blacks generally, not just between sacred versus the profane realms but also between black and white communities.

It is therefore understandable that African-American congregants display a number of sentiments regarding the black pastor: trust, pride, a measure of dependence, and even defensiveness. The black minister, for his or her part, is naturally embedded in not just a series of social roles but also, more than occasionally, in *role conflicts.* Lincoln and Mamiya (1990, 12–14) write of six "dialectical tensions" that confront the black clergy, most important for our purposes being the overlapping ones of priestly versus prophetic stances and charismatic versus bureaucratic demands. (Both pairs of concepts, of course, are based on German sociologist Max Weber's [1964a, 1964b] analyses of the sociology of religion and religious bodies' evolution.)

The priestly or bureaucratic role is one of the leaders in the established church institution that monitors worship and rituals, spirituality of members, standards of stewardship, and church maintenance. The prophetic or charismatic role, alternately, is to exhort, to criticize/judge/reform the status quo. Consider just two mundane, real-world implications of these contradictory role-demands entailed in actually pastoring, a black church. According to Lincoln and Mamiya (1990, 14):

> The charismatic tendency is also seen in the lower priority given by black churches and clergy to bureaucratic organizational forms like keeping accurate membership and financial records. From their beginnings in the "invisible institution" of slave religion, African Americans have invested far more authority in the charismatic personality of the preacher than in any organizational forms of bureaucratic hierarchy.

Thus, personality and charisma can often trump organizational or fiscal (financial) acumen for black clergy. Accordingly, the sociological consequences can shape administrative power in the group. For example, in describing such a situation of uneven leadership skills among black Baptists, Lincoln and Mamiya (1990, 42) observe:

> Once ordained and called to pastor a particular church, ministers generally are granted considerable autonomy in conducting the affairs of the church. [Pastors may also become laws unto themselves.] ... In government they may be absolute monarchs ruled by a strong pastor who, in fact, is responsible to nobody. Usually, however, some power is in the hands of the trustees and in many cases they acquire dominating power, making the church a little oligarchy. [Bracketed insert ours.]

And oligarchies, as an older literature in the sociology of organizations (see, e.g., Djilas 1957; Michels 1959; Mosca 1939) has pointed out, promote conditions of elite insulation as well as unequal power and privileges. Shupe (2007, 56–85; 2008, 51–82) has consistently argued in his "iron law of clergy elitism" that the concentration of decision-making authority within the hands of one clerical leader, or of a few like-minded oligarchs, fosters attitudes of smug omniscience, conceit, officious righteousness, and even a sense of financial or sexual entitlement.

Such leadership perspectives, coupled with the factors of a racially distinct minority church operating within a majority (and past discriminatory) society and the minority church's members' frequent trust and faith in their leaders, provide the fertile bases, or "opportunity structures," for leadership exploitation, or *clergy malfeasance*. The term "opportunity structures" originated within anomie (strain) theory in the sociological subdiscipline of deviant behavior, or deviance. It was coined by Cloward and Ohlin (1960) to account for why some lower socio-economic persons "innovate" or break laws in a discriminatory society while others do not. Their explanation was that there is unequal access to illegal opportunity situations where crimes could be committed, hence unequal patterns among disadvantaged persons in the types of crimes they commit, their arrest and imprisonment rates, and so forth. That is *not* what we mean by the term "opportunity structures." Anomie theory is a product of older structural-functionalism in sociology with a host of criticisms and weaknesses we cannot begin to explore or defend here. Suffice it to say that our use of the term specifically refers to aspects of religious organizations that render them more or less conducive to permitting deviance to become normalized (i.e., accepted by members, even considered appropriate), neutralized (i.e., explained away to members' satisfaction), or concealed (by elite perpetrators).

Finally, opportunity structures in any church, much less the black church and its unique history and positions of the pastor, are the primary source of religious *affinity crimes*. In religion the victims of affinity crimes are cobelievers embracing what they expect to be a special bond with the perpetrator whom they mistakenly believe they can trust to not take advantage of their goodwill and vulnerabilities. In the black church (written large to include black religionists of whatever stripe or denomination) the perpetrators are clergypersons (actual pastors and officers).

The victims are fellow clergy, the immediate persons directly exploited, and the larger African-American community.

Here we follow a standard breakdown to discuss these abuses (economic, sexual, and authoritative) and related victimization issues. We stress the caveat, however, that this threefold typology of abuse forms should not obscure the fact that they often occur together, or in cases where there are aspects of more than one present. While all victimization at the hands of a pastor might seem to be the result of a misuse of sacred authority, which indeed they are, nevertheless we will argue that it is useful to keep these forms conceptually distinct. For example, not all pastoral misconduct or misuse of authority is sexual or financial. Thus, we consider each variant in turn, discussing its conceptually distinctive features.

We claim no exhaustive list of contemporary scandals in the pages to come. Nor have we mounted a national survey seeking some representative sample of black churches from which to cull "atrocity stories" about abusive pastors from their parishioners. The cases presented here are simply illustrative ones, based on public reports, of clerical misdeeds supplemented by discussions with black informants published or unpublished. These instances serve to lay the groundwork for a more conceptual understanding of the opportunity structures contextualizing perpetrators and their victims' responses.

Economic Betrayals

The traditional image of the black pastor in the modern black community, above all else, has been one of success. Aside from the respect due him or her as a fiduciary link between the persons in the pew and the sacred realm, this leadership position has often been filled by persons who are charismatic and articulate, who possess at least some formal education, and who maintain model material lifestyles to some degree superior to many ordinary congregants. Hamilton (1972, 7), ruminating on pastoral images of his youth, recalls the preacher residing in a comfortable apartment in a "well-kept building," whose material lifestyle was a source of pride and inspiration to church members. Indeed, "He was one of the few black men we knew who wore a suit during the week!"

Hamilton writes of an implicit social exchange understanding between parishioners and their pastors, particularly the lesser non-celebrity urban shepherds of lower-middle-class congregations, at a material level. As a role model emblematic of their hopes and economic aspirations, says Hamilton, church members want visible signs of affluence in their leader. He observes (1972, 25):

> This has been demonstrated in the protective care some black church members show for their minister, buying him clothes, cars, food, sending him on European trips and generally seeing after him and his family's every personal need. And frequently this care is provided by church members who are themselves receiving welfare or barely eking out a living for their own families.

Writing of the Southern (not necessarily rural) black pastor, C. Eric Lincoln in *Sounds of the Struggle* (1967, 131–32), published only a few years prior to Hamilton's book, similarly states:

> There are still Negro ministers in the South and elsewhere who belong to the stereotype of ill-prepared, money-grubbing, chicken-eating, women-chasing, gold-toothed frauds, but they are, as I have said, a vanishing breed. Here and there a Baptist congregation still shows its "appreciation" of its minister by giving him a new Cadillac and a "love offering" of several thousand dollars a year, but such behavior is fast becoming obsolete.

Lincoln's prognostication of such pastors and congregational expectations is overly optimistic. The trend of black church members wanting to see their pastor (as their proxy) enjoy material comfort has not waned. This sincere and understandable desire, born out of members' high salience identity with what both the pastor and what he/she stands for, can serve as a shield to obscure pastoral malfeasance when it occurs. It is church members' satisfaction in identifying with and vicariously experiencing the leader's outward signs of affluence that can collide with considerable fiscal leeway and autonomy traditionally allotted to the black pastor [as Lincoln and Mamiya (1990, 42) and Hamilton (1972, 158–59) have noted], thereby promoting critical opportunity structures for deviant personal aggrandizement.

For example, Hamilton analyzes in some detail a complex (if older) case from the late 1950s–early 1960s bearing all the classic earmarks of parallel modern scandals. It dealt with Bishop D. Ward Nichols of the African Methodist Episcopal (AME) Church and a relative lack of close financial monitoring. Nichols (initially along with the president of Edward Waters College, an AME school in Florida) faced charges of financial misconduct in 1957. After a church judicial trial and some internal political maneuvering in 1958, a bureaucratic suspension and later ecclesiastical reinstatement occurred for Nichols. But there were further (separate) charges made by some ministers in the denomination that Bishop Nichols illegally and with duplicity appropriated church funds "for personal gain," in particular that he failed to account for almost $200,000 over a four-year period. A grand jury investigation resulted, indicting Nichols of "fraudulent conversion and embezzlement." It was learned by 1964 that Nichols had diverted church funds and donations toward a nonapproved fund in reality financing an office building that Nichols had bought at a sheriff's sale. Moreover, money was laundered, involving Nichol's daughter as "director" of a virtually nonexistent New York community center and through Nichols' wife who managed a bookstore. In April 1964, Nichols was convicted by a Philadelphia jury of embezzling at least $100,000. Ironically, a three-judge court later overturned the conviction. No one denied that Nichols had duped or misled many and funneled the money away from its declared uses, but since donors were aware of the ostensible fund to which checks were sent (though they did not know they were underwriting Nichols' real estate interests) the judges ruled there was no secrecy, hence no conspiracy to defraud, hence no "true" embezzlement.

The moral, according to Hamilton (1972, 159): "It is probably the case that more internal accountability should be enforced initially and continuously, and more scrutiny given to the legal operations of the clergy." Now, in the twenty-first century, Hamilton's words are still pertinent. Consider the following.

The Corrupt Politico-Pastor

The Reverend Ron Sailor, Jr., a former four-term Georgia state representative, son of a prominent Atlanta pulpit minister-media evangelist, and pastor of that city's Greater New Light Missionary Baptist Church, created a trail of illegalities, including fraud, wire fraud, money-laundering, public corruption, and drug-dealing. The full extent of his deviance became apparent in mid-2007. An arrest warrant for him was issued in August after Sailor bounced a $1,111 check on a utility bill, was found driving with a suspended license, and failed to appear in court (Smith and Chidi 2007). With a record of failing to pay state income taxes, he also neglected to file a dozen mandatory campaign donation disclosure reports for 2006 and 2007 (sums, it was learned, totaling over $25,000) and owed Georgia's state Ethics Commission $900 (McWirter and Perry 2008). As a result, Sailor resigned his legislative post the following March in 2008.

But Sailor's real problems actually began the previous year when he became involved in an undercover law enforcement sting. He took $375,000 in alleged cocaine profits for purposes of laundering the money to make it appear as legitimate from a man he believed to be a drug dealer but who in reality was an undercover federal agent. In a quid pro quo deal with FBI officials to avoid any future punishment, he agreed to cooperate in an ensuing public corruption investigation.

However, days before pleading guilty to the drug-dealing charge, Sailor took out a fraudulent $25,000 loan using his 2.5-acre Atlanta church complex (unbeknown to church members and officers) as collateral. To obtain the loan, Sailor had to falsify the church's corporate structure, altering the by-laws so as to pass himself off as its chief executive fiscal officer. He claimed that he had hoped to use the loan to cover his personal expenses and numerous debts. (Indeed, Georgia land records revealed that Sailor had a history of bad real estate dealing, borrowing, and defaulting on loans more than once, with at least eight or nine defaults totally at least one million dollars—Vogell 2008).

Discovered at essentially embezzling from his church, Sailor's credibility as a federal witness with political corruption investigators was, in the words of U.S. Attorney David Nahmias, "impaired pretty significantly" (Smith 2008). "At the same time he was working with the government and looking the FBI in the eye, he was working a new scheme," concluded Assistant U.S. Attorney Elizabeth Hathaway (Rankin 2008).

In April 2008, Sailor was removed by his church as pastor (McWirter and Perry 2008); in September he was sentenced to five years and three months for both the drug money-laundering and the defrauding of his church (Rankin 2008). He agreed to forfeit all property traceable to his offenses and pay restitution to his victims. With his long list of debtors from past bad deals, that last promise seemed unlikely.

Selling the Church Out from Under Parishioners

The Reverend Sailor is not the first black entrepreneurial pastor who schemed to use his church congregation's assets as collateral to finance his lifestyle. The Reverend Randall Radic, decade-long pastor of Ripon, California's oldest church, First Congregational, doctored documents so that he could literally sell his church for $525,000 (without members' knowledge) along with the parsonage and then, with more forged documents, another church-owned home. He used the collateral monies to take out loans and purchase a $102,000 BMW automobile and laptop computer. Radic eventually pleaded guilty and faced eighteen months in prison, except for a curious twist in his story: while the fifty-four-year-old pastor sat in the San Joaquin County jail over six months awaiting trail, he heard an alleged murder suspect's confession. Ray Gerald Smith, a known sex offender awaiting trial for the 2005 slaying of a woman, spoke to Radic of his deed. Radic then struck a deal with prosecutors in which the latter dropped nine charges against Radic in exchange for Radic pleading guilty to embezzlement (with no jail time) and testifying against Smith. (Radic was not Smith's pastor.) Fleeced church members were irate, but Radic avoided prison—and went on, as a "redeemed sinner," not only to create a blog for himself but also publish a book (not about his embezzlement) in 2007 entitled *The Sound of Meat* (Helgeson and Bearden 2007; Philadelphia News 2007; Winkelman 2007).

Around the end of the same year, the Reverend Donald Ray Robinson was released from a Pennsylvania prison after serving time for wire fraud associated with a real estate scam in Mississippi. His congregation at Lane Metropolitan Christian Methodist Episcopal Church in Cleveland, Ohio, had no idea that he had been incarcerated, however. He had simply told church members that he was "going away for ten months" with no more specific explanation. In his absence, some church members learned that since 2005 Robinson had used church property as collateral to take out loans and had laundered money he pilfered through outside bank accounts, to wit: he had embezzled approximately $300,000 from a variety of church sources, including funds earmarked for poor relief. He had also helped himself to a $5,000 grant from the Cleveland Foundation intended for a computer training program as well as engaged in identify theft of certain church members to illegally obtain credit cards. Robinson claimed that he was using the church property to obtain loans used to try to repay some of the funds he stole in the earlier Mississippi land fraud. But according to receipts of cash transaction found by Cuyahoga County, Ohio investigators, Robinson had in reality gambled much of the money away at casinos in Mississippi and California (Associated Press 2008; McCarty and Briggs 2008).

Arson, Alleged Government Conspiracies, and Insuring the Dead

In 2008, the Reverend Charles Koen, former civil rights activist and copastor of Christian Hope Church in Chicago, Illinois, was back in court *again*. During the 1980s, Koen defrauded a federal job training partnership program and then in 1985 tried to burn down the bank where records of his phony transactions were stored. He had used the embezzled monies for car payments, also siphoning off funds supposed to be used to pay the Social Security taxes for employees of the social service agency, United Front, Inc. (which he cofounded in 1969). In 1991, Koen was sentenced to twelve years in a medium-security federal prison in Memphis, Tennessee, on twenty-four counts of arson and embezzlement and ordered to pay $637,000 in restitution to an insurance company and the federal government. In addition, Koen was handed another three years' prison time (to be served concurrent with the twelve years for arson–embezzlement) for failing to pay income taxes during 1982–84. (Koen's case was handled by the same U.S. attorney who prosecuted the Reverend Joseph Davis of East Saint Louis, now serving a thirty-year sentence, for using *his* church as a front to money-launder and process cocaine deals—Bosworth 1994).

A spokesperson for the Charles Koen Legal Defense Fund at the time claimed that Koen was the victim of an unnamed conspiracy (*Chicago Daily Law Bulletin* 1992). Koen himself reiterated the conspiracy charges, saying:

> I see it as an overall conspiracy against African-American leadership in this country. It is a continuation of the (former) President Richard Nixon 'dirty tricks.' (Sorkin 1989)

In 2008, Koen was back working in United Front, Inc., and repeated his financial deviance. This time he was charged with being part of a scheme with several others, "knowingly allowing a company, United Front, Inc. to claim from 2002 to 2004 that it was training disadvantaged and minority applicants in carpentry skills and placing them in jobs, when in fact little or no training was being one" and collecting $4,500 for each supposed trainee (Olmstead 2008). (Irregularities about the operation came to the attention of prosecutors in 2005 when United Front's fiscal manager was charged and later convicted of embezzling money from United Front's office.) As of June 2008, Koen received a $500.00-bond awaiting trial.

The Reverend Acen Phillips directly and outrageously betrayed followers of *two* congregations, Mount Gilead Baptist Church and New Birth Temple of Praise Community Church of Centennial, Colorado, when he took out fraudulent life insurance policies on many of them (without their knowledge), making 90 percent of those policies payable to his personal ministry. Worse, some of the policies were taken out *after* their deaths but with backdated paperwork. By claiming they were employees of the churches, Phillips was able to avoid having them have to take the normal physical examinations often required. Moreover, Phillips not only took out policies on church members (living and dead) but also for individuals killed or missing in local violent crimes and named his ministry as their beneficiary, despite the fact that these individuals had never been church members nor even met Phillips.

The Reverend Phillips was accused of seven counts of defrauding the AIG Life Insurance Company (of the 2007–8 federal Wall Street bailout fame) of $575,000 and five counts of forgery. He entered into a last-minute plea agreement with the court, receiving eight months' probation, a requirement to pay $500,000 in restitution, 100 hours of community service, and compulsory attendance at a theft offenders' class and also a victims' empathy class. In return, AIG dropped a federal lawsuit, and the Arapahoe County prosecutors dropped eleven other counts against him (*Chattanooga Times Free Press* 2008; Illescas 2007, 2008). After charges were initially filed against Phillips, New Birth People of Praise Community Baptist Church locked him out, while the facilities director at Mount Gilead Baptist Church stated that his congregation would pray for Phillips and his family.

Phillips' forgery of member names for purposes of insurance fraud is reminiscent of the phony membership lists fraud perpetrated by the Reverend Jeffrey Lyons, pastor at a St. Petersburg, Florida church and one-time president of the National Baptist Church, USA, a black denomination. Lyons, featured in one of the two vignettes which began Chapter 1, sold bogus lists of his denomination's members to companies for their own commercial purposes, pocketing the sum of at least $4 million. Lyons, it will be recalled, was tried in a Florida court during the late 1990s and sentenced to five and one-half years in prison and ordered to pay $2.5 million in restitution. He spent the money from the companies (among other illicitly gained funds) on expensive cars, multiple lavish homes, and several mistresses (Shupe 2008, 50–51).

Bad Checks, Kickbacks, and More Forgery

The "Robin Hood" phenomenon, of course, is stealing from the rich to give to the poor. In a way that is what the Reverend Maurice Joseph Easley, property manager of the Mission Galleria Apartments complex in Scottdale, Georgia, and also pastor of Sanctuary Church of the Living God, was doing. Except that the residents of the apartment complex were mostly senior citizens (and hardly affluent) and the beneficiary of his *largesse* was the church he was "growing" in a unique manner. Over a period of two years, Easley redirected $70,000 in rent money (and security deposits supposed to be returned to past residents) from the apartment complex to his church's checking account. Many of the residents had been about to be evicted for nonpayment of rent before the thefts were discovered. Easley pled guilty and was sentenced to serve five years' probation and to pay $4,000 in restitution as well as complete 150 hours of community service. A spokesperson for NuRock Cos., which owned the complex, commented: "I find it horrendous and incongruous that a man that [sic] calls himself a Christian would steal from elderly and poor people to try and build his church" (Mahone 2008).

Pastor C. Eugene Overstreet possessed a colorful history of financially fraudulent acts. Around 1990, Overstreet, a Baptist minister, was ousted from his church in New Jersey after the discovery that he had a fifteen-year addiction to heroin and alcohol (McIntyre 1996). In 1997, Overstreet drew attention for becoming an adamant supporter of the Reverend Henry Lyons when officials of the National Black Convention, USA, held a closed-door meeting to decide the fate of their adulterous, larcenous pastor, Henry Lyons and offered both an emotional prayer and a five-minute argument on behalf of retaining Lyons as denominational president (McClellan-Copeland 1997). Then a year later, Overstreet was removed as pastor from Thankful Baptist Church after he and several members quarreled with church deacons over financial matters (Shah 1998).

Overstreet emerged soon after to start his own house of worship, Cathedral Church, in Decatur, Georgia. But in 2006, Overstreet was charged and convicted of passing worthless checks (a Class D felony) and given a four-year sentence with probation and victim restitution. To make things more complex, the pastor became entangled with a local sheriff in a truly bizarre pair of illegal affairs: first, a "scheme to extort money from store owners whose country of origin was India," and second, a macabre plan involving smuggling drug proceeds to Mexico via cremation urns in which the money would be hidden under cremated human remains.(Lazenby and Gregory 2008). Apprehended by FBI officials, Overstreet turned informant on the sheriff and became a witness against the latter in his trial. Later, all drug charges against the pastor were dropped by agreement with federal officials (Mercer 2008).

Lastly in this economic fraud sampler, we mention the Reverend Nigel Osarenkhoe. Osarenkhoe was also an employee of the Administration for Children's Services in New York City, specifically an adoption supervisor. In that role he conspired with two other child welfare officials between 2004 and 2007 to funnel sham adoption subsidy payments out of the agency $32 million-per-month budget to selected persons, many of whom were not really foster parents, in individual amounts as large as almost $80,000. In return, Osarenkhoe received kickbacks. One single mother in Queens, who worked for Osarenkhoe, pocketed $250,000 altogether. Additionally, it appeared likely that Osarenkhoe was counterfeiting checks and passing bogus subsidies on to pseudofoster parents who were members of his congregation, prosecutors were learning during the ongoing investigation. Once Osarenkhoe's supervisor confessed and pleaded guilty to charges including embezzlement, fraud, and money-laundering, the others did as well. The reverend and several other employees then agreed to cooperate with prosecutors (Lucadamo et al. 2008; Weiser 2008).

Sexual Deviance

Elsewhere it has been noted:

> Just as white-collar/corporate secular crimes receive much less media attention than street crimes yet are responsible for more widespread damage, the media pays more attention to sexual exploitation by clergy than to clergy economic exploitation, which affects a larger number of individuals and institutions. (Shupe 1998, 7)

Perhaps this is true in terms of direct victims, but entire congregations and denominations, not to mention families, nevertheless have their image of the pastor shaken and trust eroded by revelations that a cleric has violated a sacred norm held by most to be sacrosanct: that of the marriage covenant. It is a covenant considered special, or enshrined, by both civil statutes and religious communities (and enshrined in the latter's commandments). And adultery is only one possible form of sexual deviance.

Defining Sexual Deviance

Sexual malfeasance by pastors is often compounded with other forms of misconduct (deliberate fiscal misappropriation and excessive use of authority). The Reverend Henry Lyons of St. Petersburg, for example, used the monies that he stole when he sold fictitious denominational lists to commercial organizations and embezzled at least $244,500 from funds donated by the Jewish Anti-Defamation League (among other contributors) to help rebuild burned southern black churches to support several mistresses in sumptuous lifestyles. He bought a $700,000 waterfront home near St. Petersburg for one mistress, Bernice V. Edwards, and was negotiating with her to buy a palatial $925,000 mansion in Charlotte, North Carolina, it was learned by investigators (Shupe 2007, 68–69).

But sexual deviance is distinct enough to be considered in its own right. One sometimes hears the phrase that "pastors are only human," but that fact does not obviate the harm of their sexual deviance. We leave it for those who insist on placing their religious leaders on pedestals to ponder the implications of this ironic inconsistency. Flings and affairs, philandering and adultery are, to be sure, not against any civil laws. Not all pastoral sexual deviance is illegal, just immoral and dishonest by clear religious standards, but it is with criminal behavior that we are concerned here.

Let us be clear in our definition of pastoral sexual malfeasance, a definition consistent with both the Judeo-Christian culture of the society within which black churches operate and hold their theologies. The social responsibility of a pastor is breeched in circumstances when

1. the married preacher has sexual relations with persons other than his/her legal spouse;
2. the pastor, as a person empowered by sacred tradition to perform sacraments, executes the latter in ways that contradict legal statutes and pose disadvantages to the well-being of followers;
3. the minister engages in personal sexual behavior that is not only illegal but also contrary to church mores and would be regarded by church members and nonmembers alike as a sign of mental or emotional illness, obsession, or gross immaturity; and
4. violates or endangers the nurturing intimate nature of the marriage covenant.

This is an inclusive net, for human sexuality often takes various orientations and objects of interest.

Assorted Cases in Sexual Deviance

Clearly the much publicized Lyons case is an example of the first type of deviance defined above. Lincoln (1967, 131) and Hamilton (1972, 5) make general reference to this kind of infidelity problem with some pastors. (No estimates of proportions or percentages are given). Hamilton also provides one anecdote of clerical infidelity that the reader is left to regard as not atypical (23). This form of sexual misconduct by a pastor is undoubtedly the most pedestrian type of interpersonal deviance, in large part because of the exalted and trusted role the pastor, black or white, performs in the church. Remember that this leader is often accompanied by degrees and higher education, age and the presumed wisdom of experience, brokerage authority with the divine, personal charisma, and "gifts" of exposition/oratory, not to mention being believed by members "to be called" by God Almighty to this sacred office. Combined with these factors is the further possible issue of lay-pastoral "transference," a phenomenon long recognized by therapists and fiduciaries wherein a vulnerable person in need of assistance from a trusted professional with special expertise develops a view of the latter akin to infatuation, hero-worship, or adulation. It is a problem first named by psychoanalyst Sigmund Freud (who in the beginning of his private practice kept believing his female patients were falling in love with him). It is encountered not infrequently in client–professional relationships among psychologists, professors, physicians, lawyers, and clergypersons. Peter Rutter, a Jungian psychiatrist, in *Sex in the Forbidden Zone* (1989, 1–2), regards transference as a particular snare in relationships when the male professional holds fiduciary power over a woman:

> Twenty years ago I began my psychiatric practice with the unchallenged belief that having sex with my patients was completely out of the question.... It took me nearly a decade to stop believing in the myth of the beneficent doctor. I discovered instead that sexual exploitation by men of women under their care or tutelage is not unusual and in actuality is quite common. [He notes: by teachers, lawyers, physicians, psychiatrists, professors, clergy, and "workplace mentors."] ... These highly eroticized entanglements can occur, behind closed doors, in any relationship in which a woman entrusts important aspects of her physical, spiritual, psychological, or material welfare to a man who has power over her.... sexual violation of trust

is an epidemic, mainstream problem that reenacts in the professional relationship a wider cultural power imbalance between men and women. [Bracketed insert ours.]

But there are other less "garden variety" forms of sexual misconduct more specific to the preacher's role. In 2000, the Reverend Robert Eckert, an African Methodist Episcopal minister in Grand Rapids, Michigan, confessed to, and was sentenced to incarceration for, sexual involvement with a fifteen-year-old babysitter (Ostling 2000). Eckert was an *ephebophile* (having an erotic fascination with postpubescent minors) rather than a *pedophile* (having an erotic fascination with a prepubescent child). Or consider the case of the Reverend Arthur Allen, Jr., pastor of the all-black nondenominational House of Prayer in Atlanta, Georgia. When state investigators stepped in to remove some minors from the congregation's families because of alleged mistreatment of the children in church, including violence, one fifteen-year-old female testified that she was beaten when Allen married her to a twenty-three-year-old man and she refused to have sex with him (Wyatt 2001). Perhaps more shocking, Allen had so "normalized" this sort of illegal marriage arrangement within his congregation that when a judge told parents he would return forty-one children of church families back to their homes *if* the parents agreed to only spank their children with their hands (no implements) and not permit girls younger than sixteen years of age to marry, *the parents said they would refuse to observe the restrictions* (Firestone 2001).

The Reverend Jerald Schara, age sixty-four, pastor of two Evangelical Lutheran Church in America congregations in the rural towns of Berry and Marxville, Wisconsin, first ran afoul of the law when he encountered trouble with his computer. It was running slowly and locking up, so he took it to a technician who began deleting files to fix a virus-related problem. In the process, the technician discovered thirty-five child pornography images, fifteen of which displayed prepubescent girls. Schara had installed Ghost Surf, a program that allows a user to surf the internet anonymously. But Schara did not realize that Ghost Surf only disguises the identity of the consumer and does not prevent later retrieval of such images from the computer's memory. Schara was reported to authorities.

Ultimately, there is no way to know just how much pornography Schara viewed or for how long a period of time. However, he clearly violated not only state laws but also his denomination's pastoral mores.

Bishop George Carlson of the South-Central Synod of Wisconsin (ELCA) said in a statement: "... I was deeply saddened to hear of the arrest of the Rev. Jerald Schara. The Evangelical Lutheran Church in America does not tolerate sexual exploitation or misconduct, and we consider the charges very serious" (Elbow 2005). Indeed, this particular Protestant denomination has for some time been proactively in the forefront of addressing clergy sexual misconduct (Shupe 1995, 103).

The result was that Schara resigned from the ministry in 2006 and pleaded guilty to two counts of possession of child pornography. He was sentenced to four years of probation, during which time he was forbidden both to have contact with girls (including his female grandchildren) without permission of his probation officer or to use the internet (again, without the PO's permission), ordered to forfeit his computer, and required not only to pay $363 in court costs but also forced to register on the state's sex offender list (Elbow 2005; Metro 2005; Metro CT 2006).

Sometimes the full extent of a pastor's involvement in a specific instance of sexual deviance is not so clear, but a past record of misconduct raises suspicion. That is what happened when the blood-soaked body of Latrese Curtis, a twenty-one-year-old married North Carolina Central University student, was found at 1:30 a.m. near I-540 outside Raleigh, stabbed at least forty times in the neck, face, chest, and abdomen (along with considerable blunt instrument-trauma) *and* when police discovered that night a 2004 Chrysler Pacifica registered to Robert Lee Adams Reeves abandoned nearby.

Robert Reeves was a Pentecostal bishop with the Living in Favor with God Network Ministries in Goldsboro, North Carolina. It did not help his status as prime suspect when police investigators found cuts and scratches on his hands soon after the murder, or that he had been the pastor of Pleasant Hills Baptist Church near Bentonville, South Carolina, but left that calling in 1987 when he was convicted of a third-degree sex offense (McDonald 2008a). Since that time his criminal record had expanded to include financial card theft, larceny of a motor vehicle, possessing a stolen vehicle, and solicitation to obtain stolen property under false pretenses (Chambers 2008). Prosecutors drew on Reeves' past record and evidence (they claimed) that Reeves had established a pattern of making homosexual advances toward other men and, when rejected, took revenge on their girlfriends. It did not help that Reeves could at best provide an inconsistent account of his movements and whereabouts the night of the murder.

Soon after his arrest, prosecutors drew the following hypothetical scenario:

> Reeves felt spurned in his romantic advances toward Curtis' husband. (They had known each other prior to the murder.) Reeves therefore saw Latrese as an obstacle. In frustration, he tried to remove her from (in his view) the love triangle and, as one prosecutor claimed the evidence supported, "went to a store and bought a turkey roaster, stuffed it with the clothes he was wearing during the attack and set the garments afire." (McDonald 2008b)

While we have no special insights or information concerning the Curtis murder case, the entire Reeves example is one of a pastor's personal criminal legacy returning to bedevil him by casting over him serious, credible suspicion of committing a heinous sexually motivated crime.

Our penultimate item of sexual clergy malfeasance involved domestic violence between two married pastors. We maintain that such violence (technically assault) fits our earlier criteria of sexual deviance since such an act "violates or endangers the nurturing nature of the marriage covenant." Specifically, this case concerns the evangelist couple Thomas Weeks III and Juanita Bynum. Before marrying in a highly publicized 2003 ceremony, Weeks and Bynum had their own separate ministries, Weeks pastoring a Washington, DC, church and Bynum herself a nationally prominent Pentecostal evangelist, speaker, and author. However, unknown to many, they were actually married in a small private Las Vegas ceremony in 2002. (The "secret" lasted until an anonymous note was left on Bynum's car that someone knew, and a televised ceremony on Trinity Broadcasting Network followed shortly.) The power couple moved from Washington, DC, to Atlanta, Georgia, and established the Global Destiny Church in nearby Duluth in 2006, thereafter creating Global Destiny Ministries with other churches in Duluth, Washington, DC, Los Angeles, and London. Soon, however, the picture of progress and accomplishment in their ministry and marital relationship quickly began to fade.

Both Bynum and Weeks had financial troubles up to the point of evictions from their respective properties. However, their real sensational profile developed after a summer night in 2007. On August 21, 2007, Weeks and Bynum met at the Renaissance Concourse Hotel restaurant near the Hartsfield-Jackson Airport in Atlanta for dinner. Unknown to their congregation's members, the couple had separated earlier in June, and the meeting in August was intended to be a reconciliation dinner. But upon leaving the hotel, Weeks pummeled, choked, and kicked Bynum in the parking lot, in fact having to be pulled off her by the hotel doorman. Weeks was also charged with making "terrorist" threats against his wife (Dodd 2008).

After the initial charges were brought against the Reverend Weeks and he returned to the pulpit, he blamed the charges against him on the devil and publically maintained his innocence for many months. Soon after the violent incident, Bynum for her part publically announced that she forgave her estranged husband while dubbing herself "the new face of domestic violence" and announcing her plan to establish a special domestic violence ministry. In September, Bynum filed for divorce citing "cruel treatment" (Dodd 2007). But even the previous February one newspaper reporter who had been following the marriage woes did her own forecasting: "The stormy love affair of national evangelist Juanita Bynum and Bishop Thomas Weeks III, the power couple of Pentecostal prophesying, could be nearing an end soon" (Dodd 2008).

Support of Weeks was mixed within his congregation and churches across the nation. Weeks' own church ended up losing 1,600 members of its 3,400-member congregation (Dodd 2008). Nationally, a coalition of black and Latino churches, the National Black Church Initiative, openly decried Weeks. Although the National Black Church Initiative recognized that Weeks' Global Destiny Ministries was not a member of their 156,000-church organization nor did the group have any power over Weeks, the organization still called for Weeks' three-year suspension from ministry and asked churches and congregations not to support Weeks and his pastoring efforts. Citing the charges against him as injurious to the entire Christian community, the coalition also demanded that Weeks apologize to Bynum, his church, and all brothers in Christ (Dodd 2007). Weeks did issue an apology, but it was a blanket, generic, even vague apology at best.

As Weeks continued to publically deny the allegations against him, Bynum continued to receive media attention that spread her story further and further among religious consumers. Weeks attempted to counter this media push by doing an interview in which he specifically made accusations against Bynum that she had actually been the physically abusive one in the relationship and that he had never been violent to Bynum, despite the fact that the doorman back at the Renaissance Concourse Hotel restaurant was a witness and could testify how he had to pull Weeks off Bynum. Weeks went on the offensive and announced on his website the creation of the Faith-based Network for Domestic Violence and a planned conference on the subject.

The occurrence of the conference can neither be confirmed nor denied by us, but Weeks' planned plea did change. Weeks eventually pled guilty to aggravated assault charges and as a first-time offender received a sentence of three years' probation, anger management classes, and performance of 200 hours of community service. Bynum and Weeks' divorce was finalized later in 2008 after a two-episode appearance on the television show, "Divorce Court." The denouement of the drama, at least for Weeks, was tawdry: Weeks had begun work on producing a new "reality" show for television, its theme about his search for a new wife, but plans for the show were slowed when his local version of Global Destination Ministry was evicted from its campus in June for nonpayment of rent. As a result, the group had to hold meetings for the immediate future after November in a conference room at a local Holiday Inn.

A final case of pastoral deviance involves false accusation, a regrettable phenomenon which, given lay members' frequent strong emotional bonds to a minister and organizational-peer pressures on the congregants that make them reluctant to "whistle blow" on a malfeasant leader, seemingly does not occur with great frequency. But it does occur nevertheless. The following case is in some ways reminiscent of the false accusation in 1993 of clergy sexual abuse made by a young Ohio man named Michael Cook against Chicago's generally respected Cardinal Joseph Bernardin. Cook claimed that when he was a high school student preparing for seminary in Cincinnati some fifteen years earlier, Bernardin (then archbishop of that urban region) had sodomized him and another priest had molested him. To render briefly a complicated media and public relations scandal, it is sufficient to write that Cook actually had been the victim of "false memory syndrome" prompted by a therapist and eventually (before he died of AIDS) recanted his accusation. Bernardin, meanwhile, remained forgiving and nonretaliatory and won considerable praise from Catholics and non-Catholics alike in the Chicago area, even from victims' groups concerned with the very real problem of Roman Catholic priest sexual abuse of minors. Bernardin himself shortly after was diagnosed with terminal pancreatic cancer and passed away while a model of grace and reconciliation (Shupe 1995, 141–44; 2008, 162–65).

The case of the Reverend Dr. William Lloyd Andries was similar to Cook–Bernardin in certain respects but not nearly so clear cut. The December 1996 issue of *Penthouse* magazine featured an article entitled "The Boys from Brazil" in which it alleged that the Episcopalian Diocese of Long Island, and particularly St. Gabriel's Episcopal Church in Brooklyn, New York, harbored about a half dozen cross-dressing homosexual priests who engaged in alcohol–drug–sadomasochistic sex orgies with young men imported from Brazil for that purpose. They were supposedly engaged in swapping partners, getting high, desecrating sacraments, and did all these sordid things in St. Gabriel's darkened sanctuary at night. Said Maxa's (1996, 74) article in *Penthouse* of the young Brazilian men: "They were playthings for priests whose commitment to the Scriptures had long ago been replaced by a pursuit of pleasure that would fit nicely in Sodom and Gomorrah." Many payments were also allegedly made to some young Brazilians who stayed or returned to their country, two of whom were Maxa's primary informants.

The article specifically focused on the Reverend William Lloyd Andries, Rector of St. Gabriel's who was alleged in the article to have organized and participated (often dressed like Marilyn Monroe, complete with blond wig) in late-night parties at the church's altar, giving young Brazilians cocaine, prescription drugs, and alcohol, having sex with several of the men four to seven times a week, and who even married his favorite youth in the presence of several priests in a formal church ceremony with the officiating cleric wearing full vestments (Maxa 1996, 74). And most embarrassing for the diocese, the article featured explicit close-up pornographic color pictures: Andries totally naked hugging his new Brazilian "husband," lying with his legs splayed on a bed holding his erect sex organ, fellating another's ejaculating penis, and so forth.

Immediately after publication, the *Penthouse* article raised a mushroom cloud in the diocese. The Right Reverend Orris G. Walker, Jr., diocesan bishop, immediately launched a committee of investigation; people began looking into the professional background of the *Penthouse* article's author (who had been a gossip reporter for *The Washington Post*); conservative critics of such issues as ordination of women and homosexuals in the Episcopalian church began to howl that this incident confirmed their worst fears; an advocacy group of the Diocese of Newark for gays, lesbians, their families and friends decried what they claimed was the homophobia running rampant throughout the *Penthouse* piece's allegation and the subsequent shrill alarms rung by conservatives; and Andries sued *Penthouse*.

In the end, after some cool-headed investigation, things at St. Gabriel's turned out not quite as they had been portrayed in the lurid article. The Brazilian informants, for example, seemed to been in on the interview for the money and were not the gay "playthings" as pictured. Yes, that *was* Andries in the photographs, and he was gay. But the few facts in the article were so embellished and the rest so much fabrication that in 1998 *Penthouse* retracted the article and issued a statement regretting its publication, given that the magazine now had "new information" not available at the time of publication (such as the fact that Maxa relied almost entirely on the sensational unverifiable claims given to him by the two Brazilians, one of whom was already wanted by Brazilian law enforcement officials for unrelated crimes), and *Penthouse* acknowledged that almost all of the article's claims were "unsubstantiated" (Penthouse News Release 1998). (It was also learned that in August 1991, *The Washingtonian Magazine* had to issue a similar retraction of a 1989 article that Rudy Maxa had written about Jack Kent Cooke, past owner of the Washington Redskins. Maxa had based his article largely on "information" given to him by Cooke's chauffer, a dubious source as it turned out who had also claimed to have been held hostage by space aliens.)

But Andries was not off the hook for his pastorship. There *were* those pictures with him performing sexual acts on and with men. In 1997, Andries resigned as the diocese removed him and also renounced the priesthood. That same year Bishop Walker wrote in an open letter to his clergy and laity:

> To have allowed himself to become the subject of the intimate photographs shown in the Penthouse article was a serious lapse in judgment on the part of Mr. Andries. To have allowed the photographs to wind up in anyone else's possession is worse indeed. . . . In resigning as Rector of St. Gabriel's Church and in renouncing his Orders, Mr. Andries clearly understood the detrimental impact that his conduct and total lack of good judgment has had on his parish, this diocese and the church at large. In a recent response to the report of the investigative team, Mr. Andries has said, "I feel fully vindicated." I do not read this report as a vindication of Lloyd Andries. Yet I feel it is fair to say that by resigning as Rector and renouncing his Orders, Mr. Andries did attempt to lessen any further harm his conduct may have caused. (Walker 1997)

Perhaps the best call for justice to come out of the sex scandal was penned by The Right Reverend John S. Spong, internationally known theologian, pastor, and author:

> Perhaps equally distressing has been the effort of certain conservative elements of our Church, including many of those bishops... to use this story to attack the integrity of all homosexual people. These people assert that this type of behavior is typical of homosexual people. They suggest that homosexual people are not capable of permanent relationships. They urge punitive action and repression against all who have worked for justice for gay and lesbian Christians. These conservative Christians seem not to be aware that heterosexual behavior can also take bizarre, predatory and destructive forms that this Church would never affirm.

Spong, of course, is correct, as even our brief sample of cases has shown. But then, no one ever claimed that pastoral sexual scandal brought out the best in all aspects of any church.

Authoritarian Abuse

Religious authority is fundamentally a symbolic construction, therefore part of the social reality accepted, believed in, and reaffirmed by the given group of believers. Thus, sociologically speaking, in a pluralistic society religious authority flows upward from the congregants to the pastor, however, much that fact may seem counterintuitive when faced with a forceful or charismatic leader. For that reason, it is ironic that some ministers, deliberately or not, invert the social basis of their authority and forget the original intention of their "servant" role. One important meaning of the verb "to minister," after all, is to render aid or service, to help or assist. Not dominate or control.

Authoritative abuse, or excess of exercise of pastoral power in a voluntary group like a church, is, as Shupe (2007, 36) points out, admittedly "the 'grayist' form of clergy malfeasance." Indeed, we have to be careful not to define it simply by the terms of angry or bitter ex-members' accounts nor by what members of a group have come to "accept" as normal on the part of their leader(s). To be sure, these are potentially useful viewpoints, but we can also triangulate the understanding of pastoral authority abuse with legal definitions of the actions in question.

Thus, we define pastoral authoritative abuse as a religious leader excessively monitoring and controlling members' behaviors, lifestyles, and physical persons for the enrichment of the leader and/or to increase/reaffirm his or her power over those members. It is most useful to conceive of this third form of pastoral exploitation as a *continuum* of actions, ranging from rapacious exploitation, control, and violence at one extreme to questionable, at worst subtly manipulative actions at the other pole.

Some examples will illustrate the different gradients of authoritative abuse. Some can be considered sadistic or barbaric while others shade into something more akin to marginal morality and dishonesty.

At one extreme pole of this abuse continuum are the cases which feature outright physical coercion, involuntary restraint, infliction of pain, and intimidation. The most notorious example in the late twentieth century was the Peoples Temple of the Reverend Jim Jones, an ordained Disciples of Christ minister since 1964, who had pastored in the Midwest but moved his increasingly cult-like congregation, first to San Francisco, then to an isolated rural area of Guyana in South America. Jones himself was of racially mixed ancestry (probably some Native American, perhaps some black), but his ministry that preached a millennial brand of racial integration indisputably reached and drew disproportionate numbers of black (compared to white) adherents (Hall 1989; Hall et al. 2000, 18–21). Many followers were also elderly and extremely poor. In fact, while headquartered in San Francisco, Jones was regarded for a time as a progressive leader in race relations and work with the poverty-stricken. He was named one of 100 "most outstanding" clergypersons in America by one interfaith group, lauded as Humanitarian of the Year in January 1976, and was recipient of the Martin Luther King, Jr., Humanitarian Award in 1977, one year before the Jonestown massacre in Guyana (Shupe and Bromley 1980, 209).

Enough analysis has been written of Jones the preacher, the administrator, and the man to say that in his last days Jim Jones regularly ingested quantities of stimulant drugs (hence he was sleep-deprived), had cultivated a messianic stature for himself among his followers, and these factors, plus mounting criticisms of his church by families of some of his church members (Shupe and Bromley 1980) understandably lent him and his encapsulated group more than a dose of fear and paranoia from possible outside intervention.

For our purposes it is enough to cite Jones as an excessive authoritarian. His leadership style during the mid-to-late 1970s quintessentially fit our definition of excessively "monitoring and controlling members' behaviors, lifestyles, and physical person." The Reverend Jones routinely used incarceration, physical punishment, and intimidation to command compliance and perversely develop identification within his followers. Consider just the one brief excerpt below from the vast social science literature written in the aftermath of the 1978 Guyana massacre (hardly a "mass-suicide" when many adherents drank cyanide-laced Kool-Aid at gunpoint) by attorney-sociologist James T. Richardson (1982, 27):

> Jonestown was virtually a prison camp; no one was allowed contact with the outside world without permission and most outsiders were not welcome either, as Leo Ryan's party found out. Torture was employed as a way of maintaining control of members; adults were sometimes put for a week at a time in a wooden prison called "the box," 3/3/6 feet, and children were dropped into a water well for even small rule infractions. No other recent religious group of which we are aware visited such terrorizing action on its members . . .

Previous mention of the Reverends Thomas and Allen has been made. Our vignette on Thomas began Chapter 1, and we discussed aspects of the sexual deviance of Allen earlier in this chapter. But both men were also authoritatively abusive. Allen particularly had a penchant for claiming biblical justification to apply corporal punishment to those he termed "unruly children." In 1993, he had served a thirty-day jail sentence for child abuse after he had beaten a church member's daughter (Martz 2001). Besides performing marriages for underage girls with adult men, he also encouraged other adults to "discipline" children in front of other church members and with them helping. For example, one ten-year-old boy told police investigators after a raid on the congregation that as one adult beat him on his back another adult held his arms and two men held his legs (Judd 2001). It would risk banality to say that Allen and Thomas were simply "small-scale" Jim Joneses, but if the latter Guyana pastor was, say, placed at the extreme far left end of a continuum of pastoral authority abuse, then these two preachers would be somewhere only slightly to the right.

Somewhat less overtly abusive of spiritual authority, thus further to the right on our continuum, are the many cases of excesses committed in the name of *shepherding*. Sometimes the phenomenon is also called *discipling*, which seems to have taken hold as a conservative Christian "fad" in California among evangelical Christians in 1982 (though such a form of control as we describe below has probably never had one specific historical origin). Shepherding is a practice of supervision premised on the belief that some religionists in a congregation (the shepherds) are further advanced spiritually than others (the sheep, who not surprisingly make up the bulk of the congregants). Therefore, the latter need to be advised and monitored, alone or in small groups, on a spiritual level for their own moral development. A key emphasis is on the covenant of obedience between mentoring shepherd-fiduciary and the person voluntarily submitting to his or her spiritual authority. Chadwey (1990, 3–4) describes the relationship:

> There is an intense one-on-one relationship between the discipler and the Christian being discipled. The discipler gives detailed personal guidance to the Christian being discipled. This guidance may include instructions concerning many personal matters of a totally secular nature. The person being discipled is taught to submit to the discipler.

At best, shepherding is a sincere mentoring system that focuses strictly on spiritual issues and provides the sort of reflective religious solace that some persons desire as they face moral dilemmas, doubts, and daily stumbling blocks. It is somewhat akin to the notion of sponsorship in Alcoholics Anonymous and other self-help voluntary groups addressing addictions. At worst, obedience to a shepherd itself becomes an addiction, and a consuming one that can get out of hand, particularly if one self-aggrandizing central shepherd such as a Jones, a Thomas, or an Allen becomes tyrannically preemptive of all other authorities.

The problem, as shepherding's founders began to realize, is that a Frankenstein monster may be created. The minister's or other shepherds' authority becomes dictatorial, and in churches which stress that their narrow interpretation of doctrine is the only acceptable version, then fear of criticism, condemnation, or expulsion for disobeying shepherds creates a lockstep or group-think conformity that can inhibit rather than nurture spiritual development. The accompanying danger repeatedly experienced is that few persons without the necessary psychological–spiritual outlook and professional training possess the maturity to know where to draw the line in mentoring. The supervision of the sheep begins to spill over into various otherwise private aspects of secular life for submissive congregants.

As the founders of the shepherding movement found out to their dismay, many shepherds do not know (or reflectively pause to wonder) where their control should stop. As a result, one sees the cases of a Reverend Arthur Allen, Jr., whose parishioners were being told by him how to cut their hair, what books they could read and what movies they could watch, and so forth. The means to achieve the ends can even turn violent, as they did for the Reverend Wilbert Thomas, Sr., when he instructed an inner core of supporters, or "elders," to use tree limbs and rubber hoses to discipline congregational members and threaten them if thy thought of defecting. Ironically, Thomas forbade his church's members to read anything about Peoples Temple leader Jim Jones and the latter's own use of violence, corporal punishments, and intimidation among his followers. (See Hoffman 1983.)

Given the lynchpin position of many black pastors in their congregants' lives and in their churches within the black community, often supported by a pastor's personal charisma and the understandable charisma (or call it awe and respect) of office, a micromanaging style of ministerial supervision is fraught with the opportunity structures for abuse. Observes Blood (1986, 35–36), a critic of the entire shepherding practice:

> [Former members in shepherding groups and churches have recounted that they] were required to submit details of all aspects of their lives, from their financial positions to their sexual activities, to scrutiny by the elders in order that the latter might better "know" their sheep. In addition to regular tithing, usually set at 10% of income, sheep were expected to contribute directly to the well-being of the shepherds by providing such services as cooking and house cleaning. [Bracketed insert ours.]

In sum, the opportunity structures aspect of shepherding has been revealed repeatedly over time in a wide range of churches and congregations, Roman Catholic or Protestant, mainstream or sectarian, black *or* white (Shupe 1995, 62–67).

It need not involve sex or violence, but always an excess of intrusion. We leave it to biblical experts and theologians to nuance the differences from monastic and other traditional religious practices, such as fasting, normally associated with normatively acceptable ways to practice religion in a disciplined, submissive format that is not exploitive.

Finally, while many cases cannot typically be placed at precise points along our hypothetical continuum of authoritative abuse, some can be located in the general vicinity of the rightward pole. We have saved a pair of somewhat related cases to illustrate this contention. Both items cluster around the larger scandal of the Reverend Henry Lyons, former pastor of St. Petersburg, Florida's Bethel Metropolitan

Church, former president of the 8.2 million-member National Baptist Convention, USA, and former convict sentenced for fraud and racketeering, embezzlement, and income tax evasion.

After Lyons' conviction, there was some lingering support for him at Bethel Metropolitan Church. Eventually, however, the church leadership realized that someone would need to replace Lyons. In 2000, after endorsement by the board of deacons, the eligible active members of the congregation voted 200–49 in support of the Reverend Joaquin Marvin. Members reportedly felt elated and celebrated their new pastor, congratulating one another on a successful new start made for the church (Moore 2000). It is true that during the job interview Marvin disclosed to Bethel's deacons that he had a criminal past. In 1991, he had been caught passing bad checks, yet this information was never revealed by the deacons to the congregation as a whole. Later the deacons would claim that full disclosure outside their board was unnecessary since Marvin had been so forthcoming about his past.

However, within four days of Marvin's pastoral appointment, the state's Department of Corrections announced that it had research showing Marvin's past convictions for forgery and numerous arrests for petty larceny, possession of crack and marijuana, shoplifting, assault, displaying a weapon, and violating probation. In addition, at the time he assumed the Bethel ministry, Marvin had two outstanding arrest warrants, both issued in 1991. Incredibly, despite this history the church's deacons continued to support Marvin as he turned himself in on the outstanding warrants (He claimed he was unaware of them.) and was later released without further incident. Only then, after Marvin assumed the pastorship, did the deacons reassure the general congregation.

But the Reverend Marvin apparently had a temper. By early 2003, the deacons placed him on a four-week suspension. He had reportedly been guilty of angry outbursts directed at church leaders and congregants. Marvin began to claim there was a plot to oust him in preparation for Lyons' return after release from prison. The deacons denied such a plan, Marvin was fired, and subsequently the former pastor filed a lawsuit against Bethel citing a breach of contract (Moore 2002, 2003a, 2003b).

Who misused authority and good faith here? The deacons for withholding details of Marvin's criminal past (such as they initially knew) from the congregation, thus biasing the favorable vote to support him as pastor? Marvin, for not disclosing all details of his extensive offense record? Those who might actually have been planning to restore the malfeasant Henry Lyons to the pulpit? At least it could be credibly said that fiduciary responsibility was not met on several fronts.

In a tangentially related case, prior to Henry Lyons as president of the National Baptist Convention, USA, the Reverend T. J. Jamison had filled that post for twelve years. (Jamison was the black Baptist pastor convicted of lying under oath as to whether he had tried to offer a beauty pageant contestant $1 million in hush money to recant her sworn testimony that she had been raped by American heavyweight boxing champion Mike Tyson [Associated Press 1992].) After he stepped down from the presidency, Jamison unsuccessfully backed W. Franklyn Richardson against Lyons in the convention's presidential contest. Later, Jamison and allies (composed mainly of some Alabama-based convention members) were accused in a lawsuit of fraudulent attempts to keep Jamison's favorite officers in control while delaying Lyons' transition into office. While Jamison piously denied any conspiracy or administrative foot-dragging scheme, in 1995 the judge in a Washington, DC, Superior Court hearing a lawsuit over this issue ruled that Jamison and his allies had committed an "egregious" judicial fraud in his alleged administrative deeds, involving "despicable, conscious, and collusive conduct." The judge ordered a $150,000 fine levied against Jamison and several other convention members (McKinney 1995).

The details are complex, but evidence clearly showed that Jamison had been closely entangled in the political skullduggery. Was this whole affair merely administrative infighting or an authoritative abuse of denominational delegates' electoral wishes, all hidden behind closed doors and cloaked with sanctimonious protestations of innocence? Jamison claimed he was just a "by-stander," which infuriated the court. The federal judge ruled quite the contrary, railing against Jamison's innocuous version of events, interpreting Jamison's pastoral administrative actions as obstructive and deliberately inappropriate, if not illegal.

At any rate, the Jamison case was nowhere near same scale of interpersonal harm and illegalities seen in this chapter's previous examples. Yet, the court arbitrated the lawsuit to give an independent and rather scathing interpretation of Jamison et al.'s actions. Therefore, a case this "gray" should find a place on the authoritarian abuse continuum, but in some realistic minor position due to its less severity.

Final Remarks Regarding Pastoral Abuses

Our previous two chapters attempted to set the historical and sociological contexts within which pastoral deviance occurs. This chapter has presented a sufficient sample of economic, sexual, and authoritative misuses of status and authority to provide readers with a flavor for the various forms of clergy malfeasance. These three categories, it should be noted, were developed in the analysis of pastoral misconduct generally (and for mostly white churches) but apply equally to the American black church.

Two interesting constellations of conclusions can be drawn.

First, many of the pastors mentioned earlier possessed previous records of criminality and questionable behavior. Their immediate sins of sexual abuse, and fraud, and excessive control were not episodic but rather simply the most recent incidents in established patterns of malfeasance. Ironically, in some cases, such as those of the Reverend Joaquin Marvin, who church deacons knew of past pastoral misdeeds and criminality, they did not see fit to inform the congregations and/or simply overlooked these facts. This was a reneging of their fiduciary responsibilities to the congregations, compounding the malfeasant situation and making them accessories to the abuses. The situation is similar to the "geographic" cure practiced by many twentieth-century Roman Catholic bishops who covered up priest sexual abuse in one parish and simply moved the given priest to a new parish without forewarning the new parishioners of Father's previous malfeasant activities (Shupe 2008, 53–54). We do not lack for Protestant denominational equivalents (see Fortune 1989; Stockton 2000a, 2000b).

Second, when black pastors, virtually autonomous of outside oversight or control, have managed to "normalize" excessive deviant behavior in the eyes of their followers, such as did the Reverends Allen and Thomas, the congregation's survival itself is in some jeopardy. The collapse can be predicted either through intervention by outside control agents (prosecutors, police, child welfare officials, and so forth) or through the weights of complainants' lawsuits and the accompanying rapid disillusion. Such a situation is also similar to white church counterparts that enjoy "congregational-centered" authority structures. Such was the case with Community Chapel in Seattle, Washington. There pastor Donald Barnett, who started a modest Bible group ministry in 1967, eventually built a megachurch with a $10 million forty-four-acre church campus that included a kindergarten-through twelfth grade academy, Bible College, and extensive worship facilities. He also introduced a host of eccentric norms beyond the importance of his personal prophecies. These included bans on any facial hair, celebration of traditional Christmas holidays, and any hymns not personally composed by members of the congregation. Barnett also instituted the creation of "spiritual connections" among separate partners of different marriages that eventuated in touching, stroking, and kissing. These in time led to Barnett having over thirty female congregants among his personal "spiritual connections" as well as, finally, rampant sexuality and adultery among members. A much-publicized death and mounting bitter lawsuits against Barnett and the church virtually ended Community Chapel by 1990. Even the deacons thought better of what was occurring and abandoned the church (Shupe 1995, 62–63; 2008, 112).

Such autonomy for *any* pastor, and particularly for a black pastor within a black subcultural church, where his or her prophetic status is prized more than practical administrative acumen, creates a situation ripe with potential for minor and major pastoral abuse. With no one to answer to for behaviors and decisions, particularly if deacons and/or trustees are accessories to the deviance and provide the cloak of invisibility for the pastor, the resulting lack of accountability indicates an even smaller chance of internal control. That factor, coupled with the uncritical, or forgiving, admiration of the pastor by congregational members who have a specific social identification with their subculture's church, does not ensure but makes more probable some persons taking advantage of the opportunity structures thereby fostered.

Our cases so far have almost exclusively involved relatively low-profile local pastors. And we have dealt minimally with the reactions of congregants and the black community, among other audiences, to revelations of black pastoral misconduct. Now we turn in subsequent chapters to several higher-profile national ministers, and then, employing the lens of identity salience at several levels, to the social reactions to such controversies.

4

Authority and Aggrandizement within the American Black Church

Elites whose exercise of power becomes problematic are legion. In modern North American politics, for example, exploits of a large number of visible (and sometimes not so visible) elected politicians have filled the airwaves and spent unknown tons of news print. We could, say, start arbitrarily with

- Gary Hart, Democratic U.S. senator from Colorado during 1975–87 and presidential candidate in 1984 and then again in 1988. His presidential aspirations came apart when he was caught red-handed in compromising photographs showing him smirking as he cuddled lanky, smiling blonde Donna Rice on his lap aboard the vacation boat *The Monkey Business*.
- The conservative career of Larry Craig, Republican U.S. senator from Idaho, was likewise cut short after he was arrested for (and initially pleaded guilty to) "inappropriate behavior" (i.e., soliciting homosexual sex) in the washroom of Denver's airport in 2007.
- U.S. Congressman Mark Foley of Florida encountered his political demise after it was discovered that he had been sending a volume of salaciously explicit e-mail messages to at least one seventeen-year-old male congressional page. (Ironically, Foley at the time was Chair of the House Caucus on Missing and Exploited Children.)
- Similarly, California Assemblyman Mike Duvall had a secret conversation exposed in which he boasted of his adulterous sexual exploits with women, and he resigned in disgrace even while staunchly unapologetic, claiming he was only culpable of "engaging in inappropriate story telling."
- In 2009, it appeared that John Edwards, boyishly photogenic former U.S. senator and past Democratic vice-presidential and presidential candidate, had at least one affair, alongside his wife who was dying of inoperable cancer, fathering a child with the former woman. He had

- apparently promised to marry her after his wife died, meanwhile arranging to pay the woman hush money provided through several Campaign donors.
- And of course there was the saga of Mark Sanford, Governor of South Carolina, who disappeared incommunicado to not only his wife and family but also his gubernatorial staff and the entire state for a week in 2009, hypothesized at first to be hiking on the Appalachian Trail but in reality off in Argentina for a tryst with a long-time mistress, to the anger and embarrassment of many constituents.

All these politicians, it should be noted, were meanwhile apparent stable paragons of conservative family values. White televangelists, such as the PTL Network's Jim Bakker, or the former bisexual Colorado pastor Ted Haggard (also former president of the National Association of Evangelicals) who was discovered soliciting methamphetamine from a male prostitute (not the same man as his secret gay lover), could be added to such a list of hypocritical leadership. But we are not primarily interested in such nonminority leaders here. In this chapter we examine the real and putative malfeasance of a type of black pastor different from the examples in Chapter 3, a type not involved in the relatively petty or "pedestrian" sins of local larceny and duplicity towards small congregations and spouses.

Rather, this new class of pastor can be seen to be potentially involved in abuses of authority that have received some, but not nearly as much, media ballyhoo about their scandals as the politicians or the white pastors mentioned above. The pastors now examined are "luminaries," a word that refers to those prestigious individuals who stand in the public eye as gatekeepers of traditional or important values and who are perceived as spokespersons at-large for entire black communities and interests. They are those clerical elites and ministers whose opinions of a person, place, or event "stamp" it with legitimacy or illegitimacy, at least in the minds of many blacks. That these luminaries are also fiduciaries in the "trusted hierarchies" of a minority religion whose believers share a legacy of greater-than-average faith and reliance on their leaders' "wisdom" renders these figures all the more important.

Luminaries as Spokespersons

Such luminaries benefit in power and prestige in large part due to the church's seminal metaphor of laity making up a flock and the fiduciary leader the shepherd. In this metaphor shepherds represent a strong, wise, benevolent parent figure with nonselfish interests for their congregants' overall betterment. Lay obedience, reverence, respect, even material support, are all exchanged for the perceived qualities in the pastors' leadership that the laity interprets as the latter's gift back to them.

Moreover, the most important role served by these luminaries for any minority constituency is as *spokespersons*. The spokesperson dimensions of a luminary's leadership deserve brief analytic attention before we proceed further. At a minimum we can lay out three axiomatic statements about the scope of influence of black pastoral luminaries.

First, in the tradition of classical German sociologist Max Weber (1964b) who developed a multidimensional model of social status, such spokespersons possess a certain (if not easily quantifiable) measure of *power* (as opposed to overt personal wealth or prestige—though they often have these as well). This power is one that symbolic interactionists in social psychology identify as the disproportionate ability to shape and define the reality of situations for loyal constituencies. In other words, they speak *for* and *to* persons who find their constructions of reality about the social world credible and appealing.

Second, spokespersons, because of the important visible, symbolic leadership they provide constituencies, also reflect the latter's hopes, aspirations, and immediate interests. As a result, they validate constituencies. And as a further result, they tend to be accorded by their constituencies and sideline sympathizers an unspecified number of *idiosyncrasy credits*, i.e., having certain personal failings, forms of worldly involvement, or peccadillos overlooked, tolerated, or forgiven. Such idiosyncrasy credits lend these spokespersons an insulation from criticism and devalue the credibility of their detractors. The emotional attachment, particularly for minority clergy spokespersons, between constituents and spokespersons unquestionably reinforces this insulation, a point we will argue later in this chapter and in Chapters 5 and 6.

Third, accompanying the idiosyncrasy credits accorded spokespersons by their constituents, and solidifying their insulation from inspections by critics, is a caste-like crew of accessories, or lieutenants, helping to elevate the spokesperson above mundane scrutiny by nonconstituents. An "iron law of clergy elitism," proposed by Shupe (2007, 56–85) develops, eroding the feasibility and likelihood of spokespersons' accountability for alliances they form, how and where resources are accrued and dispersed, and so forth. Spokespersons are thus removed from much of the inspection of their professional affairs by constituents and nonconstituents alike.

Luminaries and Clergy Malfeasance

Sociologists of crime and deviance typically sort serious normative offenses into one of three categories: *street crimes*, involving violence against persons and/or their property, or at least the threat of such violence; *white-collar crimes*, where employees and midlevel fiduciaries steal resources from their employers by virtue of guile and deception rather than violence; and *corporate crimes*, where the very executive operation of an organization is colored by corruption, i.e., where deception and/or other types of malfeasance are de facto standard corporate policy for achieving collective goals (Coleman 2002; Simon 2006; Shover and Wright 2001).

Luminary malfeasance of the clergy variation is very close to this third type of deviance, an organized structured activity directed from the top flowing downwards. *All of the aforementioned characteristics of luminary minority clergy,* as *they act in the role of spokespersons, afford them the "opportunity structures" to pursue by legitimate and illegitimate means personal aggrandizement under the cover of sacred and moral causes.* That is, religious luminaries in any minority community of faith, particularly because of the roles they play "brokering" human concerns versus supernatural intentions and services, and because they serve as spokespersons for that community with the advantages of the relative invisibility of insulation and idiosyncrasy credits awarded them, encounter situations ripe for amassing personal prestige, further power, and enrichment.

Given the advantages of such spokespersons, it can be argued that such spokespersons for the community of faith ought to be held to at least as high a standard of behavior, if not a higher one, than their secular executive counterparts as well as their less publicized clerical brethren in more local and regional pulpits. True, this is a further axiomatic assumption, but we think it is an important one, for along with superior visibility, credibility, and deference should come responsibility and accountability. The sample of luminary black clergy examined in this chapter are seldom if ever revealed to have engaged in the pedestrian street and white-collar offenses of larceny, embezzlement, and drug-running more characteristic of persons discussed in Chapter 3 Even if such luminaries do such things, "smoking guns" indicating malfeasance are nowhere so evident and usually more circumstantial.

Admittedly, taking up the matter of clergy malfeasance of such luminaries is a delicate task since such figures (according to the theoretical logic of Chapter 3) are mostly respected leaders of an entire minority community. Their images and actions touch not just the salient identities of their fellow faith-adherents but also the identities of an entire minority racial group that has had a history of being discriminated against and viciously stereotyped. These spokespersons' images also influence nonminority sympathizers in the civil rights movement and opinion-makers in the larger media. Such an important identity salience, however, does not (and should not, we argue) exempt them from attempts at analysis. In this chapter we examine three black luminary clergies: one local, one regional, and one national. All are Christian. These case studies, more extensive than those presented in the previous chapter, illustrate the dynamics of identity salience, minority clerical influence, and the vicissitudes of public and minority reactions to controversy and scandal.

A Local Luminary Scandal: The Reverend (Bishop) Terry Lee Hornbuckle of Dallas

The forty-four-year-old Reverend Terry Lee Hornbuckle was a quintessential example of a black pastor who operated what Hadden and Shupe (1988, 43–46) termed a denominationally independent "parachurch organization." Starting out in 1986 as a small Bible study group of fifteen members meeting in an abandoned Dairy Queen stand, the energetic Hornbuckle and his wife Renee built that modest congregation into the Agape Christian Fellowship Church, a "megachurch" of 2,500 members, in southeastern Arlington, Texas, occupying 4,200 square feet on a 20,000-acre lot. The church had assets of over $64 million in the mid-2000s, operating additional ministries such as shelter facilities for homeless women and evacuees of Hurricane Katrina.

Hornbuckle was undeniably a self-promoter. For instance, he claimed on the church's website that he had earned a prelaw degree from Oral Roberts University in Tulsa, Oklahoma, and was a doctoral candidate through an internet college in Indiana (claims only somewhat true). He boasted that he had played professional football in the NFL and been in at least one Super Bowl as well as served as the spiritual counselor for the Dallas Cowboys football team. He claimed (with some justification, since they attended his church occasionally) to know such football superstars as Deion Sanders, Michael Irvin, and Quincy Carter.

The Reverend Hornbuckle's ministry was personally remunerative for he and his wife, Renee, as well as for their three children: between them the couple drove a Mercedes-Benz sedan and a Cadillac Escalade, were often accompanied by private security guards, and lived in a home valued at $750,000 while planning to move to a multimillion-dollar mansion in nearby Colleyville. Indeed, Hornbuckle was a prominent "prosperity preacher," a proponent of the "health and wealth gospel" familiar to Southern evangelical Protestants (Hadden and Shupe 1998, 84–85), teaching Agape Fellowship members how Jesus Christ and biblical principles could lead them to financial security. Hornbuckle had even written two books on the subject which he sold to congregants (Mosier 2006a, 2006b).

Hornbuckle's problems with several women, three of them his own parishioners, became public knowledge in 2004 and concerned events they alleged had occurred in 2003. They basically accused him of having drugged and then sexually assaulted them. The first accuser said Hornbuckle cajoled her to meet him at a Grand Prairie, Texas motel in July "so he could give her a gift." There he allegedly exposed himself and then pinned her down in a truck while he raped her. The second accuser said that in 2003, Hornbuckle invited her to an apartment where he ostensibly wanted to talk to her privately about a rumor that she was a lesbian (a sexual orientation against Agape Fellowship teachings), slipped her a drugged drink (He told her it was a "muscle relaxant.") and while she was unconscious assaulted her sexually. The third accuser also claimed that in the same year he gave her a drink spiked with a drug after he took her to an apartment and sexually assaulted her while she was semiconscious. (Drug tests soon after partially validated at least one of the stories.)

Eight other church leaders were initially named as defendants as well, but a grand jury indicted Hornbuckle (our focus here) on sexual assault and drug charges. (At the time of his initial arrest, police found methamphetamine in his SUV.) His behavior after he was released on $3.62-million bond, however, left something to be desired of a clergyman under a cloud. He was arrested six times after being released on probation or bond for violating the terms of that release, such as testing positive for drugs, later refusing to submit to an urine test for drug, and refusing to check in with Tarrant County officials to be fitted with an electronic monitoring device. Moreover, during the time before his 2006 trial he checked into two separate drug rehabilitation centers in Texas. On May 16, 2005, he entered the first one but on May 31 released himself because, according to one church spokesperson, "there was no further reason to treat him." Curiously, the next day on June 1 he entered a second rehabilitation clinic.

In spring and summer 2006, the Reverend Hornbuckle went on trial, accused of three counts of sexual assault, three more of intimidation and retaliation against the alleged victims, plus charges of witness tampering and possession of methamphetamine. (Each count of sexual assault carried a two to twenty-year prison sentence. And in Texas, interestingly enough, it is illegal for a clergyperson to use his authority and influence to have sex with a parishioner.)

Hornbuckle and his attorneys basically adopted the strategy to discredit the female accusers. The latter were portrayed in cross-examinations as being motivated by either money, exploiting Hornbuckle's financial success, or having been spurned after inviting Hornbuckle's sexual attention. Hornbuckle's admitted sexual escapades, the attorneys claimed, was absolutely consensual on the parts of all involved. For example, one of Hornbuckle's attorneys claimed that one woman had both financial and jealousy motives and was promiscuous, showing the jury a pair of her underpants. On the panties were pictured a smiley face and the words:

> Flirt, Flirt, Flirt. I just can't help it. (Mosier 2006b)

Another defense counselor rather lamely argued that one of the accusing women was "simply horny" and was actually having sex with Hornbuckle "the man," not Hornbuckle "the minister" (Mcdonald 2006b). The defense attorneys for the pastor also claimed in defense of Hornbuckle's admitted sexual behavior a somewhat sad disclaimer or neutralization attempt for a clergyman, that while he was an unfaithful husband, he was no rapist (Shurley 2006b).

Alternately, the prosecutorial team portrayed Hornbuckle as a playboy and a predator. According to one newspaper account:

> Prosecutor Betty Arvin said the handsome, charismatic minister used his position of trust to lure women into private meetings to drug and rape them. ". . . He prayed with them and then preyed on them." (Mosier 2006c)

Meanwhile, Hornbuckle's claims to have connections to professional football proved to have some truth to them. While both the Dallas Cowboys organization and the National Football League issued separate statements denying Hornbuckle's assertion that he had ever been a spiritual counselor for either or that he ever played professional football (much less been in Super Bowls), several luminary football players from the Dallas Cowboys stepped up in Hornbuckle's defense. Legendary rusher Emmitt Smith lauded Hornbuckle as "honest and trustworthy." Cowboys start Deion Sanders, an occasional Agape Christian Fellowship attender, became a witness for the defense, though, it was learned later, he had reportedly urged the mother of one rape victim who wanted to report the assault to "hold off doing anything" (Agee 2006; Mcdonald 2006a; Mosier 2006e; Shurley 2006c). Another fellow black pastoral luminary in his own right, Bishop T. D. Jakes of the 30,000-member megachurch Potters House in Dallas, also showed up as a character witness to testify for the defense.

Most telling from the standpoints of salience identity for congregational members and the significance that the awe of the pastoral fiduciary played in their minds were testimonies by the victims. One mother named Sheppard testified that:

> She didn't think it was unusual when Hornbuckle asked to meet with [her daughter] to counsel her on July 31, shortly after her 21st birthday. In fact, Sheppard said, she considered it an honor. "If Bishop Terry wanted to talk to anybody it was like a privilege. Because of his position, I took it, if he had time to talk to you, you were special." (Shurley 2006a)

One victim similarly echoed the same awe of ecclesiastical office and pastoral person in recalling:

> "I found it to be an empowering, motivational and spiritual church. I depended on it as place where I could feel safe." ... She said it was an honor to speak with Hornbuckle: "Not everybody was able to speak to the BISHOP." [Emphasis in original.] (Mcdonald 2006b)

During the summer 2006 trial, several other interesting facts were revealed. One was that a jailhouse informant testified that at Hornbuckle's request the inmate had once traded his prescription medicine (which had mind-altering effects, since it was intended for schizophrenics) in jail to the Bishop in exchange for coffee (Shurley 2006c). Another fact indicated the extent of Hornbuckle's presumption of his pastoral authority. Lisa Fjuller, Hornbuckle's executive assistant at Agape Christian Fellowship for five years, testified that he had made it clear to her and other staff members that when they were called to testify before the jury they were to be loyal to him, even if that meant perjuring themselves. He would not tolerate their disobedience, he told them. According to Fuller, he told her (and the others) in a forceful if unpastoral manner:

> Listen here. You better sell me like the MF [mother fucker] I am. Even if you don't love me, you better act like you do—or your ass will be put out of here. [Bracketed inserts ours.] (Mcdonald 2006d)

It was all a spectacle, which unfortunately clergy malfeasance scandals often are since they make such good media copy as the reverends are brought low, in the Dallas-Fort Worth Metroplex. In an editorial column for the *Fort Worth Star-Telegram*, Sanders (2006) called the Hornbuckle events "a trashy soap opera with a plot full of drugs, sex, religion and celebrity." The judge, he opined, was evenhanded, the jury took its duties seriously, and there was good lawyering on both plaintiffs' and defendant's sides. Before the jury's verdict was issued, Sanders concluded that Hornbuckle was either a victim of "calculating women," "out for money and attention," or that the reverend was "a conniving predator who used his position, charisma and even pulpit prophecies to gain the trust of women and then betray them by drugging and raping them."

At the trial's end, after thirty-three hours of deliberation, the nine women and three men of the jury took the latter view. In late August, Hornbuckle was found guilty of sexually assaulting the three women. The jury then deliberated another eight and one-half hours for his sentence: fifteen years imprisonment for victim one, fourteen years for victim two, and ten years for victim three, to run concurrently. Hornbuckle was also fined $30,000 ($10,000 for each victim). Moreover, once released, he would have to register as a sex offender for the rest of his life. The judge bluntly told Hornbuckle at sentencing: "You manipulated . . . [religion] for the worst possible purpose" (Mcdonald and Shurley 2006).

Some time earlier the church board of the Agape Fellowship, fed up with the sexual allegations against Hornbuckle, his overbearing fiduciary style, and his obvious personal aggrandizement, fired him, forbidding him ever to return as pastor, and changed their bylaws to forestall further such occurrences. Hornbuckle's wife, Renee, who had taken over his pulpit during his travails, was being reviewed by the church board for her spiritual "fitness." Meanwhile, to help pay for his legal problems, Terry and Renee Hornbuckle had to sell their forthcoming multimillion dollar mansion. After the trial, Hornbuckle (the "powerhouse-preacher-turned serial rapist," as one female Dallas columnist dubbed him—Floyd 2002), who along with his church officials was also sued by the victims, wanted to appeal his conviction but claimed he could not afford an attorney. The attorneys who represented Hornbuckle could not be reached for comment on his impecunious state; one of the prosecutors, however, concluded:

> When you preach the gospel of prosperity and flaunt your assets before the world, it is clear that you should be able to pay a lawyer. There are people out there that need court-appointed attorneys and free transcripts, but Mr. Hornbuckle is not one of them. (Mcdonald 2006e)

Of final note on the Hornbuckle finances and possible pastoral fiduciary excess, Rev. and Mrs. Hornbuckle sold their Colleyville, Texas home, valued at $1.9 million, which was quite a bit more than the $452,000 for which they bought it. They also sold a Grapevine, Texas home, and in April 2005 Renee had bought another Colleyville home appraised at $741,800. Regarding the Reverend Terry Lee Hornbuckle's appeal to the court that he was indigent, in 2006, he and his wife also owned a home in Lancaster, Texas, valued by the Dallas Central Appraisal District at $202,320. (Mcdonald 2006e; for complete newspaper coverage of the Hornbuckle trial and associated events as they unfolded, see Mcdonald 2006a–e; Mosier 2006a–h; Shurley 2006a–c; Shurley and Mcdonald 2006).

A Regional Luminary Scandal: The Reverend Al Sharpton of the East Coast

The Reverend Al Sharpton, who has never pastored any church congregational base and who might seem at first glance to be merely a New York City phenomenon, has actually spread his ministerial activities beyond that single urban area. Indeed, twice (in 1992 and again in 1994) he ran for a New York seat in the United States Senate in the Democratic primary and even made a rather long-shot (some would say quixotic) run for the 2004 Democratic presidential nomination. But the bulk of Sharpton's civil rights and entrepreneurial activities have been focused on eastern, not national, audiences.

At the outset the difficulty of separating Sharpton from a more visible black clergyperson, the Reverend Jesse Jackson, must be noted. (Jackson is the subject of analysis in the next section of this chapter.) Sharpton came onto the civil rights scene a generation after spokespersons like Martin Luther King, Jr., Ralph Abernathy, and Jesse Jackson. But Sharpton was directly influenced by Jackson who more than once has dispensed activist wisdom to him. Respected black journalist Juan Williams (2006, 52–56), among others, has strongly suggested that Sharpton in his own career has mimicked a "Jackson model": in Sharpton's tendencies to grandstand his presence at public events (particularly symbolic protests) and even to dominate their news coverage, to "shake down" corporate entities for personal and group donations with threats of black boycotts, to employ his followers like private armies that enforce threats, even to uttering offensive anti-Semitic and belligerent execrations against critics; all are practices scarcely becoming a responsible clergyperson, Christian or otherwise.

Recalls Frank Mercado-Velez, former Sharpton backer and CEO of the Heritage Network Broadcasting Company: "[Sharpton] is obsessed with Jesse Jackson to a point almost everything he does is patterned after him" (CPI 2004). That the senior Jackson's "style" became a template for Sharpton is no mystery. Sharpton as a teenager met and went to work for Jackson at Martin Luther King, Jr's Southern Christian Leadership Conference (SCLC) arm Operation Breadbasket. When Jackson broke with much of the SCLC leadership and left in 1970 to set up his own Operation PUSH, Sharpton departed as well to found his own nonprofit group, the National Youth Movement and later the National Action Network, which became the flagship fulcrums through which he levered a number of public and less-than-public financial initiatives.

But to be sure, Sharpton is no simple Jackson clone. They may be allies in some struggles, even competitors, but Sharpton is unique as a regional black leader, even if at times he displays the signs of a national wannabe. Sharpton, whose rotund figure is as likely to be photographed wearing a jogging suit as clerical garb, once combed his long hair straight back in a pre–World War II style once termed "the conk." Sharpton early in his life was known as "the boy preacher." He began preaching to congregations and at revivals at age eight; by age ten he was ordained and licensed as a minister in a Pentecostal church and toured with gospel singers Mahalia Jackson and Roberta Martin. Now he calls himself a Baptist. In his younger days, when not involved mobilizing youth groups against drugs and other urban problems, he helped promote and set up musical concerts for soul singer James Brown in locations as disparate as Brooklyn, Madison Square Garden, England, and Zaire. He eventually hobnobbed with other celebrities, such as the legendary Jackson Family, Marvin Gaye, promoter Don King, and professional football player Earl Campbell. He claims he had as one of his early mentors New York congressman Adam Clayton Powell (also a pastor at New York's Abyssinian Baptist Church). Starting in the 1980s, Sharpton became a lightning rod in a number of sensational racial protests and incidents and later became a force as a black spokesperson in New York City politics, eventually coming to confront both New York governors Mario Cuomo and George Pataki. Further, Sharpton continued to host a syndicated radio talk show.

In Sharpton's autobiography *Go and Tell Pharaoh* (Sharpton and Walton 1996, 2), he holds no illusions that many of his detractors view him, a clergyman without even a permanent church pulpit (or the congregational/denominational accountability often therein), as a gadfly and shameless self-promoter:

> ... the media had painted me as a loudmouth, a walking sound bite, a con artist, a charlatan, and, worst of all, an imposter, with no real constituency and no true issues, a self-created media manipulator.

Such *faux* self-effacing rhetoric should not be taken at face value, for it is presented somewhat tongue-in-cheek and ultimately meant to be self-serving. There is much more that Sharpton does not put in his autobiography. Consider the following as representative of what published sources have documented in terms of Sharpton's demagoguery; Sharpton's ministry's (and personal) lack of financial accountability and his duplicity and irresponsibility, including income tax issues; Sharpton's political adventurism; and Sharpton's overall emphasis on symbols versus substance in civil rights matters.

Demagoguery

The Reverend Jesse Lee Peterson, a conservative black activist, television personality, and founder of (among numerous other black self-help entities) BOND (Brotherhood Organization of a New Destiny), is admittedly a harsh critic of liberal black spokespersons. He considers many of them opportunists and downright predators on the black community. Yet, he has a valid point in accusing Sharpton of being an inveterate media hound and on more than one occasion acting the role of a "riot king" (Peterson 2003, 124–31). Whenever a major East Coast racial incident involving black–white violence occurred during the 1980s and later 1990s, Sharpton seemed magnetically drawn to it. His tone was often bellicose, at times pushing over the line into hateful.

For example, in 1987, there was the case of a black teenage woman named Tawana Brawley, who claimed a horrific multiday ordeal of rape and degradation attack by a group of white men. (She was allegedly found covered in racist graffiti and dog feces; however, her conflicting accounts of the attacks and other inconsistencies eventually unraveled, and it is not clear that she ever was attacked.) Sharpton, however, quickly went to her defense and turned it into an offensive against largely white judicial and criminal justice institutions, claiming first a police conspiracy to cover up their own involvement and then, somewhat implausibly as well as irresponsibly (since Sharpton had no evidence to back up his statements) that one local prosecutor, Steve Pagones, was a direct accomplice in the raping. (More on Pagones, who successfully sued Sharpton for defamation of character, to come.)

Later, Sharpton's grandstanding became more dangerous and mephitic. In 1991, a car driven by a Hasidic Jew went out of control in Crown Heights, New York, and fatally ran over a seven-year-old black male. Four straight nights of black protests against Jews, in which Sharpton played a loud and prominent role, culminated in a rabbinical student from Australia, Yankel Rosenbaum, being run down by a group of fifteen black protesters (to cries of "Get the Jew!") who beat and stabbed him to death. During the protests it did little to calm tempers, and much to undoubtedly inflame them, for Sharpton to announce at one point that "If the Jews want to get it on, tell them to pin their yarmulkes back and come over to my house" (Lowry 2003). Further, Sharpton did little, by either formal or informal means, to discourage anti-Semitic epithets that could be heard being yelled from the protesters, such as "Kill the Jews!" Many of the Jews in that area were involved in the jewelry and rare gem-import business, allowing Sharpton to take another ethnic stab at Judaism: "Talk about how Oppenheimer in South Africa sends diamonds straight to Tel Aviv and deals with the diamond merchants right here in Crown Heights" (Lowry 2003).

Later, on the same anti-Semitic note, in 1995, Sharpton mobilized his National Action Network members in a protest lasting two months outside a Harlem clothing store called Freddy's Fashion Mart (Owner Freddy Harari was Jewish.). Harari's landlord, a black church in Harlem, raised his rent, so Harari in turn raised the rent on his own subtenant on the same property, a music store owned by blacks. Sharpton took it upon himself to lead his NAN members in a prolonged boycott-protest against Harari (and not against the ultimate black church landlord), accusing Harari of being "a white interloper." One of Sharpton's operatives referred publicly to Harari as a "cracker." Under Sharpton's leadership NAN protesters spit on Harari's black customers in front of the store, called them "Uncle Toms," and yelled "Burn the Jew store down!" Which they did. In the protest's violent culmination, NAN's protesters stormed Freddy's shop, shot four employees, and set fire to the building. Seven employees died in the conflagration (see Jacoby 2003).

The above cases do not nearly represent a complete inventory of Sharpton's frequently belligerent and incendiary rhetoric nor his entrepreneurial involvement in what he perceives, or believes others will perceive, as racial injustices. We conclude that Sharpton knows how to manipulate black resentments, imagery, and caricatures of adversaries in as coarse a way as any other demagogic spokespersons, including Minister Louis Farrakhan (whom we deal with later in this chapter).

Lack of Financial Accountability and Responsibility

The Reverend Al Sharpton has demonstrated two remarkably persistent themes in money matters.

First, he has employed a "shakedown" tactic (learned from his mentor Jesse Jackson) in which he mobilizes (or threatens to mobilize) his National Action Network followers and sympathizers to boycott and demonstrate against companies and economic entities from which he often demands financial concessions and personal fees and/or "donations" to his nonprofit NAN. To Sharpton's admirers this metaphoric "David vs. Goliath" style of confrontation poses a bold financial comeuppance against largely white corporate America when it is successful. To others it more closely resembles extortion, even if done in the name of civil rights.

Second, Sharpton undeniably, even contemptuously has welched on legal settlements against him, reneging on his apartment's rental payments, and recidivistically evaded his tax responsibilities at local, state, and federal levels. All this is done by Sharpton in seemingly deliberate fashion, clouding his nonprofit "ministry" ledgers with his personal income and expenses so as to obfuscate investigations and indictments. To put it somewhat more euphemistically: "Sharpton's personal and public finances have always coexisted closely alongside his nonprofit organizations" (CPI 2004, 4).

Sharpton regularly takes up "love offerings" when he guest preaches in churches, not an unusual practice for visiting evangelists, but the money that goes into his pocket also goes mostly unreported for tax purposes. However, overall Sharpton's money comes from a variety of sources.

In 2005, he loaned himself out as an ad-man, paid to do commercials for the LoanMax company. LoanMax specialized in offering loans to poor minorities with bad credit histories. Loans of money were made at very high rates, but in addition to interest persons taking out the loans had to put up their car titles as collateral (thus defaulters also lost their vehicles if they could not keep up payments—see Williams 2006, 53).

But unquestionably the most controversial source of income for Sharpton personally as well as for NAN have been Sharpton's "shakedowns," as they have been termed by his critics. For example, in 2007, Anheuser-Busch, brewer of Budweiser and Michelob beers, was handed a subpoena as part of an Internal Revenue Service Investigation of wealthy corporations which donated to Sharpton's NAN in exchange for the dubious advantage of Sharpton calling off real or threatened boycotts *and* at the same time being solicited by Sharpton for donating money to, and sponsorship of, NAN events. In 2007, the beer manufacturer donated between one hundred thousand dollars and half a million dollars to NAN. This threat-and-pay off-scenario more than a little has approached a racket. And AB was just one of many corporations that had donated to NAN under similar Sharpton pressure (Bennett 2008).

Journalist Juan Williams (2006, 54) has reported that for staging (and sometimes leading) so-called "civil rights" protests against alleged offending companies, Sharpton typically pockets a minimum of $10,000. In fact, sometimes he is paid by a company's rival(s) to stage such protests, even when racial issues are virtually nonexistent. This happened in 2002 when Detroit's white-owned Adell Broadcasting Corporation, failed to convince another white-owned cable television company, Charter Communications, to carry some of Adell's programming. Adell hired Sharpton to stage a racially trumped-up, bogus protest in front of Charter's St. Louis offices. Recounts Williams (2006, 54): "[In St. Louis] Sharpton got out of a limousine . . . to lead three busloads of protest members in chants of 'No Justice, No Peace.'"

Protesters in this instance were partly recruited from homeless shelters and paid $50 apiece plus a meal. (According to Williams, the Reverend Jesse Jackson had also been similarly paid by Adell to put pressure on Charter.)

In another 2002 media case, the EchoStar Communications Corporation and its DISHNetwork became Sharpton's targets. EchoStar carried twenty-one public interest channels offering educational and other informational programs aimed particularly at minority communities, and one year earlier was considering over a dozen applicants to be added to its programming lineup. Among these applicants was ColoursTV, a nonprofit African-American-owned-and operated network, the board of directors for which included leaders from the Urban League, the National Association for the Advancement of Colored People (NAACP), and the Black United Fund. DISHNetwork selected ColoursTV and StarNet to join EchoStar's total package. Sharpton's own Word Network was one of the original applicants but was rejected. In an obvious case of frustrated self-interest, having little or nothing to do with racial discrimination, NAN became the vehicle for Sharpton's initial protest against EchoStar in 2002, charging that EchoStar had not made its public inspection files available (as required by the Federal Communications Commission). EchoStar executives, including its Chief Executive Officer and Chair, said they had offered to meet with Sharpton and Word Network associates, but they were stonewalled. Instead, Sharpton turned to loud visual protests (Ironically, EchoStar was anticipating a merger with DIRECTV, which carried Sharpton's Word Network; by merging the two would have added six million viewers to Word Network—see EchoStar 2002).

Sharpton also took $500,000 from Plainfield Asset Management, a Connecticut-based firm, in 2008, for lending his name to the Education Equality Project (EEP). The EEP was an initiative ostensibly intended to help ameliorate the unquestioned white–black achievement gap in school. The $500,000 was actually funneled through the nonprofit Education Reform Now group and was paid to Sharpton and NAN in inconspicuous increments to help pay NAN's $1 million, which it owed the IRS in back taxes and penalties. But Sharpton's involvement with EEP was to help a former New York Chancellor, Harold Levy, who had gone on to become a Plainfield executive. At the time Plainfield was actually a major investor in gaming/gambling operation, pressuring New York City and New York State officials to approve two negotiations with hundreds of millions of dollars. For using Sharpton's name, Plainfield took its donations to Sharpton-NAN as a charitable tax donation (CPI 2004, 4–6).

Under Sharpton's leadership NAN between 1994 and 2006 saw revenues go up from $200,000 to $2 million. Little of those monies were derived from NAN membership fees, however. Rather, most came from corporate shakedowns such as Anheuser-Busch experienced and donor *largesse*, the latter particularly from entertainment and fashion industries. For example, in 1979, the biggest single NAN donor was Sharpton's old friend from show business days, boxing promoter Don King ($245,000). And that type of source is where much of the money to underwrite Sharpton's activities and lifestyle have come from.

Much of what we specifically know of Sharpton's income and various economic ventures comes often from his legal entanglements and tax woes. All in all, for a pastor, Sharpton is a terrible steward of his personal finances, a poor role model for aspiring black entrepreneurs, and a virtual absentee when it comes to taking responsibility for his personal business and nonprofit entities.

To wit: In 1989, Sharpton was indicted by a grand jury on sixty-seven tax evasion charges (but not convicted), all the while flippantly claiming that he was "now going to join the black leader tax indictment hall of fame," referring to . . . whom? Bishop "Daddy" Grace or Father Divine, who also encountered troubles over their failure to pay taxes? Prosecutors claimed Sharpton looted a quarter of a million dollars from his early National Youth Movement, writing personal checks for cash out of the group's bank account, falsifying records, and soliciting money for the group that it never received (CPI 2004, 14).

From 1993 to 2002 the New York State Department of Taxation and Finance filed eight complaints against Sharpton and his wife, totaling more than $75,000. The federal government alone held $37,449 in liens against the Sharptons, but by 2003 he still had not paid up and dismissively ignored them. Sharpton's response, tinged with mockery, was that the government should instead pay *him* (a descendent of slaves) reparations, "a position that turns his troubles into a political protest that resonates with supporters" (CPI 2004, 4). By 2008, Sharpton, his business entities, and NAN owed millions of dollars in back taxes. As of 2006, NAN alone owed $1.9 million in just payroll taxes and related penalties (Bennett 2008).

Sharpton has shown he is at times seriously remiss at paying back taxes and other debts. The Center for Public Integrity (2004, 1) has concluded that Sharpton "has been publicly branded a slanderer and faced numerous lawsuits and a few criminal charges for flaunting tax laws, refusing to pay bills, and mismanaging his nonprofits in the 1980s and early 1990s." In June 1998, for example, the owners of Sharpton's Crown Heights, New York apartment began eviction proceedings against the Sharpton family because the Reverend owed them $6,000 in back rent. A housing court ordered Sharpton to pay the money, but six months later he was back in court because the same owners claimed he still owed them the original unpaid rent *plus* another $11,000 in rent chalked up during the interim. "He attributed the lapses in rent to his increased advocacy activities, which demanded money and time that prevented him from preaching, his main source of income." Meanwhile, in 2008, he owed $931,397 in back federal taxes and $365,551 in New York City taxes (CPI 2004, 4).

Perhaps the clearest picture of Rev. Sharpton's murky financial status is provided by the slander lawsuit against him brought by Steve Pagones, a New York district attorney in the Tawana Brawley case. During a courtroom rant and likewise in the media, Sharpton wildly tried to paint Pagones as an actual accomplice in the alleged rape. Pagones sued Sharpton and two Brawley family attorneys (both of whom were later disbarred for unethical behavior) for defamation of character. In July 1999, Pagones finally won a settlement of $65,000 against Sharpton. Then, after trying unsuccessfully to garnish Sharpton's shifting sources of income and Sharpton's paying little or a nothing of the settlement, Pagones filed a second suit. This second lawsuit resulted in a number of revealing depositions from the Sharpton side that provided interesting information on the activist preacher and his finances. For example,

> Sharpton claimed that by 2000 he had last filed a U.S. personal income tax return in 1998, and he could not remember if he had sent his accountants any of the information necessary for them to request an extension for filing his 1999 return. Meanwhile, Sharpton's attorneys told the court the preacher had no savings or checking accounts, no stock certificates, no U.S. Savings Bonds, and—somewhat dubiously—that though Sharpton was not the legal owners of the clothes on his back he did indeed own his wrist watch and wedding ring. (CPI 2004, 4–5). Also in that suit's deposition it emerged that Sharpton at the time received $73,000 annual salary from NAN, that NAN paid his daughters' tuition for a private school, and that NAN gave him $1500 a month for his home's rent and utilities. Financial disclosures in 2003 showed Sharpton had received $20,000

("against future revenues") in 2002 from one of his companies, Rev. Al's Productions. From another personal enterprise, RawTalent, Sharpton received $40,000. However, Sharpton refused to hand over any of his 1995 tax returns concerning Rev. Al's Productions, saying his accountants were "in discussion" with the IRS. He also claimed that he had lost the list of individual donors who donated to Rev. Al's Productions because the relevant records were lost in a February 2005 fire at NAN's office (where Sharpton's financial ventures' records were generally kept). (CPI 2004, 5)

Note finally that, as mentioned above, NAN at one time paid his daughters' tuition to a private school. In 2001, Sharpton double-dealt with Edison Schools, a charter school corporation that had made preliminary agreements with New York City to receive $250 million of taxpayer money to jump-start five troubled inner-city schools. Sharpton initially signed on to support Edison, but as unions complained and he smelled the populist scent in the wind, Sharpton switched course and became Edison's vocal nemesis. He piously stated his public argument against public school monies being used to fund private schools: "People who want private solutions should pay for it [sic]." Yet Sharpton, as nonprofit NAN officer, *illegally* took an interest-free loan of $17,220 from that organization to help pay to enroll his daughters' in a private school!

And these represent just a sample of Sharpton's Byzantine intermingling of private businesses, cash and recorded donations, and dubious nonprofit activities. The Sharpton financial picture has had the activist repeatedly in the courts; time and again in trouble with local, state, and federal tax agencies; and all this despite the continued presence of his accountants and lawyers. The picture is convoluted and obtuse. As the Center for Public Integrity (2004) summed it up:

> Sharpton has built, with the aid of a core of wealthy contributors, a small empire of tax-exempt and for-profit companies and mingled their finances to confuse creditors and tax collector alike. When called to account, he conflates his personal travails with his civil rights crusading, turning his own questionable practices into a vehicle for self-promotion and raising his political clout.

It could be argued (as Sharpton often does loudly) that Rev. Sharpton is a victim of government scrutiny because he is a visible civil rights activist and a prominent black spokesperson who makes the white power structure uncomfortable. This charge might seem at first reasonable if one considers revelations about how the FBI leaked compromising, embarrassing information and even deliberate misinformation about other black leaders to "cooperative journalists" who would help spread deliberately contrived stories about them in attempts to undermine their public credibility. This indisputably has happened in the past with black activists such as the Reverend Martin Luther King, Jr. (Garrow 1981) and Minister Louis Farrakhan (Gardell 1996). But a closer look at Sharpton's financial wheeling-dealing belies this possibility. In the phenomenon of attracting legal and governmental attention to his finances, Sharpton is a self-made man.

This was particularly true after Sharpton was videoed in what compromisingly appeared to be an attempt to negotiate a drug deal with an undercover officer during the late 1980s. Despite Sharpton's earnest and pious denials, there is now an abundance of evidence—prosecutors would call it proof—that he did work as an informant pertaining to drug-dealing for the Federal Bureau of Investigation. He provided firsthand information, snitching on celebrities, such as boxing promoter Don King, and black politicians as well as organized crime luminaries and crack dealers. This is by his own admission and according to published interviews with him (see e.g., Taylor 1998b, 227–29).

Political Adventurism

As noted earlier, Sharpton was twice a Democratic U.S. senatorial candidate from New York and later a Democratic presidential candidate in 2004. (Sharpton also ran for the New York State Senate in 1978 but later was disqualified because he did not meet residency requirements.)

But Sharpton's meteoric rise-and-fall candidacies at any level had neither the inspirational, ground-breaking significance and impact of the Reverend Jesse Jackson's two presidential nomination campaigns nor Jackson's staying power as an important player on the national political scene. For example, Sharpton's 1992 run for the United States Senate as a democratic candidate garnered 20 percent of the New York City vote but only 14 percent of the statewide vote. (Not surprisingly, he obtained 67 percent of the black vote statewide but clearly did not attract numbers of white liberals.) His brief fling in the Democratic presidential primaries was just that. (But it did give him the visibility opportunity to stand shoulder-to-shoulder with other more seasoned primary candidates in early debates for a time.)

Two rather questionable activities in Sharpton's 2004 bid for Democratic presidential nomination illustrate his political adventurism with characteristic flamboyance.

First, during the campaign Sharpton reportedly took $200,000 from Roger Stone, a political strategist and known Republican activist. According to journalist Williams (2006, 52), Stone's previous foray into the black political arena was during the 2000 presidential election when he allied himself with those conservatives trying to prevent a recount of black and Jewish (presumably more likely to vote Democratic) voters in the controversial Miami-Dade County vote-tallying. But in 2004, Sharpton brought Stone and his money onboard his primary campaign and actually appointed Stone a top aide. It appeared to observers that Stone was really functioning as a Republican agent provocateur, pushing Sharpton's left-of-center message in order either to shift mainstream Democrats in that direction or to make Sharpton a contentious player with whom other Democratic primary candidates would have to deal—all of which would eventually help any Republican nominee's cause. Williams (2006, 52) concluded that if Jesse Jackson at least had tried to bring black persons and their issues onto the national presidential stage, enhancing black pride and such persons' interest in national politics, "Sharpton, by contrast, was running a campaign solely about his own personal ambitions to get on the national stage, even to the point of working as a mole inside the Democratic primary for the Republican Party..."

Second, during the campaign there was evidence of Sharpton's spendthrift and dissolute behavior, accommodating himself with a flamboyance worthy of an earlier Father Divine or Bishop "Daddy" Grace. According to at least one journalistic report, Sharpton and his campaign entourage lived "high on the hog" during their travels whereas most more serious candidates usually are perennially cash-strapped and economize when ever possible in such matters as travel and accommodations. Sharpton et al. stayed in the nation's more expensive and swankiest hotels. On one visit, the Sharpton party stopped at the Four Seasons Hotel in Los Angeles for a rather high-priced layover. That visit alone cost five percent of the entire cash Sharpton had raised in the third quarter of the previous fundraising period (Lowry 2008). Sharpton may have been sinking money from his tax-free "love offerings" back into his campaign, but by 2008 his failed campaign's use or misuse of funds were under federal investigation (Bennett 2008).

Conservative columnist Rich Lowry (2008) considers Sharpton to be one in a line of political entrepreneurs who gained short-run visibility and enriched themselves in the process by staging quixotic runs for the U.S. Presidency (along with others such as Pat Buchanan and Alan Keyes):

> But Sharpton has no measurable policy proposals, no distinctive ideological position, nothing but himself and his resume.... With Sharpton the dumbing down of presidential candidates is complete.

Symbols versus Substance

The overall indictment of the Reverend Al Sharpton as a black spokesperson has come with his reluctance to move beyond hoary slogans and posturing that had some true meaning during the 1950s and 1960s but now have become hackneyed, out-of-step, and more mantra-repetition (while perhaps still useful for self-aggrandizement) than reflective of the actual twenty-first-century civil rights situation. While *Wall Street Journal* commentator Al Hunt (2002) declared black leaders like Sharpton "irrelevant," black NPIR/television journalist Juan Williams (2006, 47) has been more critical of Sharpton being historically behind the times while still vocal, raising tired symbols rather than real issues of substance:

> Black politics is still defined by events that took place forty years ago. Protest marches are reenacted again and again as symbolic exercises to the point that they have lost their power to achieve change. As a result, black politics is paralyzed, locked in synchronized salute and tribute by any mention of the martyrs, the civil rights workers who died violent deaths at the hands of racists.

Sharpton, in other words, speaks with his rhetoric of iconic historical figures and old semiotics, rallying his followers with worn-out images that once possessed bite but now are only clichés. A classic but recent example of such empty posturing, with manufactured outrage that poorly reflects modern realities, occurred when the Reverends Jesse Jackson and Al Sharpton ventured to Harvard University's campus in late 2001. It had become known that Dr. Cornell West of the Afro-American studies department had taken offense at comments made generally and specifically by the school's president, Dr. Larry Summers. Summers simply urged West to engage in more scholarly research and less "pop" activities as well as to join in a Harvard problem affecting other universities in the United States, namely, grade "inflation," i.e., no longer giving "Gentlemen's C's but now Gentleperson's A's and B's" for otherwise average work. (And at that time West's most memorable recent work had been participating in a rap CD.) As a result, West and several others in his department, including his distinguished colleague Henry Louis Gates, Jr., threatened to leave Harvard and move to Princeton University.

Enter Jackson and Sharpton, both of whom claimed Summers had "dissed" West, and by extension, black studies. It may or may not be of consequence that President Summers had been giving the identical message on grade inflation generally to other units of the university. Jackson, who had never even spoken to Professor West about the alleged incident, "stormed into Cambridge demanding a meeting with Harvard's president" (which Jackson never obtained), and the grandstanding Rev. Sharpton belligerently threatened to sue Harvard (on what grounds he did not say). As journalist Hunt (2002) concluded (and presciently so when he anticipated Sharpton's next ill-fated political bid):

> Jesse Jackson and Al Sharpton often seem irrelevant relying chiefly on a press that feeds and stokes the faux conflicts on which they thrive.... The shrill and silly conduct [of Sharpton] reinforces the political bankruptcy of the national black politicos. Jesse Jackson has made important contributions to politics and civil rights; now he looks like a headline-hunting ambulance chaser. Al Sharpton may be shrewd, but this performance, coupled with his past demagoguery, make it impossible to treat his threatened 2004 Presidential run seriously.

In summing up the Reverend Al Sharpton we conclude:

Sharpton is actually a post-civil rights movement black pastor, operating in an era when activist giants have largely passed on. That cherished illusion of being an important racialist spokesperson, by itself, however, does not make Sharpton malfeasant. Rather, significant evidence of his misconduct can be found in such things as: his unpastoral hate-speech demagoguery; his cavalier disregard for courts and rule of law, court-orders, and financial responsibilities incumbent upon a pastoral steward who is also a financial fiduciary; and his personal aggrandizement in the name of higher spiritual and humane purposes.

A National Luminary Scandal: The Reverend Jesse L. Jackson, Sr.

To suggest consideration of the Reverend Jesse L. Jackson, Sr. (hereafter Jesse Jackson), within the same framework of malfeasance akin to the pastors previously described, particularly with the likes of a rapacious deviant cleric like Dallas' Bishop Terry Lee Hornbuckle, may seem, to say the least, inappropriate, if not a travesty of responsible comparison. Jackson is, to put it bluntly, an icon, one of the most readily recognizable social and political leaders in America of the twentieth and twenty-first centuries, black or white. Civil rights and antidiscrimination activist, having worked directly with the venerable Martin Luther King, Jr.; advocate for educational reform and student responsibility; living symbol of urban black empowerment; champion of black capitalism and entrepreneurial values; international mediator and moral protagonist for national and international minority causes; twice a serious contender for the Democratic Party's presidential nomination: Jackson has either been all of these or certainly portrayed himself acting in these roles.

But Jesse Jackson has not been a one-eyed Jack. He has two eyes, two sides to his persona, even if a virtual cult of respect for his public pronouncements and activities has at times obscured what is sometimes behind them and how Jackson had consistently crossed the lines of boldness and unconventional initiative into seriously questionable self-aggrandizement, cultivation of affinity with criminality, and hypocrisy. We do not intend to question Jackson's enormous importance as a moral spokesperson for the black community. We do not deny his hard-earned significance as a major player in the national political arena. We admire his undeniable key historical participation in the civil rights crusade of American history. Yet he is, by any of the accounts we cite or summarize, a complex checkered human being. As we shall document within our limited context of pastoral deviance, Jackson has not always been the exemplar of any virtue that he has preached. His episodic-to-chronic foibles and malfeasance as a pastor are matters of record, if not always generally acknowledged.

Some Consideration of Jesse Jackson's Early Years

Virtually every analysis of Jackson's activities, from apologetic treatments boarding on puffery (Stone 1984) to journalistic coverage (Colton 1989; Faw and Skelton 1986; Frady 1996; Reynolds 1975) to hostile criticism (Timmerman 2002) has backtracked to examine

Jackson's social origins, up-bringing, and experiences later as a proud, talented young black man growing up in the segregated South. This is because the infrastructure of his personality and closely-tied ambitions were laid early. His soaring pronouncements, his tendencies to stretch the truth and alternate between belligerent and inspirational rhetoric, his personal drive to carve out a niche for himself in black American history as well as beyond: all have to be linked to his formative years if any sense is to be made of his pastoral adventures.

For this reason, it is worth first briefly considering something of the factors of Jackson's youth and the times during which he grew to adulthood as they help adumbrate the facts and patterns of his later behaviors. We by no means attempt anything resembling a psycho-biography of the Reverend Jackson. We are social psychologists, not psychiatrists or psycho-historians. Nevertheless, enough reliable observations have been recorded of Jackson's early life in the segregated South, and enough of it rings true in foreshadowing his adult social, economic, and political activities, to warrant some preliminary mention of Jackson's early years and their influence on his later fiduciary behaviors.

Thus, on October 8, 1941, an unmarried black teenager named Helen Burns, who possessed a flair for music and once held dreams of pursuing an entertainment career, gave birth to a baby boy whom she named Jesse Louis Burns. The father, Noah Robinson, was already married to a woman with children of her own from a previous marriage. The birthplace was Greenville, South Carolina, a textile mill town near the Blue Ridge Mountains with a community of racial segregations as structurally severe as anywhere in the South. Helen was initially stigmatized and ostracized as an unwed mother within the local black community to the point that she was forced to leave her Baptist church.

After Jesse's birth, Noah Robinson contributed financially to Helen's single-parent household. Three years later she married Charles Henry Jackson (who gave Jesse the surname he used thereafter), a man who had once worked at a shoe-shine stand and performed miscellaneous other jobs, and had several more children by Charles. It was generally a lower-middle-class economic existence at best, and times were not always good. During that period, Jesse became estranged from his stepfather, who then and later always took decidedly more interest in his own natural children. But ironically, in Jesse's young adulthood and later years, he and Noah Robinson would not only reconcile but form a close bond, Noah—not Charles—taking parental pride in Jesse's accomplishments.

After adolescence, Jesse Jackson's emerging talents presaged many of his adult characteristics. He was brash and impatient, glib, aggressive, a quick learner, terribly self-consumed with a desire to stand out from his peers and be recognized by larger society, and therefore ambitious. For one example: Jackson became a star quarterback on Greenville's black high school football team. Journalist Marshall Frady, who wrote a fairly appreciative but balanced biography of Jackson, reports that Jackson was a teenage sensation in the black community of his hometown: "During these years of his first, local glory, he developed into a glad young prince of Greenville's black community" (1996, 118). It rankled Jackson considerably, however, as an inescapable fact of race that local media cared little for black sports (or any other black) accomplishments and virtually overlooked his athletic prowess in favor of white high school champions. There were other slights, some writ large and some grinding exceedingly thin, in Jackson's daily life in Greenville's racial atmosphere that appear to have affected Jackson's striving to escape both the lack of opportunity for a young black man and his own personal sense of ignominy. For instance, Jackson, though born with a thick stammer, became a recognized student speech competitor but found himself sometimes bypassed in favor of white students when a teacher would pick the most outstanding students for speech competition.

This second-class treatment spread throughout Jackson's young life once outside Greenville. In fall 1959, Jackson went off for his freshman year to the University of Illinois at Urbana on a football scholarship. While a BMOC (Big Man on Campus) within his narrow black and athletic subcultures, he encountered prejudice and discrimination on the larger campus, if not always as blatant as in Greenville. Blacks at U of I, for example, were once not permitted to attend a concert by the Count Basie Band. Racial slurs and discourtesies given out in the open by white students were casual and not infrequent. When Jackson came home for Christmas break during that first year, he tried to take out books from the Greenville Public Library to complete a class speech assignment but unexpectedly was refused. (He was told he could only use a distinctly inferior, blacks-only library in Greenville.) Worse, when he returned to the Urbana U of I campus to complete the assignment, white students also arriving back saw him on the way to the library and taunted him with the unprovoked

"Nigger! Nigger, your ass is grass, and we're the lawn mowers!" (Frady 1996, 139–40). With a litany of such incidents, from small slights to taunts and disguised threats persistently chipping away at his dignity, Jackson developed what Frady (1996, 129) refers to as a "submerged fury."

Jackson left the University of Illinois after his first year. He was disillusioned at the daily racist scene. (This was, after all, the state that proudly touted itself on its car license plates as The Land of Lincoln. He expected something better in terms of racial egalitarianism.) Moreover, his chance to play quarterback at Illinois, thereby recapitulating his virtuoso success at Greenville's black high school, was not materializing since Illinois already had a starting *black* quarterback. And he had neglected his studies, for whatever reason, and was put on academic probation.

Jackson returned south and enrolled in the largely black North Carolina Agricultural and Technical College in Greensboro, became a sociology major, and went on to play football again as quarterback until a knee injury in 1960 led him to drop out for a year. He returned in 1961, met another sociology major, a young woman named Jackie, whom he married in 1963, and eventually graduated in 1964. Immediately after, he was admitted to Chicago Theological Seminary on a Rockefeller Fund Theological Education scholarship. There, however, his actual class attendance and performance were erratic. Arrogant toward the disciplined academic routine of reading, going to lectures and seminars, and completing assignments, he contemptuously dismissed those "details" of graduate school as "the paralysis of analysis" and instead preferred to want to jump immediately—some, such as his professors who petitioned the administration for him to leave CTS, would say precipitously—into various sorts of activist ministries. Journalist Kenneth R. Timmerman (2002, 16), who interviewed one of Jackson's influential mentors (later president of the seminary), has referred to "Jackson's abysmal academic achievement" during that time. Jackson, for his part, apparently wanted respect, admiration, and the honors that came with recognition of achievement without doing the necessary work to earn or acquire them. Nevertheless, only six months away from graduation, dissatisfied with the "ivory tower" nature of academic life and impatient to do something more "meaningful" and more directly tied to action, Jackson rounded up fellow concerned students to help in the civil rights movement. He led them South to Selma, Alabama, where he was to meet and work for Dr. Martin Luther

King, Jr. (Jackson eventually did graduate from CTS years later, but at the climax it in fact was more an honorary degree than one earned. See Frady 1996, 204–7).

Of further details of Jackson's uneven educational career at CTS and his first minor forays into Chicago's Democratic patronage system and local protests, our purposes here have little interest. Jackson's later self-aggrandizement and what Frady (1996, 245) terms "manic opportunism," rather, constitute our focus. However, enough has been recorded from interviews with Jackson, his speeches and autobiographical statements, and discussions with his family and friends over the years by journalist Frady and others to discern two critical factors underlying Jesse Jackson's style for attracting attention to himself, claiming charismatic leadership status, and running/managing his various initiatives and enterprises:

First, Jackson was born a member of an oppressed racial minority in a fairly rigid segregation caste system, He was born illegitimate and later became a largely ignored stepson. His family, furthermore, was relatively poor. In various ways, Jackson was a "multidimensional outsider" (Frady 1996, 13). But Jesse Jackson was smart and alert, and the continual reminders of limited horizons for smart, alert minority members at his time unquestionably grated on him. He achieved a modest but tantalizing amount of success within the racial boundaries allowed, which only whetted his ambitions and accompanying sense of relative deprivation.

Second, Jackson developed a somewhat moralistically romantic or heroic ideal of what he could do on a large noticeable scale. However compensatory such an interpretation of Jackson's later-life activities may seem (and we are certainly not childhood determinists), as a young man the opportunities for revolutionary change presented themselves to him in the personage or role model of Dr. Martin Luther King, Jr. and the greatest human liberties movement in American history.

As a result,

> ever since sensing early in his youth that he bore an uncommon personal promise far beyond the bounds of what he had been born into, his obsession has been to re-create himself into someone with a meaning large enough to answer that early sense of his possibilities—that is, quite simply, to belong to that wider society in which he found himself outcast by making himself into a moral hero in its life. (Frady 1996, 13)

Later, in his social–economic–political endeavors, Jackson would act the part of a visionary and moralizing prophet. He would also all the while seem to be compulsively readjusting the focus on the public limelight on himself, seeking reaffirmation of his heroic status in the black community. More importantly, *he had a tendency to conflate his own financial self-interest with larger public causes and concerns*, often cloaking the former in hyperbole and moralistic, even biblical metaphors for which his earlier experiences of black religion and later formal theological training prepared him well. Less of an outright con-artist than the Reverend Terry Lee Hornbuckle, certainly less of a financial deadbeat and clown than Al Sharpton, Jackson, we maintain, took his own personal needs and compensatory strategies, psychological or social, into his pastorate on a broader scale, a fact which compounds the tragedies of his malfeasance.

Martin Luther King, Jr. and the Southern Christian Leadership Conference

Back in Greensboro at the North Carolina Agricultural and Technical College during the early 1960s, where Jackson was influenced by faculty members who were associates of Dr. Martin Luther King, Jr., Jackson made some tentative forays into the civil rights social movement industry. He attended, for example, some student meetings of CORE (Congress of Racial Equality) as well as a few protests. However, movement leaders there reportedly felt "a certain wary ambivalence" about him, as if he was pushing too hard too soon to move up into their leadership hierarchy (Frady 1996, 169–71).

By 1965, while a student at Chicago Theological Seminary, Jackson organized a huge proportion of its students to journey to Selma, Alabama (with Jackson as their shepherd), to join in protests against (among other things) state police excesses. There he was soon seeking a stage to demonstrate his own oratorical and leadership abilities, much to the dismay and anger of civil rights activists with greater tenure in the cause. Here, activists such as Julian Bond and Atlanta's Mayor Andrew Young did not even know who this presumptuous, uninvited grandstander was. Even when not yet even any kind of SCLC official, he appropriated such a public persona and presented himself at large as a de facto SCLC staffer (Frady 1996, 171).

In Selma, however, he impressed the Reverend Ralph Abernathy, who in time introduced him to King. King was also impressed with Jackson and soon gave him the mission of organizing black ministers in Chicago in an attempt to move the SCLC beyond its regional identity and onto a national stage. Jackson threw himself vocally in a most public way into helping organize protests and assuming the role of major SCLC spokesperson as far as Chicago was concerned. With King's blessings he began running Operation Breadbasket, a training ground for Jackson's own later strong-arm economic tactics to force mostly white-owned business entities to hire, promote, and support black businessmen and enterprises (House 1988, 7–9; Reynolds 1975, 177). All the while, Jackson kept thrusting himself, no matter how abruptly and discourteously, into SCLC affairs. His brazen and persistent self-promotion as King's indispensable aide and confidant offended many more experienced activists who had devoted larger portions of their lives into civil rights (Frady 1996, 223). Even one fairly apologetic biographer of Jackson admits that:

> He seemed to be an upstart, a Johnny-come-lately who was grabbing all the attention but who had not paid his dues. Staffers complained about him, but they were forced to tolerate him. (Stone 1984, 84)

One primary reason that Jackson's narcissistic hustling continued within the SCLC as long as it did seems to be that the older King, for whatever reasons saw promise in Jackson's energy and leadership activities and genuinely liked him (Frady 1996, 216–24). Jackson, for his part, had no intention of usurping King's iconic leadership but rather chose him as a role model and prophetic alter ego. He revered and approached King always "with an almost abject adoration and awe," as a "true, heroic father figure" (Frady 1996, 209). This virtual worship became so apparent, that—and there is no other delicate way to make this point—Jackson finally made himself more than something of a pest around King, constantly inserting and reasserting the Jackson presence whenever King was around. Jackson's needy hoverings around King increased to the extent that, according to a variety of published sources, King would periodically tell Jackson in no uncertain, exasperated terms to back off and leave him alone. To which Jackson would profusely (and probably genuinely) apologize. (See, e.g., Colton 1989, 45.)

Jackson's final connection to King was symptomatic of the tireless drive behind his ego and, finally at the end of King's life, Jackson's scurrilous grandstanding. Immediately after Dr. King's assassination at 6:01 p.m. on April 4, 1968, at the Lorraine Motel in Memphis, Tennessee, Jackson (who was nowhere near the balcony where King was shot, but rather below in the parking lot) began telling other SCLC workers not to talk to the press. Instead, Jackson appointed himself unofficial SCLC spokesperson and began a bogus spiel that he was the last man on earth to talk with King. The story was enlarged (falsely) when Jackson immediately (i.e., that night) flew home to Chicago to appear on such media outlets as the *Today Show* and in other media venues wearing (he claimed) the same shirt splotched with King's blood that Jackson supposedly wore while cradling Dr. King in his arms and receiving those last dying words. He is recorded as having said on the air: "I am here with a heavy heart because on my chest is the stain of blood from Dr. King's head. . . . He went through, literally, a crucifixion. I was there" (Frady 1996, 229).

Actually, Ralph Abernathy was the person on the balcony holding King at the moment of his death. Jackson was later to parade a photograph of himself and King on the balcony, as if to imply and confirm that it was taken moments before the assassin's bullet was fired, instead of the photo in reality being taken the day before. And the blood splotches on Jackson's shirt *could* possibly have come from King's wound if (as some later witnesses suggested) Jackson had snuck up through the motel to the balcony and, unseen by the attendants clustered around King, smeared some of the blood on the shirt before leaving town. (See for more or less hostile versions of the event and Jackson's embellishments: Colton 1989, 46–7; Frady 1996, 206–8; Timmerman 2002, 5–11.)

The consequence of Jackson's dubious assertion to have been the last person to hear King's last words, or to hold him as he claimed he did, "was nothing less than the beginning of a controversy that would eventually split the SCLC wide open . . ." (Stone 1984, 18). Jackson's much promulgated claim was a colossal outrage of improbity in the eyes of those who actually been there with King at Memphis and who had endured in the past Jackson's seemingly limitless energies to blow his own horn. It seemed like the ultimate pretention and maneuver to set himself up as inheritor of King's prophetic, charismatic leadership mantle. Other SCLC leaders were horrified at Jackson's ghoulish tall tale. Writes journalist Frady (1996, 229):

> If the rest of King's troupe of assistants had never been particularly charmed by Jackson to start with, most of these who'd been at the Lorraine Motel that evening were apoplectic when they learned of his claims. Some insisted Jackson had never come near King's body.

Jackson's report of his alleged last moments with King can be dismissed, perhaps, as a boast, an exaggeration made by an excited, stunned, over-eager aspirant to black leadership playing to a detail-desperate audience and his wanting some claim to fame, if not sympathy, for later purposes. What Jackson learned while briefly manning the SCLC's Operation Breadbasket in Chicago, however, had more far-reaching implications for his later economic ventures, including his well-known PUSH organization. And these lessons, we maintain, are more important then Jackson's bogus claims of how he attended Martin Luther King, Jr.'s death. Before examining PUSH and its involvement with malfeasance, however, we need first to discuss where the logic of black boycotts of white businesses (and gratuities returned to boycott organizers) originated.

The Roots of Black Economic Pressure and Boycotts

In his book *The $30 Billion Negro*, investment counselor D. Parke Gibson (1969, 1) lays out the economic logic underlying the visible black boycotts of white businesses that became so important a part of the American civil rights movement starting in the 1960s:

> The Negro consumer, who spends in excess of $30,000,000 annually for goods and services, is now in a position with his consumption characteristics to be the difference between profit and loss for many companies. These characteristics, combined with a growing affluence, make him an important consideration for marketing effectiveness in the future of American business.

For example, in an appendix Gibson (1969, 272–79) briefly reviews 132 trade periodical articles from the mid-to-late 1960s (appearing in publications including the *Wall Street Journal*, *Fortune*, and *Business Week*) and shows they cover such areas of black sales and consumption as: black marketing strategies; the extent of the black market; drug, chemical, and cosmetic industries; shoes and clothing; the tobacco industry; brewers and distillers; electronic appliances; jewelry; printing; and television entertainment. Written less than half a decade after Martin Luther King, Jr. began Operation Breadbasket in Chicago, and though the book's statistics and proportions of products consumed by blacks are considerably dated, Gibson's primary point is still valid.

King realized it as well: not only have black consumers been a significant element in the nation's overall economic picture of production and consumption, but in order for his dream of freedom to really take hold, the civil rights movement had to move beyond just voting rights and ending the most blatant inequalities of segregation. What race-ethnic sociologists term *institutional integration* had to be achieved. That is, blacks could not simply achieve affluence (somehow) and then be full participants in the economy. They needed to become part of both financial institutions and the corporate entities that produce and market goods and services. Blacks needed to gain entry into America's fiscal infrastructure, and not just as semiskilled and lower-tier workers. Otherwise, as King appreciated, simply obtaining civil and political rights without integration into all levels of the economic sphere "would avail little for poor blacks unless it was accompanied by measures that ensured access to the education and training required for truly gainful employment" (Ashmore 1994, 265).

Hence the rationale of black consumption as a form of leverage for true integration, and pressure brought to bear on as-yet institutionally discriminatory companies through the boycott, or threat of boycott, became its tactic.

However, neither King nor his more visible successor in this leverage tactic, Jesse Jackson, initially discovered or developed the tactical black boycott of white businesses (though King first experienced the power of the Montgomery, Alabama, bus boycott in 1955). The crucial template of the firm threat of (or actual) boycott by black consumers (and consequently lost sales) unless certain demands are met, followed quickly by offers to negotiate jobs, training, and market access/distribution arrangements for black producers, originated in Philadelphia during the late 1950s and 1960s. Its pioneer was the Reverend Leon Sullivan, a black pastor who eventually turned the racial boycott into something of an art form. (Sullivan actually based his model on an earlier boycott led by Dr. T. R. M. Howard, a wealthy physician and community activist on Chicago's South Side who successfully organized a boycott of gasoline service stations to pressure them to open restroom facilities to black customers [Beito and Beito 2009].)

Sullivan organized over 400 black Philadelphia pastors and through them used their congregations to mobilize (and guarantee to recalcitrant white business executives) grassroots black cooperation in a boycott. The rationale of the united pastors, spread throughout the church laity, was simple: "We cannot in good moral conscience remain silent while members of our congregation patronize companies that discriminate in the employment of our people" (Gibson 1969, 35). Some of the goals of the Sullivan boycotts, termed the Selective

Patronage System, embraced specifics no longer at issue by the latter half of the twentieth century, such as racially integrating lavatories and lunchrooms at places of business. But the economic heart of the SPS consisted of more jobs (and training for those jobs) for blacks and broader market access for products manufactured or produced by black companies, particularly if these could be distributed by white-owned chain stores. The SPS first went after a major bakery company, then the Pepsi-Cola Bottling Company, then successively and successfully the Esso Standard Oil Company, the Gulf Oil Corporation, the Sun Oil Corporation, and the Great Atlanta and Pacific supermarket grocery chain, among others (Gibson 1969, 37–47).

But there was something more to the successful institutional integration template than just breaking down racial barriers, at least as Rev. Sullivan (and later Jackson) was/were concerned. Within a few years of actualizing effective boycotts and/or pressure through threats thereof, Sullivan had built up "a personal patronage network" using the grassroots contacts of SSP. "He also demonstrated that boycotts could be personally lucrative, as he was subsequently appointed to the board of directors of General Motors" (Timmerman 2002, 23), a feat of considerable upward occupational mobility for a clergyman. In 1966, when Jesse Jackson took over Operation Breadbasket in Chicago, he may or may not have anticipated all the details of Sullivan's cultivation of economic clout, both for the black community and for Rev. Sullivan, including the well-nigh cronyism for the latter, but there is no question Jackson came to use this same template as his personal self-aggrandizing tool.

Operation Breadbasket, PUSH, and PUSH-Excel:
Shakedown and Kickbacks

In 1965, Dr. Martin Luther King, Jr. put Jesse Jackson, the youngest of his aides at the SCLC, in charge of King's prime northern civil rights initiative: Chicago's Operation Breadbasket. The mission of OB, like that of Philadelphia's Sullivan, was to reverse the "economic colonialism of the black community" (Frady 1996, 197). At the outset the naïve, bombastic Jackson was not much more than an apprentice to more experience civil rights activists. Recalled one:

> Jesse didn't know what the hell he was talking about, because he was just a theology student. So we taught him business. (Frady 1996, 199)

The activist veterans explained to Jackson the dynamics of racial discrimination in hiring, staffing, and operating the largely white-owned businesses taking dollars out of the black community. Jackson was swift to learn about the realities of the Chicago economic scene and a quick read of the Sullivan model. Soon he bellicosely boasted of the newly energized OB philosophy:

> We are the margin of profit of every major item produced in America, from General Motors cars on down to Kellog's Corn Flakes ... If we've got his margin of profit, we've got his genitals. (Stone 1984, 74)

The basic formula Jackson employed, whether it be called justified economic pressure or a thinly veiled protection-racket "shakedown," depending on one's point of view, was honed in Chicago before Jackson took it national a few years later. It consisted of five key phases, the last of which was relatively unpublicized but well known in Chicago and within Jackson's inner circle. (The fifth phase was never mentioned in more apologetic summaries of OB and later PUSH; see, for examples of these, Ashmore [1994, 265–66, 274]; Colton [1989, 7–10, 144–7, 55–56]; Stone [1984]). These phases were:

First, send a corporation's top executive a questionnaire claiming that the Jackson organization "had heard complaints" of racial inequality and discrimination against it; demand details of the total percentage of black employees, numbers of blacks in managerial positions, and so forth (Frady 1996, 254ff); and then threaten an embarrassingly prolonged boycott with visible and vocal demonstrations if executives demur or ignore the questionnaire.

Second, boycott; or, assuming the executives are intimidated by the threat of a boycott or simply want to avoid pragmatically the possible costs of such an economic siege, offer for an OB team to meet with executives to negotiate for such concessions as more black employees, more black managers, more distribution of black-produced products, redirection of the corporation's insurance and investment business to more black-owned financial institutions, and so forth.

Third, call a press conference where a statement, largely crafted by OB or with its significant input (down to specific wording) but allegedly written by contrite white executives, will be read by them. As part of this orchestrated event, executives will repeatedly voice mea culpas of past discriminatory behavior and earnest wishes to mend their ways and their intentions to avoid the errors of the past by implementing policies to better serve the cause of racial equality.

Fourth, OB vowing to return for periodic checkups on the actual outcomes of executive promises (which only sometimes occurred) were one kind of follow-up. The press conference, however, was the main moral and symbolic victory. Another, most important form of follow-up, was when the corporations were expected to make financial donations or "reparations" to OB and its designated recipients.

Fifth, grateful beneficiaries, mostly black businesspersons (often called by the Jackson team "donors" and "benefactors") who profited from the white concessions, were expected, in a sometimes unspoken, often more explicitly spelled out agreement, to provide services and material as well as financial gifts and business opportunities directly to OB, Jackson himself, and Jackson's immediate family and inner circle (Frady 1996, 254; Timmerman 2002, 62–92, 121–36, 181–208, 321–71). The arrangement operated as a kind of "fee-for-service" brokerage that left the benefactors "prepared to reward Jackson personally and handsomely for his services" (Timmerman 2002, 25). It is reported that Jackson crassly told one group of black businessmen before a boycott what was expected of them in this understanding of reciprocity:

> We're all family here, but you have to pay to play. You cannot ride to freedom free in Pharaoh's chariot. (Cited in Frady 1996, 280)

These are harsh accusations, particularly the last. In discussing Jackson's considerable if pastorally questionable aggrandizement from OB and PUSH, of which we are only providing an outline and representative illustrations, it is important to point out that virtually all sources for data on his enrichment are mainstream journalistic, sources while to some academics and rarified ivory tower scholars are somehow less reliable or even déclassé. (This was an initial criticism encountered by one of us [Shupe 1995] during the early days of analyzing church organization patterns in clergy malfeasance when many journalists and hardly any professors were following this form of elite deviance.) It should be noted that unlike many scholars, who must satisfy an academic editorial board and only very seldom any attorneys, most journalists (*not* tabloid writers or rogue internet bloggers) are held to a high evidentiary standard in publishing for fear of libel lawsuits and often must pass more rigorous editorial standards than many academic writers, whether in journals or books. Even when the journalism coverage is critical (and the following sources on Jackson more or less are), the reporters have generally answered to a bar of legal proof raised higher (in our experience) than it generally would be for much academic publication. This caveat about our direct journalistic sources and summaries of such sources by other writers is not meant as an apology for our reliance on journalistic sources, but rather as an explanation.

At first, of course, white executives had no apparent reason to feel intimidated or pressured by OB and either ignored or rejected the questionnaire gambit. The first target for Sullivan's boycott tactic, Country Delight, Inc., a dairy, thought they could call Jackson's bluff. Jackson immediately mobilized one hundred Chicago South Side black churches, and the boycott only lasted three days before executives gave in. Then came the boycott of High-Low Foods, a grocery chain; that boycott lasted ten days before negotiations began. High-Low committed itself to bringing 183 blacks into a range of positions. The OB boycott of the much disliked Red Rooster, Inc., a market chain accused of selling inferior quality, even spoiled meats and produce to its "captive" urban black customers (". . . like a slum landlord of food"—Stone 1984, 76), held out and was finally driven into bankruptcy. The boycott of the Great Northern Atlantic and Pacific (A + P) grocery chain, which had forty stories in Chicago's black neighborhoods, eventually pledged 970 jobs for blacks after a *sixteen-week* boycott. Furthermore, A + P contracted with a black sanitation firm to collect the garbage from the chain's stores as well as agreed to carry twenty-five-plus items produced for black consumers by black companies, from orange juice to spray deodorant, on its shelves (Frady 1996, 202; Stone 1984, 74). Another chain, Jewel Tea, pledged 662 jobs for blacks.

Jackson's operation (no longer thought of as Sullivan's tactic, except by scholars) was undeniably successful in Chicago. One estimate of this success was that just after the first two years under his leadership, between three and four thousand blacks directly found employment; two black-owned banks found their deposits growing from resources funneled their way by recently boycotted or threatened-with-boycott white companies, from some $5 million to $20 million; and annual income and revenues for Chicago South Side blacks rose approximately by $22 million (Frady 1996, 202); among other victories.

Jackson and OB went on to use the boycott-threat tactic on a number of other companies operating in the Chicago area, including the Borden Milk Company, Bowman Dairies, Wayne Dairies, Coca-Cola distributors, and Del Farm Stores. After the initial successful boycotts, however, the threat of boycott became usually all the leverage Jackson needed (at least within Chicago). Soon the mobilization of foot soldiers, many of them black Chicago gang members (from violent gangs such as the Blackstone Rangers and the Black Disciples, with whose leaders Jackson had become friendly for mutually beneficial and pragmatic reasons) were often functionally unnecessary. The gangs, in particular, were used as "filler" protesters for crowd effect and "body guards" as well as for their less-than-subtle, menacing physical presence in crowds and at such places as construction sites (Frady 1996, 250–1; Timmerman 2002, 26–30, 78–80).

Once negotiations with white executives had been completed and the latter had agreed to eat public crow as formerly racially oblivious louts, the settlement would be publicly announced at press conferences in moralistic language characteristically Jacksonesque. For example, the settlement itself would be referred to by both sides as "a covenant." (Within six months of OB's first boycott, all major food chains on Chicago's South Side had established "covenants" (also known as "treaties") with OB (Frady 1996, 255).

To say, these "covenants" represented true changes of heart by formerly insensitive white executives (instead of what social psychologists term *public compliance*) would be disingenuous. At the same time, public announcements made by corporate leaders could not easily include feelings that they had been victims of extortion nor could they cynically say later they became "covenant" partners to buy off Jackson and the OB. Nor did many publicly air their later complaints that some blacks foisted on them were patently unqualified (Frady 1996, 255). But in fact "some white businessmen began privately referring to Jackson and his preacherly squads as 'the moral mafia,' and indeed their suasions were sometimes perceived to be not altogether spiritual" (Frady 1996, 254). In fact, the executives' staged public contrition statements resembled nothing so much as the old-style Stalinist-era Moscow show trials of alleged politically deviant dissidents. These Chicago events were really orchestrated to provide two psychological functions. For Jackson's OB black followers, the press conferences were empowering, vindicating their sense of having been wronged and now achieving redress. For other nonboycotted executives and their enterprises, the press conferences and statements of capitulation served, in criminological terms, as forms of indirect deterrence, i.e., pay us now or pay us (more) later, but the advantage of paying us now is that you will at least salvage perfunctory positive publicity amounting to vague claims of newly found humanitarian enlightenment.

Jesse Jackson and Operation Breadbasket were a visible success in terms of the economic justice goals envisioned by the late Dr. King. Indeed, as one *Wall Street Journal* observer (Jenkins 1998) wrote about Jackson at the helm of OB and the later PUSH: "Nobody has shaken the money tree of corporate America more vigorously or more successfully in favor of his constituents." But King likely did not anticipate Jackson's personal aggrandizement as a result of adopting Rev. Sullivan's boycott model. Recalls journalist Frady (1996, 25), "In the course of his Breadbasket campaign, Jackson had also rapidly established a small dominion of his own in Chicago, assembling around him a prestigious company of patrons," a coterie in which Jackson himself prospered.

Jackson also became a celebrity in his own right. At his Saturday morning Breadbasket radio broadcast "services," which often had 2,000 OB sympathizers in attendance, a legion of black luminaries not infrequently stopped by to laud Jackson and OB. These included stand-up comedian-turned-television-sitcom star Redd Foxx, actor-musician Isaac Hayes, composer Quincy Jones, movie actor Richard Roundtree, "The Greatest" heavyweight champion Muhammad Ali, and the singing Jacksons (including young Michael), not to mention various African politicians and visitors.

By the start of the 1970s, Jackson had become too high profile and independent spokesperson for running a mere wing of the SCLC. There had long been animosity between Jackson and the older SCLC civil rights leaders, such as the Reverend Ralph Abernathy, exacerbated by Jackson's grandstanding behavior in the limelight as some kind of self-appointed heir apparent following King's assassination. Jackson was also resented for sending relatively little of OB's revenues down to the SCLC in Atlanta. (Abernathy once "suspended" Jackson as OB's director for sixty days.) Jackson's accounting of earned OB revenues was vague, cursory, and (many suspected) incomplete. The same could be said of the allegedly considerable monies raised by Jackson's several inspired Black Expo convention in downtown Chicago (Timmerman 2002, 37–44).

On Christmas Day, 1971, Jackson made his move for independence from the SCLC by announcing that he had dissolved OB and was creating his new organization, PUSH (the acronym for his ambitiously named People United to Save Humanity). In most ways PUSH was a continuation of the Jackson-run OB, minus any ties to the SCLC. What Jackson had literally done was to loot the SCLC's Chicago office, taking *all* of OB's files and office equipment, most of its membership who now had a personal loyalty to Jackson, and twenty-five former OB staff persons as well as five of OB's board members (Frady 1996, 255). It was a bold coup within the black civil rights social movement industry.

Kickbacks from grateful black businesspersons prospering from OB boycott maneuvers came directly to Jackson. They also flowed to his family and his friends through OB in the form of "supplementary monies," material gifts, property use, vehicles and services, all of which might nominally be made in the name of OB but which were virtually reserved for Jackson's exclusive use. (A similar arrangement of titular "nonownership" but actual wealth for a religious leader occurred with South Korea's Rev. Sun Myung Moon, alleged messiah and successor to Jesus Christ, when he came to the United States starting in 1965. See Bromley and Shupe [1979].) These gifts or "donations" began coming almost immediately, certainly early in the two years of OB's aggressive campaign. For a relatively young man, a social activist who did not even seek the line of work for which he went to graduate school, and who had not long before lived with his wife and children in a dingy one-bedroom walk-up apartment while obtaining free groceries from a church's charity food line, Jackson's "own personal situation improved significantly." Soon A. R. Leak, an undertaker and part-time preacher, moved the Jackson family into a more upscale nine-room apartment with sun porches on both the front and back (Frady 1996, 257–58).

Later, such "benefactors" provided Jackson with a Lincoln Continental (with chauffer) for his exclusive use. He was to receive other cars, such as Cadillacs and SUV's. Jackson received a great many clothes from merchants. His children's tuition to an exclusive private educational academy was likewise paid. Eventually in 1970 he was even provided a fifteen-room house on Constance Avenue in an older-money section of Chicago, along with free yard service and upkeep. The financing on that house, i.e., specifically who put up the loan money for the mortgage, was not an obfuscated fact by the FOJ—Friends of Jesse (for details, see Frady [1996, 269–80]; Timmerman [2002, 35–36]). Journalist Kenneth Timmerman (2002, 36) notes about Jackson that "he knew how to get others to pick up the tab for his expenses." One FOJ "benefactor," George Jones, who owned a milk company aided by a boycott, recalled:

> We paid his salary, We took care of whatever bills he had. If he or somebody in his family became ill, we had doctors for them. We got him his house, took care of fixing it up. Carpenters worked gratis, painters worked gratis, carpenters put in carpets gratis. And he wasn't bashful at all if he wanted something specific; he would call one of us up . . . If he needed clothing, a car, a trust fund for his family. . . . (Cited in Frady 1996, 270).

Jackson carried this quid pro quo logic straight out of the SCLC's OB and, after he recast the group as his own, PUSH. PUSH's quest for black economic empowerment began to involve a growing list of national corporations approached with the Sullivan tactic. Jackson's boycott ambitions expanded considerably beyond the Chicago metropolitan area. He and PUSH began to take on (with success) an impressive array of enterprises. Here we list only a small number of corporate entities that included Coca-Cola, 7-Eleven stores (owned by the Southland Corporation, headquartered in Dallas, TX), Burger King, Heubelein Distilleries, Avon Products, Miller Brewing Company, The Joseph P. Schlitz Brewing Company, Quaker Oats, Flagstar (owners of the Denny's restaurant chain), Texaco Oil, and the General Foods conglomerate. In the case of General Foods, Jackson negotiated a "covenant" that brought blacks and minorities into over 360 jobs at all levels, increased General Food's deposits in exclusively black-owned banks by half a million dollars, redirected another $20 million of insurance policies to black companies, convinced General Foods to steer more advertising to black-owned agencies, and pressured the company to give more business to black law firms and black construction companies (Frady 1996, 279–80). Spoils of these "covenants" not only went to black businesspersons who now "owed" Jackson personally but also to PUSH and Jackson's cronies. "At the same time," remarks journalist Frady (1996, 280), "in the course of extracting these agreements, Jackson also continued to compile from their beneficiaries a growing legion of indebted backers, from whom he not incidentally expected a "tithe" back into the organization that had gained them admittance into the corporate firmament." And all such "covenants" brought agreements of future business deals among the largely white corporation and black companies, which meant future "royalties" to the Jacksons. Investigative reporter Kenneth R. Timmerman, who wrote

Shakedown: Exposing the Real Jesse Jackson (2002), is quoted as having said in a media interview about his book: "I've had a number of CEOs come to me and say paying Jesse Jackson $400,000 or $500,000 was the price of doing business" (Cited in Peterson 2003, 100).

One example of how this largesse was shared by the inner circle was Jackson's half brother, Noah Robinson, Jr.

Noah Robinson, Jr. is only worth mentioning here because he was a consummate con-artist operating under the OB and later PUSH umbrellas as an inside crony who benefited from the OB's Sullivan tactics and later from all the federal government money sought by Jackson through PUSH. Noah came north to Chicago to work with his half brother when the latter was put in charge of the SCLC's economic initiative. Noah was a bold talker and shrewd. Previously he had earned a MBA degree at the Wharton Business School and had started a consulting firm in Philadelphia where he reportedly engaged in a series of questionably legal business deals (Frady 1996, 122). At OB he became a manipulator with a headstrong opinion of himself. (Ralph Abernathy once referred to Noah as "a chronic troublemaker"—Frady 1996, 122). When Jackson abandoned OB and moved on to navigate PUSH, Noah took over OB briefly as its head but then also moved on to join Jesse.

Noah profited considerably from the Jackson "donations" and from the business opportunities offered by the "covenants" with white corporations. Thus, he became the first black distributor of Coca-Cola, received a Kentucky Fried Chicken franchise, and later received franchises from Wendy's Old Fashioned Hamburgers and Bojangle's Chick and Biscuits, claiming to be starting far more than a dozen restaurants in Chicago and New York. Noah later was discovered to have embezzled $650,000 (with at least one other Robinson brother) from his own Wendy's fast-food restaurants, for which (along with other shennanigans) he was convicted on thirty counts of racketeering, mail and wire frauds, bankruptcy fraud, and tax evasion and went to prison for six years (plus having to pay $125,000 as partial restoration of unpaid taxes). He also had padded his employee "staff" rosters with Chicago black youth gang members as "security guards." (His half brother Jesse had provided his introductions to the world of Chicago gangs.) Noah later started the Robinson Group which defrauded the federal government of tens of millions of dollars. During the administration of President Jimmy Carter, racial quotas or "minority set-asides" to help provide grants for minority companies were established. Noah created a number of bogus front organizations, ostensibly owned and operated by blacks, which were really used to obtain government contracts that were then given as subcontracts to white firms. For example, Noah received a $155,000 per year grant from the Office of Minority Businesses, then used it to obtain $1.4 million from Chicago sanitation officials to carry away garbage. The money was supposed to be used to pay minority firms and workers—which never happened. White companies with white workers received the money. In essence, Noah funneled federal monies intended to stimulate minority businesses and provide jobs away from the black community and provided the contracts to white businesses that then paid him kickbacks. Between 1979 and 1984, Noah Robinson, Jr., through the Robinson Group, received $33 million in government contracts meant for minority firms. Many of these were arranged through PUSH, and some with Jesse Jackson's direct help and contacts. Also, through Jesse's contacts, Noah fell into criminal relationships with Chicago gangs, particularly the Blackstone Rangers. After being investigated numerous times by federal and state governments as well as by the *Chicago Tribune* and other local media, and after more than a few criminal indictments, Noah was convicted in 1988 of murder for hire, drug trafficking racketeering, criminal conspiracy, and suspected soliciting and arranging the stabbing of a federal witness. In 1992, while serving felony sentences in a federal penitentiary for defrauding the IRS and having been an accessory to attempted murder, Noah was further convicted of drug-racketeering, murder, and attempted murder (though these last three convictions were ultimately overturned—Frady 1996, 120). Noah blamed political enemies, business rivals, and government harassment. But no one ever disputed that his commitment to civil rights or economic justice were overshadowed by his urge to get rich. (For further details on a complex, at times almost bewildering network of misrepresentation, fraud, boycott kickbacks, hustles of the federal government, and gang interactions, see Frady [1996, 121–29]; Timmerman [2002, 62–67, 81–84, 193–95], among other available compilations of sources.)

Jesse Jackson, on the other hand, embedded his personal enrichment within a biblical, even pastoral role. Jackson's logic echoed back to the time-honored Gospel of Prosperity, i.e., that part of god's Providence is good fortune, in terms of health and finances, for those who follow His Principles, which Hadden and Shupe (1988, 131–35) maintain has been a running theme in American Protestantism from the Colonial era to the fundraising appeals (and self-serving justifications) of modern "televangelists." Citing himself as a "servant to his people," Jackson has argued that of the many (material) blessings he has received from his followers, there was something sacred:

> There're all kinds of by-products for the great servants. People want you to stay in a comfortable house, want you to wear nice clothes, have the car of your choice—with bulletproof windows.... It comes out of service. It's like some divine law of reciprocity.... I cannot help you without helping me.... But ... you cast that bread upon the water, it'll return to you toasted, with *butter* on it. (Emphasis Jackson's; Cited in Frady 1996, 270)

All quid pro quo notions of social exchange aside, the eagerness of Jackson's supporters to shower him with material benefits and multitudinous services and his comfortable willingness to accept them conforms to what we said earlier of the role and social status of the preacher/pastor in black congregations. It is not a matter of mere gratitude. The preacher is the alter ego of the group: his appearance in public and his visible lifestyle are symbols of the layperson's own hopes and aspirations.

The salient identity of the black pastor in the view of congregants overlaps with their own close identification to the life of the sacred community. What in other circumstances might seem excessive or inappropriate enrichment at their expense, or at least violating the norms of distributive justice when he lives lavishly while they do not, are actually reversed in this situation. It is important to followers of a charismatic black preacher that he manifestly live better than they do. It is confirmation of the ultimate legitimation of the black community's struggles up from scarcity, oppression, and discrimination. When he "makes it," all who identify with the church community vicariously "make it" as well.

But at some other personal level, despite Jackson's pious denials of personal wealth (for example, that his PUSH annual salary was only $200,000 considering all that he had to do) and his nonownership of many of things that he was provided without cost, he knew how things looked—the expensive cars and clothes, the homes, his children's private schooling, first-class travel accommodations—to the outside non-black society he so assiduously cultivated. He was in fact following precisely the same pattern of enjoying wealth, privilege, and comfort while denying he really possessed it of two twentieth-century messiahs, South Korea's Rev. Sun Myung Moon, and Harlem's Depression-era

Father Divine. Jackson himself was sensitive about this issue and even declared in a 1973 *Penthouse* magazine interview:

> I'm no Father Divine. I have not amassed a great fortune. I have a modest income. (Ewing 1973, 108)

Jackson went on to found PUSH/Excel (PUSH for Excellence) in 1975, a moral crusade led by Jackson to promote the socialization of middle-class values of honesty and self-discipline, personal responsibility, the work ethic and delayed gratification, self-confidence, and education in poor and minority youths. Jackson's group took millions of dollars from corporations and philanthropic groups ($260,000 total in 1977), from state legislatures ($300,000 from Louisiana for a New Orleans project), from cities such as Chicago, Denver, Kansas City, and Los Angeles ($403,000 from LA alone), and from federal government agencies such as the National Institute of Education, the Office of Education, and the Department of Labor ($445,000, $700,000, and $500,000, respectively, just in 1979—see House 1988, 27). Jackson became on outspoken champion of the Protestant Ethic and also, building on his Sullivan tactics work in Chicago and later nationally, a symbol of capitalist entrepreneurship. The media called this entire effort "Jesse Jackson's crusade" (House 1988, ix) and at first lionized him.

But much of PUSH/Excel was, to put it politely, empty rhetoric, otherwise "smoke and mirrors." PUSH/Excel was fundamentally run by civil rights social movement activists, not experienced bureaucrats, hence there was sloppy bookkeeping and minimal accounting for how money was spent, poor follow-up of results from programs in schools, and a decentralized structure that exacerbated all of the above problems (House 1988, 3, 20–25, 101–13). As a result, three years later

> the program was in shambles; the mass media that had lauded it only a short time before now proclaimed it a failure. Jackson himself was accused of various misdeeds and chastised for his demagoguery and lack of follow-through. Jackson defended himself by asserting that his political enemies had sabotaged the effort. (House 1988, ix)

Jackson had been warned up-front by the director of the National Institute of Education (among others) that he would be accountable for not just observable results of the programs but also for tracking expenditures. She told him that "if you take federal cash, then you have to be able to account for how the cash is spent, and you have to specify what it is you're going to do with that cash." (From the transcript of an interview in House 1988, 23.) Jackson, however, was blasé about such concerns; he was, after all, an inspiring orator capable of generating crowds, peppered with celebrities, of tens of thousands, perhaps even a prophet. But he was no bureaucrat. As a result, Jackson treated PUSH/Excel in many ways just as he had used PUSH and Operation Breadbasket: as cash cows to fund his lifestyle, for the extensive and expensive travels all over the nation and eventually all over the world for his showcasing of himself and his ambitions.

Jackson had always overlapped personal and social movement cash flows so as to make his true financial worth ambiguous and not easily investigated by outsiders, but this time there were more than local journalists snooping around his assets and expenditures. During the post-Carter Republican Reagan administration when a private set of evaluators from the American Institute for Research that had contracted with the federal government began to examine PUSH/Excel's books as well as its results, they judged the entire program to have been a disaster. PUSH/Excel had no way to show much of any impacts on the youth cohort it was supposed to help, and it was obvious its stewards had squandered considerable monies. To be fair, AIR used a business model evaluating "investment behaviors," i.e., how personnel's time, money, and energy were expended, in a hard-nosed analysis of what immediate outcomes were produced. Yet, PUSH/Excel was clearly more interested in the long-range intangible benefits of educational preparation and character-building. (And AIR's head evaluator was Charles A. Murray, an arch-conservative hostile to social welfare program, in general, and who had also coauthored the thinly veiled racist book *The Bell Curve* which claimed that scores on intelligence tests, on which blacks usually fared worse than whites, were the product of genetic inheritance—see Herrnstein and Murray 1994).

Concludes Ernest R. House in his thorough analysis of the rise and fall of PUSH/Excel (1988, 74):

> If it was a "program" at all, PUSH/Excel was a symbolic, religious, motivational program . . . It was decentralized; there were few discrete, standard, uniform activities. Program activities were local, opportunistic, and adventitious, and more often "one-shot" events. The evaluators' conceptual scheme could not accommodate this type of program.

By the late 1970s, PUSH/Excel was finished, Jackson somewhat disgraced by its much ballyhooed promise and then its fizzle. PUSH as well was moribund and broke due to Jackson's neglect. By 1976, the latter group was in debt for $400,000, thanks in part also to Jackson using its monies for travel expenses as he kept up his frenzied pace crisscrossing the country. And the IRS began to look at how PUSH spent its approximate total of over six and one-half million dollars government grants, an investigation that eventually earned PUSH back-tax penalties (Frady 1996, 290ff; Timmerman 2002, 87–92).

But there was an important function that the notoriety of PUSH/Excel served: "PUSH/Excel helped Jackson to build a national political base at the expense of the U.S. taxpayers" (Timmerman 2002, 69).

Hymietown and the Love Child

We do not intend to consider Jesse Jackson the candidate for the Democratic presidential nomination in 1984 and again in 1988 except to mention the significance of that political involvement for our malfeasance analysis along three lines.

First, the campaigns (particularly the first) understandably raised interest in Jackson's financial affairs from local and regional levels to a national plateau. Some of the interest was retrospective, including reviewing the early Operation Breadbasket and later PUSH "covenant"-construction process. White liberals applauded the financial gains for blacks, conservatives deplored the process as blatantly coercive in a manner unbecoming a pastor. Neither camp made much of the kickbacks initially, but Jackson's personal enrichment gradually came to light, hence we know now what corruption the Sullivan tactics actually unleashed in Chicago and elsewhere.

Second, Jackson's 1984 precampaign relations with American Jews had been gravely strained by his 1979 adventuristic, if unofficial (and possibly illegal) "diplomacy," as they watched him jet overseas and hobnob with Fidel Castro, various African dictators, and particularly Middle Eastern leaders with histories of terrorism and hating Israel, such as Libya's Colonel Muammar Qaddafi and Palestine's Yasser Arafat (Colton 1989, 83–7; Timmerman 2002, 107–20, 147–54). And there was as well his increasing associations with the Nation of Islam's anti-Semitic Minister Louis Farrakhan who had previously referred to Judaism as a "gutter" and "pig" religion. Then in January 1984 during the presidential primary, in what he thought was an off-the-record conversation with a black reporter from *The Washington Post*, Jackson complained of bad press coverage in New York City by referring to Jews as "Hymies" and New York City as "Hymietown." This was an ethnopaulism more worthy of a localite of modest formal education like Al Sharpton than coming from a well-educated (undergraduate sociology major, ordained seminary graduate) presidential candidate with serious aspirations to overcome the racial, ethnic, and other divisions separating Americans. Jackson offered profuse Mel Gibsonian apologies to the Anti-Defamation League and other wings of the American Jewish community, once among blacks' staunchest white allies in the civil rights movement, but the damage was irreparable.

Third, the two campaigns again raised Jackson's PUSH/Excel persona as a moral exemplar for youths, a black spokesperson for strong families, male parental responsibility, and integrity. The announcement on January 17, 2001, that he had had an extramarital affair with staffer Karin Stanford and fathered a daughter with her in 1998 occurred after Jackson's second presidential campaign, but it likely played a part in his decision not to pursue a third run for the nomination. The news contrasted with his image as a motivator of black youths to hold themselves sexually accountable.

Jackson only made the announcement when he learned that the tabloid *National Enquirer* was going to publish the news after conducting a two-month investigation, and soon after he canceled a protest of George W. Bush's inauguration that was to occur just a few days later (CNN.com 2001; York 2001). Journalist Kenneth Timmerman (2002, 388–89) recalls: "Jackson's sexual escapades had been widely rumored for years. The wonder was not Jackson finally got caught, but why it took so long." Ironically, journalist Marshall Frady (1996, 166) reports an interview with Jackson's wife some years earlier in which she prophetically acknowledged the likelihood of such infidelity. She said:

> Of course I know what happens out there. I'm no *dummy* . . . But I don't believe in examining the sheets . . . I can't spend too much time worrying about other women if I am to develop myself.

Mrs. Jackson revealed that she was aware of his extramarital activities but did not want o hear about them. That interview was virtually a decade before the "love child" announcement.

Human failings and hypocrisy are understandable. But there was a higher standard to hold Jackson as (1) a black luminary, spokesperson, and civil rights hero whose moral integrity formed a large part of his currency with followers and admirers; (2) a leader and role model providing guidance and moral exhortations to young black males against thinking that fathering babies out of wedlock was some sign of mature manhood; and (3) a pastor in the black community who accepted the rights and privileges that accrue to that status. He ran for president, not sainthood, but he was the actor, more than any other person, who aggressively raised himself up on that tall moral pedestal.

Conclusion

To many black and white Americans, the Reverends Jesse Jackson and Al Sharpton are beacons of inspiration, icons of courage, opponents of racism, and economic entrepreneurs. They preach a gospel of hope, self-empowerment, and symbolic pride. To some black and white observers who have examined their biographies, however, the behaviors of Sharpton and Jackson are hypocritical and remind one of the forgotten Christian notion of what it is to "minster" and to "serve." Advises conservative Christian author Blue (1993, 31, 33):

> Jesus stated clearly that the only legitimate spiritual authority is servant authority.... Positional authority carries with it the power to be coercive, to compel. Servant authority, however, cheerfully forfeits this power, so that those who submit to it can only do so freely and voluntarily.

This servant humility is lost in the Sharpton/Jackson adoption of the Sullivan strategy to strong-arm and intimidate corporations. Moreover, given the personal enrichment both gentlemen have experienced in the course of their economic pressure adventures, and their personal hypocrisies in advocating capitalistic entrepreneurship but relying on a different mode altogether for their lifestyles and fortunes while mobilizing mass groups to do the hard work, one is reminded of Jesus rebuking the Pharisees in Matthew 23 when he admonished them:

> you must do what they tell you [on the authority of Moses] and follow their instructions. But you must not imitate their lives! For they preach but do not practice. *They pile up back-breaking burdens and lay them on other men's shoulders—yet they themselves will not raise a finger to move them.* They increase the size of their phylacteries and lengthen the tassels of their robes; they love seats of honour at dinner parties and front place in the synagogues. *They love to be greeted with respect in public places and to have men call them* "rabbi!" (Phillips 1972) [Italics ours.]

Sharpton and Jackson are both guilty of financial misdeeds, unsavory and less-than-ennobling activities, and personal behavior unbecoming pastors and unworthy of the goals set forth by Dr. Martin Luther King., Jr. The only reason we bring up King's name in this conclusion to luminary malfeasance is that both Jackson and Sharpton themselves regularly invoke King's name as a kind of holy imprimatur on their own activities. Their overall clerical malfeasance can be summed up in one word: self-aggrandizement in the name of pastoral activism. Moreover, such acts of aggrandizement seem to be pyramided for their value in future enrichment and prestige.

Yet how could either man, Sharpton now a media fixture as a pundit in 2012 with his own hour-long show on the MSNBC cable network and Jackson a frequently sought-after commentator for the "black perspective" on virtually every network, have risen to prominence in spite of the misdeeds enumerated in this chapter? Part of this reason is the personal charisma of each which helped blind followers to, or encouraged them to ignore, the facts of such unpastorly behavior. The salient identities of lay church laypersons, or social movement activists, with their religious and racial traditions do not encourage seeking out or accepting negative information about touted leaders. To be fair to the latter followers, many followers simply have not had access to information about their leaders' actual day-to-day activities, past or present. And, to be fairer still, such ignorance has been the state of many other outside observers. (The next chapter discusses media blinders, deliberate or otherwise, to clergy malfeasance conducted by minority luminaries.)

One correct impression that ought to be gleaned from our sources is that it has taken a host of historians, biographers, internet bloggers, investigative reporters for mainline media outlets, and watchdog agencies to parse out the details of the above instances of clergy malfeasance. Such information of clergy misuse or excess of authority have obviously not been forthcoming from the leaders themselves. Moreover, the narratives at time become complex, if not convoluted, and require patience to unravel like some spiritual/economic/political knot. Nor is popular mythology easily challenged or replaced by facts.

Yet about both Jackson and Sharpton there is still that liminal area where, for all their faults, they have had positive impacts on youths, civil rights, politics, and black businesses. Depending on one's interpretation, this polar judgment can be considered a paradox, a contradiction, a mystery, or a tragedy. About the Reverend Terry Lee

Hornbuckle of Texas, however, whose behaviors have approached the sociopathological, there is no paradox, contradiction, or mystery, much less any tragedy of disillusion, except for the parishioners who put their beliefs and gifts in the hands of his ministry. They confided their faith in him as a pastoral fiduciary and came to accept his lies, his superinflated ego, and his ruthlessness; consequently they were duped for this faith. Unlike Jackson and Sharpton, Hornbuckle was the lowest sort of clerical malfeasant, who abused religious trust with conscious and determined regularity and squandered his true ministerial capabilities.

Thus far we have dealt with the part played in black pastors' malfeasance by identity salience. That is, we have examined the identities of pastors and church congregants within their church communities and how these identities lead the former to confuse their own self-interests with those of true ministerial service. What we have not done more than touch on is how these black church social identities "filter" news of abuses to allow both pastor and followers to fit the identity of clergy malfeasant into a larger identity hierarchy. In the next chapter we turn to such matters, including the identity salience factor in how society, in general, and the media, in particular, deal with the awareness of black pastoral misconduct through resolution of cognitive dissonance.

5

Black Pastoral Misdeeds, Charisma, and Identity Salience

Thus far we have referred to the social-psychological concept of identity salience as this is employed by black parishioners to ignore, downplay, and/or rationalize malfeasant actions by their black pastors. For such persons in the pews, their racial sensitivity and their role relationships to their minority church congregation represent two prominent forms of self-awareness in a hierarchy of identities. These identities often encourage them to excuse the minister of his or her moderate-to-even-serious transgressions or overlook these in ways that would not be so forgiving or charitable in more secular contexts.

In this chapter we extend the notion of identity salience beyond the congregation and its immediate members to the community writ large. We are interested in examining why some observers of the black church, particularly in both the black and white media, so often give certain black pastors, for whom there is a documented record of exaggeration (if not mendacity) and less-than-spiritual behaviors, a nonskeptical "pass" on accountability. In answering this question we will ultimately turn salience identity outward, that is, to the noncongregational audiences of the clergy behavior. This will involve issues of racism, racial myths, fears of being called racist, and white guilt. But to do this we must first examine a purported trait of many black pastors that is often claimed, attributed, and loosely thrown around as if it were some tangible, easily measurable, objective personal characteristic: *charisma*.

Charisma and Identity Salience

Late nineteenth-century German sociologist Max Weber (1964a, 1964b) maintained, as true now as then, that we live in the age of legal–rational, or contractual, role-related authority. Traditional authority, the mode of regal aristocracies and inherited privilege to command obedience, is rapidly on the way out or allowed to linger only for symbolic and/or nostalgic value. Bureaucracy is the context of our modern era.

But *charisma* (from *charism*, or gift, in Greek) continues to reassert its presence. Weber defined charisma as a perceived exceptional quality of leadership of certain persons, derived from any one of a number of possible sources, such as ascetic illumination, divine revelation, exceptional skill or wisdom, or any origin transcending ordinary life. Weber (1964b, 328) asserted that "it is the charismatically qualified leader as such who is obeyed by virtue of personal trust in him and his revelation, his heroism or his exemplary qualities so far as they fall within the scope of the individual's belief in his charisma." Charisma, in other words, is *perceived* as an inherent endowed character trait of the leader by those followers who claim they feel or recognize it. Charisma is fluid, and its dynamics overthrow the staid routine of bureaucracies and dismiss tradition as irrelevant (even pernicious). It is the stuff of revolutionaries and social movements. Charisma excites, inspires, and mobilizes. It stands apart from ordinary, mundane status quo authority.

Charisma also creates loyalty to the leader, which is to say it reorders internally the primacy of role attachments within hierarchies of identities for followers who are attracted to such a leader. Writes House (1988, 117), who has Rev. Jesse Jackson explicitly in mind, most charismatic leaders

> are expansive, dominating, powerful personalities with strong convictions who impose themselves on their environments by their courage, decisiveness, self-confidence, fluency, and energy. . . . They generate a collective excitement to which masses of people surrender themselves.

Indeed, consider elements of Stone's (1984, 152, 163, 164) admittedly laudatory profile of Jackson, one illustrating the description of charisma by Weber and House. Jackson, Stone writes,

> is a high flyer, a swinger who jets back and forth across the country, mingles with the beautiful people . . . He dresses sharply and expensively. . . . When he walks on stage, everyone in the house knows that he is one black cat who has made it. . . . What people want is

a man who looks, acts and walks as if success is his, as if he is the shining example of his own work. That is precisely the role that Jesse Jackson fulfills.... Jackson was a strider, an athlete, and his mere physical presence seemed to bring the attention and respect of the crowd. Men who have a strong sense of purpose and a powerful body seem able to do that.

Similarly, in a less apologetic vein, journalist Frady (1996, 5) has referred to Jackson's "swashbuckler's carriage," with the "flair of a cavalier," a "populist John the Baptist" (44), but also, in the opinion of some, "an insufferably sanctimonious swaggerer" (23).

The strong identification of followers and admirers with the charismatic leader merges his or her purposes and modus operandi with those of the followers, until they can be legitimately said to act as extensions of his or her purposes. There is no need to posit slavish, zombie-like obedience or some mythology of brainwashing. Identification with a charismatic leader is simultaneously an emotional, rational, and even spiritually motivated phenomenon. It is a sociological truism that dynamic social movement leaders have this charismatic flavor. (Flavor is defined here as a social exchange between follower needs and leader demeanor. The leader's demeanor is a symbolically symbiotic reward to followers for support and loyalty.) Charismatic leadership justifies to followers that their short-run sacrifices and the hard work entailed in their willingness to be mobilized are worth it.

But charismatic leadership is Janus-like. The downside of charismatic authority is that the leadership may be erratic, likely as much symbol as substance. Charisma is necessary and functional to stimulate innovations and even civil disobedience or revolution but is a poor resource to sustain an organization over time. Charismatic leaders can create a myriad of exciting projects, for example, even shot-gunning them at followers and raising high expectations. But without the savvy to transform "prophetic" aspirations into the details of more "priestly" mundane day-to-day operations, many of these may turn out to be quixotic efforts quickly spent, leaving a host of projects gradually fading away, as one analysis of the charismatic Asian pretender-to-messiahship, the Reverend Sun Myung Moon and his Unification Church with its numerous short-lived initiatives, found to be true (see Bromley and Shupe [1979]). Moon was a grandiose prophetic and dreamer of initiatives but poor on details to implement his inspirations.

There are, as House (1988, 133–36) notes, limits to charisma besides the fact that charisma in a leader is ultimately a perception based as much as followers' needs as on anything absolute or objective. Charismatic leaders are frequently intense motivators but middlin-to-lousy administrators. Ironically, as Weber (1964a, 1964b) pointed out, there must be a successful "routinization of charisma" wherein the idiosyncratic nature of "prophetic" leadership shifts or is transformed into "priestly" or hierarchical, bureaucratic authority for stability in achievement of goals. (Whether or not this transformation becomes oligarchic, as Michels [1959] and Shupe [2008] maintain, is not our concern here.)

Suffice it to say that charisma, so historically embedded in the role of the black pastor in the American black church, from preaching to often somewhat personalized authoritarian management styles, as we noted in Chapters 2 and 3, is the root source of the black layperson's salient identity both as a congregational member *and* as a "brandname" follower of this pastor or that minister. Salient identity of members with the pastor who heads up a minority church or cause, in other words, is grounded in his or her perceived charisma as much as, or more so than, any other factor. That is why, as House (1988, 15) observes, Jackson ran his terribly disorganized PUSH and PUSH-Excel missions, long on rhetoric but short on sound fiscal management, into the ground. Jackson directed their operations like an autocratic Black Baptist church preacher—and his followers were comfortable with such a style, until the houses of cards fell (but never all at once).

Black Identity Salience and Black Media

Though the American black church has always served as a major crucible within which black identity salience is forged, reinforcement of this overarching racial identity is not limited to the domain of that institution. There is also the important black public media, historically print rather than electronic (at least in order of importance). Indeed, journalist Henry Lee Moon (1967, 133), press secretary for the National Association for the Advancement of Colored People in the 1960s, at the time flatly declared: "Among the host of organizations, institutions, and social forces now actively concerned with various aspects of the civil rights issue, the Negro press, in point of seniority, yields only to the Negro church." Therefore, a brief review of the "race beat," as Roberts and Klibanoff (2006) term it, is in order.

The Black Press

The Reverend Samuel Cornish, a black freeman from Philadelphia, is credited (along with a friend) with having established this country's first black (likely also its first *minority*) newspaper, *Freedom's Journal,* in New York City in 1827. Its stated purpose was "improvement of our injured race," and the editors grounded their abolitionist and equal justice sentiments solidly in the U.S. Constitution (Hunt 1967, 12). There were also white abolitionist newspapers circulating during that era, such as William Lloyd Garrison's famous *Liberator* (started in 1831), but Cornish's paper began a legacy of black periodical publications funded, written, and edited by blacks and intended specifically for black audiences. In fact, an *independent* black voice was *Freedom's Journal's* credo: in the first issue the editors proclaimed: "Too long have others spoken for us" (cited in Roberts and Klibanoff 2006, 13). The newspaper only survived three years, and that precarious existence presaged the fate of many future newspapers. But hundreds of such black publications were to follow (many as short-lived as the *Journal*) between 1827 and the beginning of the civil rights movement in the 1950s.

That first black newspaper illustrated a future pattern of such publications covering ordinary subjects of interest to ordinary black people but ordinarily ignored by nineteenth- and later twentieth-century white newspapers. One predominant subject of the black print medium was continual outspoken recognition and nonacceptance of racial inequality and injustice. Incorporating this theme for the most part made the black press unique. Local, regional, and national black newspapers, daily or weekly, openly wove themes of protest and discrimination into their other topics covering economic and political issues, social activities, jobs and housing, public and private transportation opportunities, and the arts. On this issue of persistent racial protest, journalists Roberts and Klibanoff (2006, 13) wrote:

> The earliest newspapers, both Negro and white, were primarily advocates and special pleaders. But long after white papers had turned to coverage of general-interest news, their Negro counterparts remained loud, clear instruments of protest, by turns advocative and provocative. And for virtually all of their history into the 1950s, they had the race story all to themselves.

During the great wave of internal migration during World War I, when droves of Southern, previously rural blacks, came North to work in the factories of such industrial cities as Chicago, Detroit, Milwaukee, Cleveland, Pittsburgh, and Buffalo, the black presses thrived. Some newspapers drew truly regional as well as national readerships. Many Northern newspapers found eager Southern subscribers as well.

These publications had names like the *Chicago Defender* (which at one time had a circulation of more than 150,000 and sold two-thirds of its issues outside the Chicago area), the *Afro-American, Journal and Guide*, and *The Pittsburgh Courier*. They did not eschew patriotism during the War but at the same time unflinchingly reported on discrimination against black troops in the military branches. Meanwhile, the presses provided understandably anxious families with news about sons in uniform and information about the War; they also brought Northern news back home to the relatives of the migrants who had headed North to work. Report Roberts and Klibanoff (2006, 16):

> All the newspapers found a common result from their coverage: readers wanted more—from the front line, the sidelines, and in between the lines. Negro papers, with few limits on the infusion of drama and parochialism, filled their pages with personal and effusive stories about the essential importance, valor, and loyalty of Negro soldiers. The war was a marketing bonanza.

All post–World War I black papers settled down to the stuff of modern media: entertainment news, politics, artistic personalities and reviews, celebrities, sports, and so forth. But all inescapably were laced with the running theme of life in segregated America and its resented injustice by black citizens.

The importance of this black print media legacy is twofold. First, when precipitating events of the late 1950s led to the formation of the Southern Christian Leadership Conference, the first boycotts and demonstrations, and the coalescing of long-standing grievances into a true social movement industry, black Americans were cognizant enough to make use of the newest journalistic innovation available: television. During the early-to-mid 1950s, for example, Southern radio and television stations as well as newspapers (all the former and almost all the latter being *white*) carried minimal mention of blacks (except when the news covered crime). It took the *national* television networks and press services to bring black resentment to the electronic media. Recalls William B. Monroe, Jr. (1967, 85), former chief of the Washington News Bureau of the National Broadcasting Company (NBC):

> The first time many Southern whites saw Southern Negroes standing up and talking about their rights was on network television. They just plain did not believe it.

Monroe remembers some whites believing that the national networks "manufactured" these unhappy black citizens in the same way (we recall) that some cultic extremists in the United States believe that this country never really accomplished a manned lunar landing in 1968, but instead NASA only filmed it on a sound stage. Nevertheless, Monroe says the national news finally punctured "the magnolia curtain" and television became the tool of choice, or "the chosen instrument" for advancing the civil rights movement.

However, such a statement should not dismiss the important role that the black print media always played, and still plays, in reinforcing the salience of racial identity to black readers before the Civil War, during the Southern Reconstruction era, during both the world wars, and thereafter throughout the Truman, Eisenhower, Kennedy, and Johnson presidential years into present times (see also Klein 1967; Moon 1967; Young 1967).

Second, as has been pointed out earlier, the black press along with the black church helped create fora wherein uniquely black concerns in a segregated society could be openly expressed and dealt with pragmatically. While many whites, Northern and Southern, seemingly were oblivious to continual black resentment of second-class citizenship and the white hypocrisy of democratic ideals of equality, undergirded as it was ultimately by the threat of white coercion, the black press did not dodge the reality. The racial conflict, however muted, the black press acknowledged in its we–they worldview. This coverage had the sociological function of creating solidarity and a unit of shared understandings among blacks (Coser 1956).

Media Constructions of Black Charismatic Leadership

There have been many genuine black leaders who rose to recognition as such by virtue of their bold, stirring oratory or their social positions that placed them in the historical arena of change at moments when their accomplishments and rhetoric resonated with the black community and marked them for notice. This list has included Samuel Cornish, Denmark Vesey, Nat Turner, Frederick Douglass, Booker T. Washington, Marcus Garvey, Father Divine, Martin Luther King., Jr., and Thurgood Marshall, among many others. But what of the host of lesser black "luminaries," particularly clergypersons, who periodically crop up in the media, some enduring and other passing relatively quickly? Who can be considered "authentic" spokespersons for black interests and who have at best been briefly identified in that role by journalists merely needing an interesting sound byte to flesh out a story?

Within the first decade of the civil rights movement, journalists and their editors found that trying to discern the legitimate black spokespersons from the scoundrels, grandstanders, and adventurers was sometimes a difficult task. Part of the problem was that for white newspersons, even the most well-meaning and conscientious, the entire cultural–historical context of the black civil rights movement was a foreign place. George P. Hunt (1967, 19), former managing editor of *Life* magazine, wrote:

> There are no set rules for an editor to follow in the treatment (or avoidance) of racial news. The situations are different, the environments are different, the people involved are different, and so are the editor's alternatives—silence, partial silence, story positioning, balance, the ring of crusading journalism, and so on.

The particular problem of identifying and vetting "authentic" black leadership was keenly felt. For example, Martin S. Hayden (1967, 35), former editor in chief of the *Detroit News* wrote:

> For reporters, Negro or white, there is always the question of the reliability of their Negro informants. Specifically, there is the problem of sorting out Negro "leaders." Some who claim to be Negro leaders are genuine; some are little more than self-promoters with a letterhead and a fancy organization name; some are simply charlatans. I think every white editor, Northern or Southern, has to guard against a temptation to accept so-called Negro leaders at face value ...

Arthur B. Bertelson (1967, 61), editorial-page editor of the *Los Angeles Times* during the 1960s, raised the same note of wariness about identifying black leaders based on his own experience:

> Here we committed the honest error of putting too much faith in the avowed purposes of what was at first the revolving leadership of that [black] community. Those leaders, who came to strut and fret their brief hours on the stage, were in part charlatans and demagogues, and they quickly faded. Our mistake, the mistake of the press, was in not applying the astringent of objectivity to the words of these people. [Bracketed insert ours.]

Respected reporter for the *New York Post*, Ted Poston (1967, 70–71), observing black myths in politics and civil rights, similarly criticized journalists for these sorts of errors in legitimating bogus black leader-wannabes that his colleagues above warned against:

> But there is an increasing and dangerous tendency for Northern papers to create their own versions of Negro leaders in the Harlems of this country. How do they do this? Simply by giving front-page coverage to and designating as a "leader" any nonwhite citizen who makes preposterous statements about race relations. [Post termed the practice] ... giving respectability to irresponsibility ... [Bracketed insert ours.]

Finally, Thomas W. Young (1967, 131–32), editor of the Norfolk (VA) *Journal and Guide* (a venerable black publication), repeated the same theme from the standpoint of established black media professionals:

> One other vital role that the Negro press had assumed fell to it because the white press failed to demonstrate its responsibility in the matter of identifying and evaluating Negro leadership. A frequent criticism is that the white press "creates" Negro leaders in such cities as Chicago, New York, Philadelphia, and Los Angeles. The problem is not limited to the cities listed. Examples could be cited from almost every community where there has been civil-right activity.

Young decried the instant raising-up of essentially nonentities, whatever their fleeting moment of notice by journalists, to alleged "spokesperson" status and claimed it was more a white than a black sin of commission. He affirmed that "... the Negro publisher knows who the Negro leaders are, the sources and the extent of their strength. The Negro press does not invent or create community leaders." And he denounced that "proliferation of spokesmen and chieftains eager to head a march at the drop of a hat or the click of a newsman's camera."

The evolution of the civil rights movement did produce some leaders more enduring than others. Some, like Ralph Abernathy, modestly eschewed more attention than their activities warranted. Others deliberately and continually cultivated publicity. A good example is Jesse Jackson, who proved adept at inserting himself into the media limelight until he became an accepted spokesperson fixture in the eyes of journalists. Stone (1984, 148) recalls that in the early years of Jackson's aggressive entry into the Southern Christian Leadership Conference, he had a photogenic preoccupation:

> When journalists were shooting photos of King, somehow the unknown Jesse Jackson would appear standing next to the great leader

as though he belonged there. When there was a lull in a civil rights rally, Jesse would leap onto the stage and begin making a speech.

It was a skill that improved with experience, so much so that though Jackson was fundamentally mistrustful of the media due to his limited ability to control the images of him it projected, by his second run for the Democratic presidential nomination in 1988, Jackson nevertheless tried to create the impression with journalists that he was their simpatico, a candidate who was finally candid with them and trustworthy for their purposes (Colton 1989, 145). Other black leaders, with admittedly their share of charismatic presence and strong emotionally charged messages, such as Al Sharpton (who was an admirer and junior understudy of the older Jackson) and the Nation of Islam's Malcolm X and later Minister Louis Farrakhan (Gardell 1996; Singh 1997) were astute vicarious students of how to play to the camera with dramatic staged events, memorable impassioned images, and shock-value rhetoric.

But grandstanding is not the same as outright criminal mendacity. The demise of the Reverend Henry Lyons, once pastor of a black St. Petersburg, Florida megachurch and past president (1994–99) of the National Baptist Convention USA (NBCUSA), was due in part to his extravagant lifestyle (several homes and expensive automobiles), his adultery (several mistresses and a vengeful wife), and his fraudulent activities. Lyons had conspiratorially inflated the membership rolls of his denomination, at one point claiming he represented thousands of members more than actually existed, in order to sell the bogus list to commercial companies for their own marketing uses. He bilked those companies out of four million dollars. Lyons also pocketed over a quarter of a million dollars donated by the Jewish Anti-Defamation League (and other charitable groups) supposedly to be used in rebuilding burned black churches in the South. In 1988, Lyons pled guilty to five fraud charges as well as forty-nine *other* charges including racketeering, defrauding banks, and failure to pay the IRS taxes on almost one and one-half million dollars income. He was eventually sentenced to five and one-half years in prison and court-ordered to pay two and one-half million dollars restitution. So powerful was his denominational members' identity salience with their leader that the NBCUSA voted in annual conference the same year as his conviction to continue paying Lyons his $100,000 annual salary for the duration of his incarceration (see Peterson 2003, 4–6; Shupe 2008, 50–51).

Pastoral scandals continued to plague the NBCUSA, as we indicated in Chapter 3. Many of the other "minor league" pastoral malfeasants in that chapter, it will be recalled, were not the national-level or even regional-level luminaries on a par with a Texas-based Terry Lee Hornbuckle, New York's Al Sharpton, or Chicago's Jesse Jackson. In the minor luminaries' cases it was largely their criminal deeds and internal church scandals that attracted outside media attention rather than those pastors having, as Sharpton and Jackson did, assiduously sought the media limelight and then, under press scrutiny, have the publicity backfire and cause exposure of their ministries' less-than-savory aspects.

Several modern black writers, journalists, and others, have taken the black media (and other "observers") to task for lacking the very discernment that journalist-editor Thomas W. Young (cited above) claimed was a black specialty. As a prime example, Juan Williams, a politically moderate Fox Network television commentator, recently bemoaned how charisma and simply loud exposition have substituted for substance or true leadership direction. In his book *Enough*, Williams (2006, 27) accuses Jackson, Sharpton, Farrakhan, and a host of other black spokespersons for simply parroting the time-worn-out clichés phrases of an earlier civil rights era purely for their crowd-catching emotional value and failing to advance any *meaningful* civil rights or black grassroots initiatives, locked as they are in the mind-set of the 1960s. In Nation of Islam's Louis Farrakhan's case he espouses with great and sometimes hateful noise the utopian, antihistorical drivel of early black nationalist movements in the first part of the Twentieth Century. Indeed, the subtitle of Williams' book, *Enough*, lays his thesis out in stark terms: *The Phony Leaders, Dead-End Movements, and Culture of Failure that Are Undermining Black America—And What We Can Do About It*. Worse, claims Williams (2006, 67–85) during the 1970s and 1980s these spokespersons distracted black Americans from striving for meaningful gains with the empty and impractical chimera of white financial reparations to blacks in compensation for centuries of slavery. And some like Jackson and Sharpton, Williams bluntly accuses, have used black civil rights rhetoric as a dodge to enrich themselves personally in the short run with a "take-what-you-can-get-now" cynical mentality that attempts to loot white corporations (2006, 44–66). Says Williams (55): "Under Jackson and Sharpton, the high moral standing of civil rights has eroded, slid downhill. . . ."

An even harsher critic of the same charisma-*sans*-substance vein is Rev. Jesse Lee Peterson, an unabashedly conservative critic, admirer of Booker T. Washington's self-help philosophy, sometimes media pundit, and president of the nonprofit organization BOND (Brother Organization of a New Destiny). In his book *Scam* (2003, 4), Peterson attacks pastoral con-men and hypocrites like Rev. Henry Lyons ("The corruption of the black church starts at the top and trickles down into the congregations."). He has further condemnations for others mentioned in previous pages above with no punches pulled:

> Black Americans have been scammed: what's worse, they've been scammed by their own folks. . . . If some blacks wonder why things don't improve despite this "leadership," they need to wake up to the fact that these leaders profit by creating hatred and animosity between the races. (ix)

Peterson refers to such leaders, for all the reasons discussed earlier in this chapter, as "problem profiteers" and "scam artists," "self-appointed leaders," "self-proclaimed leaders," and "arrogant elitists," many of whom "display little or no personal integrity in their own lives." In similar hyperbolic terms he concludes that "blacks don't need leaders. What they do need, however, are good role models" (11–37) minus "delusional thinking" and the self-pitying mind-set of being encouraged to embrace victimization.

The foregoing description may seem harsh and certainly unfair to the majority of black pastors who conduct their ministries with integrity and sincerity and who go about a regular routine of ministering to congregants' constant spiritual, emotional, and even physical needs without all the grandstanding proclamations and occasional personal enrichment. But, as in any sociological study of deviance, we are engaged in analyzing the exceptions, the noticeable but nevertheless influential (and at times, predatorily harmful) pastoral malfeasants who, due to the inconsistency of their words versus their deeds, suggest the need for analysis.

"Spoiled Identity" and the Black Sellout

There is one further aspect in the media of black identity salience and charismatic (pastoral) leadership to be examined: the concept of the "sellout." Harvard University law professor Randall Kennedy, an author who has written about topics ordinarily considered taboo among his black colleagues, devoted an entire book to the topic of his title,

Sellout: The Politics of Racial Betrayal (2008). In this book Kennedy deals frankly with the image of a "corrupt, acquiescent" black person attempting to curry favor among whites once he or she has achieved some position of privilege or celebrity status. The concern of blacks, he says, is that such a hypothetical black person will sellout for white establishment attention and rewards at the expense of neglecting fellow blacks' attempts at social improvement, equality, and even that individual's racial identity. In Kennedy's words (2008, 4–5):

> When used in a racial context among African Americans, "sellout" is a derogatory term that refers to blacks who knowingly or with gross negligence act against the interest of blacks as a whole.... someone who is dangerously antagonistic to blacks' well-being. He is worse than an enemy.

Examples of such alleged sellouts would be black persons who rise to prominence, particularly in government but also in other institutions, and then seem more interested in mingling within those multiracial corridors of power than serving purely as advocates for black causes. Kennedy mentions black politicos (who also committed the "sin" of becoming Republicans or working in federal Republican administrations), such as former General Colin Powell, Vernon Jordan, former U.S. Secretary of State Condoleezza Rice, and U.S. Supreme Court Justice Clarence Thomas. Also included would be intellectuals such as libertarian economist Thomas Sowell. Prominent blacks who were accused of selling out in the nineteenth century would include Martin R. Delany (an exponent of black nationalism during the 1870s but who broke with the Republican Party, became a Democrat and campaigned as a former Confederate general) as well as the venerable abolitionist Frederick Douglass who married a white woman; in the early twentieth century, black leaders labeled as sellouts by fellow blacks included famous sociologist W. E. B. DuBois, who outspokenly criticized black protest actions against American's involvement in World War I and Harlem's apotheotic Father Divine, who spurned his black wife and married his white secretary (Harris 1971; Kennedy 2008, 6).

Sellouts are condemned by the black media as Quislings, betrayers, even saboteurs of racial equality, members of the "I've-got-mine-and-screw-you!" club. They are called "Uncle Toms," "oreos," "Stephen Fetchits," and so forth. Persons tarred with the cognomen "sellout" have, in sociological terms, a stigma placed on their reputations, or are each reduced to having a "spoiled identity," meaning their racial identity (as a normally important part of a minority member's salience hierarchy) has conflicted with, and been lost in, their quest for upward mobility and personal aggrandizement. They have been bought off and seduced from their racial duty. (Stigma comes from the Greek for mark or sign; in sociology, it is a negative moral status that influences other persons' views and treatment of an individual so-labeled—see Goffman 1963.)

As far as the black media and other black spokespersons are concerned, attacking or critically reviewing the actions of black celebrities (with the exception of addictive or libidinous black athletes) *by other blacks* in the media is often considered selling out. This reality forces some black journalists to walk a delicately strung tightrope (Newkirk 2002). Jesse Lee Peterson (2003, 123), conservative black author, cleric, and critic of many contemporary black luminaries such as Jesse Jackson and Al Sharpton, puts the matter bluntly:

> Black people tell each other that a black should not criticize a fellow black in the company of whites. These blacks who do have clear vision and state the truth plainly are called "sellouts," "traitors to the cause," or "Uncle Toms." We have been made to feel guilty if we dare to disagree with black ministers of whatever stripe.

House (1988) has discussed the fine line that has to be drawn between racial unity within a minority group for the sake of achieving collective benefits versus the tyranny of (in our words) racial identity salience over the individual's right to critical discernment and disagreeing with leaders. But fundamentally he concurs with Peterson's complaint, particularly as it involves charismatic leaders and airing their "dirty laundry":

> Furthermore, debate and dissent within the minority community are often interpreted as disloyalty to the minority cause; consequently the leadership that develops is often not based on a rational discussion of issues but on direction imposed by the leader. Minority charismatic leadership is often antidiscursive and antidemocratic and tends to be authoritarian. This tendency is further complicated by the fact that the traditional leaders of the black church have been authoritarian preachers certified by white elites. (163)

An example of this "certification" by the white elite media can be seen in the political career of Jesse Jackson. Unquestionably Jackson has been lionized as the successor to Dr. Martin Luther King., Jr., the last standing leader of any consequence of the civil rights era, even a champion of black capitalism (a claim we dispute in the final section of this chapter). The media rarely deny that he is charismatic, forceful, earnest, and commanding; often he is portrayed to blacks as larger than life and indomitable. Starting during the 1970s, and particularly in the 1980s, Jackson was featured in major articles in *Time*, and *Life* magazines, most major urban newspapers like the *New York Times*, and even was the subject of the coveted *"Playboy* Interview."

In one academic study, Nannetta Durnell of Florida Atlantic University performed a content analysis on 184 articles on Jackson (She counted 2,100 assertions about his leadership.) in *Time, Newsweek*, and *U.S. News and World Report* for an entire year (January 1 to December 31, 1988). She asked the research question, "[Did these three national news magazines] portray the Reverend Jesse Jackson as a mythical hero in their coverage of the 1988 United States presidential campaign?" [Bracketed inserts ours.] Her conclusion was that these three leading national magazines (none of which is especially liberal) presented Jackson and/or his presidential quest the majority of the time as "mythic" and Jackson himself as the "mythic hero" in the textbook sense understood by anthropologists and classical folklorists. Durnell (1988, 209) writes that "This mythical component has significant implications for African American leaders." The media in effect became a "storyteller," and its repetition of the "mythical motif" of a leader like Jackson, snowballing from publication to publication in a sort of (our term) "self-fulfilling focus" built the charismatic legend, or halo. Says Durnell (1988, 209):

> This study also reveals that to be regarded as a mythical hero means power.... to be identified as a Black leader in America, one needs to be more than articulate, charismatic, and religious oriented,... this individual should possess the constructs of a mythical hero.

When the criticism of such a black mythic hero does come, especially from a minority journalist, opprobrium as a sellout and the stigma-affixing ensues. The quintessential case is that of Milton Coleman, (black) journalist for the *Washington Post*. In 1984, during his first campaign for the Democratic presidential nomination, Jesse Jackson took a break with Coleman in an airport lounge and after asking if "he could talk black" between them uttered his famous reference to Jews as "Hymies" and New York City (where he was having some campaign headaches) as "Hymietown." Coleman published the remarks, and a mushroom cloud rose up from fellow black journalists as Jackson's currency with Jewish voters (hard-hit already by his recent pro-Arab meetings in the Middle East) headed downward. Black journalist-professor at New York University, Pamela Newkirk (2002, 147), observes that Coleman was pilloried as a black Judas. He "was assailed by blacks across the country as a sellout who, for career advancement, was attempting to derail Jackson's historic campaign." Minister Louis Farrakhan denounced Coleman in terms of "filth" and "traitor" (Newkirk 2002, 147).

Al Sharpton made the same accusation about General Colin Powell, adding Powell to a "spoiled identity" list along with conservative black academics, black district attorneys, and prosecutors that Sharpton did not like, and government officials who were not stereotypically liberal "black" in their professional roles, political leanings, or stated attitudes. And journalist Kenneth R. Timmerman (2002, 42–43) recounts the case of black *Chicago Tribune* reporter Angela Parker, one of the pioneers in revealing Jesse Jackson's clergy malfeasant corporate kickbacks as head of early Operation Breadbasket. Jackson lambasted and embarrassed her personally in a gathering of fellow reporters, verbally abusing her in plainly sexist ways, and had her home picketed by OB followers. Even if he was not directly involved, his condemnation of her indirectly resulted in her receiving death threats and professional harassment for years. (See also Timmerman [2002] on black journalist Barbara Reynolds and Reynolds [1975] herself for details of her own experience with hostile black responses and the "sellout" accusation due to her investigative reporting that to an extent delionized Jackson.)

In closing this brief section on black charismatic leadership and the black media, it should be reiterated that while charisma is commonly (and mistakenly) understood as a personal attribute of a leader, like his or her inherent character or a possession, in reality charisma is relational. Charisma is in the eye of the beholder. And followers exchange their gifts of time and energy, their loyalty and some portion of their autonomy to the demands of any charismatic leader in exchange for the promised benefits (like IOUs) and immediate reassurances provided by the leader. This is the fundamental social exchange occurring within the black church between pastors and laypersons. Charisma is more than really good oratory. It is heroic images fed by a media—particularly a minority-based media—eager to cultivate charisma in the leader both directly for their own commercial value and indirectly for their audience. Charisma can be eroded or lost, but it often has staying power in the face of evidence that should otherwise discredit it.

White Guilt and Reverse Identity Salience

If it is sometimes difficult for black journalists and observers to cast themselves in the role of counter-identity salience critics of other black spokesperson lest they be accused of betraying some general minority cause, it becomes more so the case for white critics who wish to avoid being stigmatized as racists. Journalist Marshall Frady (1996, 9) in beginning his thorough biographical examination of Jesse Jackson's career and its socio-political meaning, questions whether it is possible for a white person to empathize sufficiently to comprehend a black leader's odyssey through segregation and then into a post-civil rights movement era. Frady concludes that it is possible, within limits, but also asks further whether there are "special reaches of human experience," sacred or exclusive to any group, that are ultimately beyond the comprehension of even sensitive outsiders. He concludes obviously in the negative, as he demonstrates in his 566-page book on Jackson.

But, however, the debate on the feasibility of attempting to do research on an in-group other than one's own (for example, "It takes one to know one" versus "Can only Nazis write about Nazis? Does one have to have been a battered woman to write about domestic violence?"), there is (or ought to be) a certain indirect humility that occurs to most fair-minded whites when they analyze black activities within a worldview and meaning context that they cannot readily or conventionally interpret at first glance. This was particularly a problem for white journalists during the early days of the civil rights movement, at least for the more discerning members of that profession who were alert enough to guard against knee-jerk parochial reactions to an emotionally charged social movement. The movement emerged, after all, out of a social environment that was quite foreign to aspects of their own experiences. For many white journalists it was all a learning experience. For example, journalist Harry S. Ashmore writes in *Civil Rights and Wrongs* (1994, 411) of whites reporting on blacks in print newsrooms during the 1960s:

> Until the 1960s blacks were portrayed in print and on radio and television by demeaning stereotypes that certified their inferior

social status. When I was breaking in as an apprentice journalist, the style sheets in effect on most newspapers designated members of the minority as "negro" with a lower-case "n." "Colored," having been incorporated in the title of the NAACP back in 1913, was acceptable, but "black" was proscribed, along with such palpably offensive terms as "nigger," "darky," and "coon."

Ashmore remembers when "Negro" became capitalized "to put it on a par with such terms for other 'races'" such as the Irish or the Italians or the Japanese. Only later (some would say reluctantly) did newspapers, particularly in the South, begin to use "Mr." or "Mrs." or professional titles for black newsmakers. Ashmore correctly notes that the dual psychological effect of employing (or not employing) such titles of courtesy on both black/white readers and white writers was profound. In the ensuing years, particularly beyond the 1960s, a "marked revision" (his phrase) in references to blacks occurred across a variety of media outlets.

True enough. But the case can be made further that, as the media coverage pendulum swung away from demeaning stereotypes of blacks and more subtle dismissing of respect for black social actors, a sort of *reverse identity salience* began to evolve in white reporting on black leaders. This reverse was not just a matter of using courtesy titles. It also dealt with questions of motives and the criticisms of behaviors, things that whites felt comfortable imputing and describing about white offenses but not when they belonged to black leaders.

The reputations of the latter, in effect, have now become somewhat sacrosanct. It takes truly egregious activities, too frequently or flagrantly committed to ignore, for white criticism to be applied to black leaders. This has never been true, of course, for the most extreme groups and their spokespersons. Witness the Nation of Islam and the host of denunciations of Minister Louis Farrakhan, a man representing a group espousing open racial superiority themes and who has not been lax to hand out racial and hateful epithets to Jews and many whites. But for spokespersons of apparently black mainstream organizations and churches, there has been a reluctance by the media to "play up" or focus on their more malfeasant sides.

A prime reason has been white guilt. Black author Shelby Steele (2006, 21) claims that blatant white racism has evolved counterclockwise into white guilt that is often seen by some black leaders opportunistically as an opening to press the case for black victimization and white payback: "A moral ambivalence and guilt around race had opened in white America that could be worked on by anger." Not only is racial prejudice "utterly illegitimate" but now white guilt

> makes the moral authority of whites and the legitimacy of American institutions *contingent* on proving a negative: that they are not racist. The great power of white guilt comes from the fact that it functions by stigma, like racism itself. Whites and American institutions are stigmatized as racist until they prove otherwise.... [White guilt, writes Steele] depends on their fear of stigmatization, their fear of being called a racist. (27) [Italics in original.]

Black political scientist Andrew Hacker, in his book *Two Nations* (1992, 50), observes that the white liberal sense of white guilt (liberal, of course, recognized as a broad spectrum made up of nonconservative ordinal points) is nonetheless "a white coherent outlook concerning what white American owes to its black citizens." It involves public and even private forms of discourse about blacks, particularly for journalists, politicians, and academics. Hacker operationalizes white guilt in terms of being especially felt by those educated whites in the broad middle class:

> general empathy for the less economically well-off; free-floating altruism; accepting "personal responsibility for racial conditions that prevail in their country" regardless whether the white person is of Southern or slave-owning heritage; growing ambiguities about the accomplishments, primacy and value of Western culture and civilizations; concerns that the negative aspects of modern technologies toward indigenous cultures and the environment are somehow inherently "white"; a personal and indiscriminate psychology of *mea culpa* "atonement" toward blacks in general (i.e., as a category); a decided, almost driven cultivation of African American music, art and theater; and a relentless search for black approval.

On this approval issue, "White liberals," says Hacker (1992, 55),

> want to be liked by black people, as if having this goodwill is a seal of approval.... Liberals hope blacks will acknowledge that some whites—themselves, as it happens—are not The Enemy, but rather can be counted as friends and allies. For blacks to grant this, if only by bestowing a smile, serves to certify one's moral status.

Contrarily,

> Liberals stand in dread of black disfavor, which must be mollified by admitting to oversight or error. This is especially evident when blacks charge whites with racism. Rather than deny the indictment, the liberal tendency is to admit to such bias, and pledge renewed vigilance against future errors. (55)

The upshot, these two authors agree, is a consequence we term *reverse identity salience*. Many liberal whites, including some unknown proportion of journalists and many academics, have incorporated guilt from belonging to a racial category that formerly included some oppressors into their hierarchy of personal identities. They purchase the argument that they should identify with former blacks' former literal oppressors and internalize the guilt thereof. Both Steele and Hacker see this reverse of identities as useful for some exploitive black leaders. It is what enabled Jesse Jackson, first in Chicago and then nationally, to put the fear of stigma of being labeled racist into the hearts and pocketbooks of so many corporate executives. Not explicitly mentioning Jackson and his Operation Breadbasket in Chicago, Steele's (2006, 35–36) description of the situation nevertheless seems keenly on target with the logic behind Jackson's corporate shakedown:

> Thus, while guilt made racism into a valuable currency for black Americans—a currency that enmeshed whites (and especially white institutions) in obligation *not to principles* but to black people as a class.... White guilt had inadvertently opened up racism as the single greatest opportunity to blacks from the mid-sixties on—this for a people with no other ready source of capital with which to launch itself into greater freedom.... white guilt began to make racism into an opportunity for blacks—an occasion for "demands."... [Emphasis in original.]

Steele calls it all "blackmail by white guilt," leading politically correct (and therefore wary) whites to be "afraid of racism's hyped-up and bloated reputation."

Thus, to return to a Jesse Jackson (and by parallelism to regional Sharpton-type charismatic leaders), Elizabeth O. Colton (1989, 186–88), press secretary for Jesse Jackson's second (1988) run for the Democratic presidential nomination, recounts how Jackson, who had long had a love–hate attraction for media coverage, after his spectacular win in the Michigan Democratic primary was treated with a double-standard by largely white press members concerning the "scrutiny" he received as a candidate:

> Soon after Michigan the media began a campaign of "scrutiny," but their examination of Jesse was still not the same as it would have been for another successful candidate. The new "scrutiny" was more publicized and talked about than real. The media's spotlight on Jackson seemed to elevate him still more instead of raising the questions that needed to be addressed.

Colton also notes the white guilt/fear-of-being-called-a-racist factor in white reporting on Jackson:

> Unfortunately, reporters feared that any criticism of Jackson would be construed as racism. For most, there seemed no solution, no way out. Even those traveling with Jackson, who knew more about his mercurial personality, would not dare write about it. And the more powerful he became, the more they realized that they would have to temper any criticism if they were to be allowed to continue following him, not only in this campaign but in the future.

One national television network correspondent confessed to this fear of stigma as a racist and told Colton:

> I know I'm not a racist, but I also know that it would be very easy to do and say things now vis-à-vis Jesse that could easily be interpreted as racism. I'm willing to do tough pieces on Jesse, but you can be sure that we'll look at every damn syllable. It's absolutely clear to me that if Jesse were a white man, he'd probably be getting... kicked around rather royally by the press.

In the same way, despite his image of being a champion of black entrepreneurship, including being promoted as such in a book he wrote with his son, U.S. Congressman Jesse L. Jackson, Jr., *It's About the Money! (1999)*, the bulk of Jackson's assets and his income from his various groups has either come from government grants (that he often mismanaged) or kickbacks he demanded from real black entrepreneurs, often moderately sized businessmen, when he squeezed concessions from white corporations. Jackson in fact has typified a trend observed by Earl Ofari (Hutchenson), namely, that black people in the United States have historically had a weak commercial tradition and that it has been rarely ameliorated by spokespersons for their financial empowerment. Rather, a black elite, often involved in politics, has benefited at the expense of most blacks. Says Ofari (1970, 10): "This elite has, when politically active, pressed black capitalism upon the black masses as a program to solve their problems, but never with significant results." Instead, the "programs" end up helping those elites. The same could be said for the majority of black Chicagoans and Operation Breadbasket. Cronyism is never democratic in its fruits.

Critics of this reverse identity salience argument may point to the avalanche of criticism, black and white, of the pre–World War II charismatic black leaders Father Divine, Bishop "Daddy" grace, and the other "black gods of the metropolis," as Fauset (1970) labeled them. But these men were nonmainstream religious leaders, beyond the pale of "respectable black churches," and white guilt was still a thing of the future. Existing critical media treatments of Sharpton, Jackson and others have generally been written by avowedly conservative writers (such as journalists Al Hunt and George Will), published by notably conservative presses (such as Timmerman's 2002 *Shakedown*, Regnery Press), or, particularly if the journalists like Chicago's Angela Parker and Barbara Reynolds are black, hounded as sellouts and, insofar as possible, marginalized by both the white mainstream media and/or efforts of the targets of their critical reporting.

Concluding Remarks

It is ironic, but explainable, that the malfeasant activities of some charismatic black leaders have been ignored, minimized, or pushed aside out of most public awareness. White guilt, or fear of accusations of being racist, are primary among the motives of observers who choose to "look the other way" or blithely dismiss "pedestrian" acts of clergy malfeasance, such as flirtatious or even adulterous behavior by black clerics.

By way of summary, there are three social conditions within which the white media will largely overlook such behaviors:

1. There is white guilt, which does not exempt pre-civil rights reporting and conservative outlets but seriously curtails modern mainline media reporting in the way of a self-fulfilling prophecy: fear that reporting black clergy malfeasance may call down accusations of racism, which discourages such reporting, hence later reporting minority clergy misconduct makes it even more sensational and subject to increased fears of being called racist.
2. The black leader is clearly embedded within and identified with a mainstream black church tradition. (Remember that Depression-era

Father Divine stepped over the line when he claimed that he *was* God, not even the Son of God.) White leaders and outside critics are adverse to promoting criticisms of "sister" black denominations that bear a strong ecclesiastical affinity to white ones.

3. The misdeeds of the black pastor are believed to be purely local, and evidently the results of idiosyncratic motives such as greed, lust, or pride (as we sampled in Chapter 3). Thus, these revelations of misconduct are perceived as merely episodic and not indicative of anything more fundamental or systemic in much the same the mass media misinterpreted earlier reported Roman Catholic priest pedophile scandals of the 1980s (and their cover-ups) as something anomalous rather than phenomena endemic in the American Church hierarchy (Berry and Renner 2004, 74ff).

It is as if the more nationally prominent a leader's persona, the more easily he (usually a he) receives a "pass" by the media for actions that would otherwise call down a scandal. White guilt seems less impressed with street crime and local bad pastors than with national luminaries.

These are conclusions pointing toward the more general theoretical statements we wish to make in the concluding chapter. But there are still further empirical generalizations to be made before that denouement.

6

Understanding Black Pastoral Malfeasance and Laity

Until recently, the study of clergy malfeasance as a special subtype within larger elite deviance has almost exclusively focused on white pastors and their churches, with a few Asian group exceptions. True, some black pastors have been "caught" in elite deviance's published analytic "net," but only incidentally or anecdotally and with almost never any consideration of the place of black ministerial leadership misconduct within the black sacred community, black culture generally, or in light of black religion's history.

At the same time as observed earlier, studies of pastoral malfeasance in older groups, Western and Eastern, abound. Consider just a short sample of sources (not including numerous social science journal articles) for Roman Catholic priest abuse from the 1980s and 1990s *before* the 2002 Boston Archdiocese megascandal (Berry 1992; Burkett and Bruni 1993; Greeley 1992; Hopkins 1998; Hopkins and Lasser 1998; Horst 1998; Kennedy 2001; Shupe 1995, 1998; Shupe et al. 2000; Sipe 1995, 1998; Stiles 1987; Vaillancourt 1980). For Protestant, Mormon, and Jewish groups there are also a number of reliable sources stretching back decades, as there are for Asian spiritual groups, new or traditional, in the United States. For example, in one particular modern Zen Buddhist scandal involving power, sex, and money (among the three things Zen believers are supposed to put in relativistic spiritual perspective) in San Francisco Zen Center, an American teacher-successor to a Japanese Zen missionary engaged in rapacious adultery and sexual exploitation of female devotees, audaciously padded his lifestyle with luxurious perks such as limousines and sumptuous living accommodations, and authoritatively demanded deference from followers (Downing 2001).

Such case studies are legion in North American religion.

Some of this social exchange of obedience/reverence-for-spiritual comfort/assurance transaction, one can obviously conclude, is due to adults consciously seeking new religious wisdom and lifestyles and willing to undergo sacrifices to achieve spiritual clarity. (See e.g., Balch [1995] on one West Coast charismatic cult with such a spiritual transaction that went terribly wrong.) Some of it, on the other hand, is systematically conditioned, or socialized, into congregants of mainline groups at a young age. For example, Roman Catholic journalist and editor Daniel Callahan (1965, 77) writes of church socialization within the highly pyramidal church's parochial school system when he was young, and its discouragement of looking critically at elites, in the 1960s:

> [A Catholic student's] religious education is accompanied by a thoroughgoing indoctrination in the etiquette and demeanor required of the layman in the presence of nuns and priests. He is taught to pay elaborate homage to the dignity and lofty status of those in the religious life. He will learn that normally it is not proper for him to challenge them, especially on religious matters. He will learn that deference to their religious authority, and the purported wisdom which goes with that authority, must be the norm to be followed at all times. What training cannot accomplish in this direction, the garb of nuns and the collar of the priest often can. These are signs of authority, signs that those so adorned are figures deserving of special respect.

However, beyond possible similar anecdotal reasons for the countenance of black pastor abuse as we have presented among parishioners, there remains the task to draw out and discuss the fundamentals of an inductive theory of minority congregational response to this phenomenon. (Recall that we are not interested in the various psychological motives of perpetrators. This is the task of psychotherapists and clinical psychologists.)

According to our previous axioms in Chapter 2, the black congregant reaction to scandal should not represent merely some anomaly of the pre and postslave American historical experience. Rather, as sociology maintains, the general ought to be located and perceived in the specific. History ought to be preserved in the present. And the black experience ought to be worth something more than the sum of its miserable and glorious parts. Thus, the black pastoral malfeasance phenomenon ought to resonate more broadly beyond Afro-Americans to larger domains of social identity and allegiances in more minority cultures and religions.

One way to develop a set of theoretical propositions about minority congregant responses to clergy malfeasance is to employ a systematic examination of clergy scandal *as an evolutionary process rather than as an event*. In other words, how do the seeming regularities of discovery, shock, elite resistance, and later public reaction coalesce into something more meaningfully larger instead of only being regarded as freakish or episodic? To do this we can turn to other subdisciplines in sociology already possessing well-established conceptual schemed for our purposes.

It is tempting to make use of the lens of Neil Smelser's (1962) six-stage "value-added" theory of collective behavior. This approach was originally developed to provide patterned predictability in analyzing the life cycle of riots, demonstrations, and similar types of collective behavior that previously were otherwise regarded as chaotic, totally without structure, and even irrational. Smelser concluded that collective behavior was not caused by mysterious or unknowable, irrational, asocial forces but rather by understandable social structural strains and rationally sought, if even violent, outcomes in a stepwise development.

However, Smelser's approach is limited due to its fundamentally structural–functional assumptions and that fact that it is purely descriptive, whereas our approach is obviously conflict oriented, and we strive for general predictive theoretical propositions. Instead, we turn to a more recent branch of sociology in a three-part syllogism.

Toward a Logic Model Approach

We believe a more fruitful orientation for making empirical generalizations about clergy scandals, or a pretheoretical path on which to first embark, can come out of evaluation research in sociological practice. Sociological practice, let us axiomatically state, is that form of applied sociological research aimed at intervention or amelioration of policy/group procedures. With that formalization end in mind, Davidson (2005), a premier exemplar of this approach, advocates a preinterventionist inventory of conceptual and theoretical assumptions of the problem to be addressed, the causes and strategies which will presumably alter the course of events, mechanisms that will operate as anticipated, and the expected outcomes. This inventory, she maintains for practitioners (particularly those wanting to sort out the operations of a complex organization) is best summarized in a pictorial illustration of independent, intermediate, and dependent variables sketched out in a chronological flowchart ordered by boxes, arrows, and so forth. Davidson (2005, 242) describes this approach as

> A diagram that illustrates the cause-and-effect mechanism(s) by which an evaluand [the entity being evaluated] meets (or is supposed to meet) certain needs or produces (or is supposed to produce) certain effects. [Bracketed words ours.]

We think this "logic" of the logic model is heuristically useful, though we trust to the literacy of our readers to dispense with boxes and arrows. Instead, we proceed as follows: We first examine a recent example of apparent black pastoral malfeasance (or at least a scandal if no malfeasance could be legally proven, with the "evaluand" perhaps being the congregation or its ministry) in its purely descriptive form. Then we perform the construction of a logic model through a narrative that highlights the generic aspects of the scandal, i.e., aspects relevant to similar scandals within the black (and other) communities. Finally we will present a set of inductive propositions for a theory of minority clergy deviance.

Description of a Scandal

We have chosen the 2010–11 clergy scandals of Bishop Eddie Long, pastor of 25,000-member New Birth Missionary Baptist Church in Atlanta, Georgia, as an apparent episode of black clergy malfeasance. In particular, we will focus on reactions from three audiences: the congregational members themselves, the outside black community (secular and sacred), and larger societal reaction.

There is an enormous journalistic literature on Bishop Long's scandals (unrelated to the separate literature on health, sex roles, and so forth generated by Bishop Long himself as an author), from *Newsweek* magazine to numerous theological publications and regional newspapers such as the *Atlanta Journal-Constitution* and *The Washington Post* to an enormity of internet blogs and independent reportages. We have sampled from each pool, content here to outline the Long scandals as illustrative of the minority pastor situation central to our concerns. Our interest lies not in judging Bishop Long or making decisions about the validity of accusations against him. Rather, his case, as much as others more briefly referenced, can ultimately inform theory.

The Bishop Long Case: Background

As we stated in Chapter 2, in part a review of the origins of the black Christian church in North America (and concomitantly the importance of the black pastor as an emerging leader and spokesperson), Christianity was in a very literal sense foisted on black slaves along with other burdens by white owners with the hope that this religion would subdue them, make them perhaps more other-worldly in their aspirations, and therefore more docile. The plan eventuated otherwise. Christianity gave slaves a crucible within which their own leadership and separate subculture could be cultivated and thrive. It was ultimately, judged in hindsight, the most dysfunctional thing the slave owners could have done. Blacks sorted through both the biblical story of liberation in the saga of the Hebrews and the message of equality and justice in Jesus' life to mold a special sustaining motif of hope and inspiration. It endured through situations of enslavement, then afterwards in the precarious time of Reconstruction and Jim Crow segregation, and finally into the more liberating era of the 1960s and 1970s civil rights movement.

The tension of being a racially minority church in a racially majority society never dissipated, however, and the black pastor was always a key gatekeeper between the minority church and larger society. He and she were the power brokers, the representatives, and luminary lightning rods for progressive change aiding the black community, no matter how secular the latter. The historical legacy of any caste system, based on race or whatever criteria, from India to Japan to the United States, is never easily forgotten or disengaged by laws or time itself.

Bishop Long shared in the legacy of the black pastor's dual personae, priestly and prophetic, in his shepherdship role.

The Bishop Long Case: How He Set Himself Up for Scandal

In 1987, Eddie Long took over pastoral responsibilities of the New Birth Missionary Baptist Church in Atlanta, Georgia, with its modest 300 members and tiny church building and thereupon instituted a campaign to revitalize it into a megachurch. A former college business major and failed sales representative for Ford Motors, Long turned to theology and before New Birth had been briefly the pastor of another small church in Jonesboro, Georgia. Soon Long adopted a hip-hop image, sought younger congregants, and like other black ministerial role models on cable television began New Birth's transformation (Walton 2009). Soon, also, Long began to attract well-known rap artists and other celebrities as well as the alliance of other black megachurch pastors such as Dallas' T. D. Jakes as his enterprise flourished. By the time of Long's 2010 scandals, he had literally created a pastoral fiefdom, complete with a 25,000-member congregation meeting in an amphitheater-like cathedral, as well as church-related businesses and charities that Long supervised, a private church-run academy, a cable television ministry reaching 170 countries, a private jet he used to travel around the country and the world, and a major sports/fitness facility called Samson's Health and Fitness Center. The issue of physical fitness played a major role in Long's ministry, or as he termed it, "muscular Christianity." Indeed, church-related sites on the internet still abound with photographs of Long in skin-tight shirts revealed broad, well-defined shoulders, Schwarzenegger-style pectoral slabs, and a tight stomach. The image of a washboard stomach and well-pumped shoulders became a surrogate image of Christianity in Long's church.

Meanwhile, Bishop Long lived ostentatiously in the manner of a Daddy Grace, one source of criticisms outside the ministry from both other black as well as white clerics. He frequently was driven in his Bentley accompanied by an inner cadre of lieutenants and bodyguards; wore Gucci sunglasses, gold necklaces, diamond bracelets, and Rolex watches; flew in that private jet; and was paid by the church board a $3 million per annum salary that included a $1.1 million five-bedroom house with other amenities. Long cultivated celebrity "guests" visiting the church, including nationally known rap artists and politicians. Indeed, Long's church became a magnet for politicians seeking endorsement and currying favor with evangelical middle-class blacks. Long could even boast that he personally knew several U.S. presidents, including President George W. Bush (a political fact, besides his flamboyant lifestyle, which irritated other black pastors and leaders, mostly Democrats—Butler 2011). While enjoying his own celebrity status, Long's New Birth church attracted young, single affluent blacks so much so that it came to be jokingly referred to as "Club New Birth."

Self-effacement was not the Bishop's style. He bragged once to the media:

> We're not just a church, we're an international corporation. We're not just a bumbling bunch of preachers, who can't talk and all we're doing is baptizing babies. I deal with the White House. I deal

with Tony Blair. I deal with presidents around the world. I pastor a multimillion-dollar congregation. (McKinley and Brown 2010)

Long was correct. But aside from his taste for hobnobbing with music celebrities, politicians, and professional athletes, his rich lifestyle, and even his hubris, there were three aspects to his ministry—or the "Long theology"—that caused his ministry strains due to outside criticism (and, as we will shortly mention, internal inconsistencies). These three aspects also laid the groundwork for his subsequent scandals.

First, Long imitated the "prosperity gospel" of many other black and white ministers (particularly on television), past and present. This theological slant maintains that Jesus' emphasis on the virtues of the poor and the accusations against the rich have been misunderstood, that God's providence for true, faithful Christians is wealth and health, that *that* is God's intention for us. It is not the financially meek who will inherit the earth. This apologetic neocapitalist strain of thought has a rich history in American Protestant Christianity. (For a brief but succinct summary, see Hadden and Shupe 1988, 131–32.) In his flashy display of jewelry and expensive automobile and other aspects of his lifestyle, Long was in keeping with the hoary belief of many black parishioners, discussed earlier, that the pastor is an exemplar of success and ought to live as well, or better, than his most successful congregants.

Second, coeval with Long's "prosperity gospel" message, he preached an extremely male-centered viewpoint (congruent with his fitness interests and personal muscular physique which he even displayed by wearing his muscle t-shirts in the pulpit) that Walton (2009, 215) calls the myth of the "Strong Black Man," a heroic and virile hero who must channel his "wild instincts" into family-supportive behavior, but which the price is a wife's submission to him. One of Long's several self-help books he claimed to have written is entitled *What a Man Wants, What a Woman Needs* (McKinley and Brown 2010). Long even had a celebrity "faith-and-fitness guru" Donna Richardson, once a member of the U.S. President's Council on Fitness, Sports and Nutrition (and wife of well-known black morning radio host Tom Joyner, the latter a strong Long-supporter even during his scandals) who helped literally introduce aerobics into New Birth church services. She often would address the congregation by means of video feeds and Skype. "The energy of the worship went to another high," Long is reported to have said (Butler 2011). This almost macho emphasis in Long's theology is interesting, given the later dimensions of his scandals.

Third, consistent with his emphasis on heterosexual virility, Long preached an unrelenting, even virulent antihomosexuality message couched in terms of "traditional" family values. In 2004, Long and Bernice King, daughter of Coretta and Martin Luther King, Jr., marched at the head of a 5,000-strong throng through downtown Atlanta, decrying gay marriage. The demonstration was entitled "Reigniting the Legacy" (Butler 2011). Long was denounced as a homophobe and of pandering to black American Protestants' traditional antipathy to the homosexual lifestyle.

In hindsight, observers can see in these three aspects of Long's practical theology and activities contradictory issues that could cause strains and further preconditions for scandal if contradictions in his behaviors came to light.

The Bishop Long Case: What Precipitated the Scandal

The precipitating factors emerged abruptly in 2010. Social conservative and outspoken proponent of Christian heterosexual virility, Long was accused of having committed sexual improprieties on four former male members of a youth organization that Long had chartered and even mentored. Specifically, the men claimed Long had repeatedly coerced, cajoled, and seduced them into homosexual acts, violating his clerical authority and fiduciary responsibility to them. During the years of sex he had purportedly offered them new cars, cash, exotic trips, jewelry, and free living accommodations in church-owned houses. The young men all had attended New Birth's Longfellows Youth Academy (Butler 2011; McKinley and Brown 2010).

According to the fourth of the young men to sue New Birth's pastor, 22-year-old Spencer LeGrande of New Birth's Charlotte, North Carolina satellite church, Pastor Long had told LeGrande in 2005 that he (Long) would be his "dad." Long had LeGrande accompany him to Kenya on a trip during which Long allegedly gave LeGrande a sleeping pill and then had the two engage in sexual activity. ("Engaging in a sexual relationship was a healthy component of his spiritual life," LeGrande recounts Long telling him.) The next year LeGrande accompanied Long to South Africa where the sexual relationship continued. Long discouraged LeGrande from displaying interest in girlfriends and urged him to move to Atlanta to be closer to New Birth's mother congregation. The relationship, LeGrande maintained in his lawsuit, continued until 2009 when LeGrande returned to Charlotte (Chivvis 2010).

The pattern was similar for all four men. Long purportedly was helping each in his "masculine journey" with mutual kissing, oral sex, and masturbation. All the while Long called them his "spiritual sons" and provided them with biblical passages and spiritual urgings that rationalized the behavior as definitely *not* homosexual (Chivvis 2010; Jabali-Nash 2010).

By 2010 the four plaintiffs were joined by two more lawsuits: one prosecuted by a bank alleging that Long and two associates had defaulted on a loan to buy a gym in Jonesboro, Georgia, and owed $2 million, the other by a former New Birth female employee who claimed a male member of Long's pastoral staff had showed her a picture of his penis and demoted her when she protested (Butler 2011). Thus, in one year these somewhat interwoven factors, colliding with many of the masculine, even "macho" public images within a heterosexual Christian context Long had sought to promote, precipitated a set of malfeasance scandals for the reverend.

The Bishop Long Case: The Reaction

The precipitating revelations alleged about Bishop Eddie Long in 2010 generated a bifurcated set of reactions (not including those of merely by-standing voyeurs and observers such as ourselves). The first reactions were from those who chose Long's low point in public relations to attack him personally and pastors—particularly prominent megachurch pastors—generally as hypocrites. The second set of reactions originated from those who rallied behind him, with various degrees of enthusiasm.

Editorials in Southern newspaper not-so-subtly laced their texts with cynicism, similar to what was seen, say, in the Dallas media during the Terry Hornbuckle scandal (see Chapter 3), denouncing Long as a false prophet, liar, and hypocrite. Internet blogs were downright caustic, even vicious.

But the second response, that of enthusiastic-to-qualified support, was telling. A few supporters outside New Birth quickly and without reservation arose to Long's defense. Manifesting a classic case of appeal to social/racial identity in refusing to cast the first stone, nationally prominent Dallas black evangelical pastor T. D. Jakes, who previously had rallied to support the now-disgraced Dallas, Texas sociopath Terry Hornbuckle, proclaimed that such scandals, even if true, "should be under the blood"—that is, should not be discussed, much less exposed by blacks about blacks (Butler 2011). Such a response acknowledges salient social identity defensiveness in not betraying or "selling out" other blacks, regardless of their actions, as we discussed in Chapter 5. (Interesting, perhaps out of consideration for their public commercial images, the hip-hop rapster celebrity friends of Long whom he liked to parade in front of his congregation uniformly kept silence during the scandals.)

Part also of the reluctance to support fully Pastor Long, with conflicted emotions, lies with the long recognized but subterranean existence of homosexuals active in the black ministry. The unspoken question that remained plagued some members: "Was Pastor Long, despite his bold heterosexual preaching and ostensibly macho attire, actually gay?" Thus, "The long-standing issue the scandal hooked into was homosexuality in the African American community" (Butler 2011). Homosexuality was traditionally been anathema to evangelical black Protestants. Yet, gays have always been active, from pasturing churches to playing other important roles while maintaining a double life within the church. Conclude two journalists (quoted in Mellov 2010):

> The prevalence of gay men in black church choirs and bands, for example, is accepted but not widely discussed. The unspoken agreement is that gay men get to act as Seraphim, so long as they are willing to shout in agreement as they are being flagellated from the pulpit. It's an indignity gay men subject themselves to each and every Sunday.
>
> The true tragedy in the black church and its persistent inability to deal openly and frankly with matters of sexuality before [a scandal] where what comes to the surface is that which is underneath.

Thus, the spectacle of a megachurch minister suddenly shown possibly to have feet of clay and unclean hands, an example of the fallen cleric always a delight to the secular press and skeptical observers of religion everywhere, split the responses to accusations against Long. Left in the middle, however, were parishioners who had to deal with the cognitive dissonance caused by their membership and their social identity with the New Birth congregation and its shepherd, on the one hand, and the rather stark information being brought forward, on the other. Typical was the reaction of one member:

> "My heart just kind of sank," said Cheryl Jenkins, 43, who owns an accounting firm. "If he says he didn't do it, we believe in him. If it turns out that he did and he apologizes, we have to accept it. No one is above reproach." (McKinley and Brown 2010)

Such attitudes, however, are not easily mobilized when the pastor's posture alternates between denial and belligerent defense and then eventual legalistic capitulation to accusations of malfeasance.

The Bishop Long Case: The Short-Run Denouement of a Scandal

The defenders and critics of Bishop Eddie Long mobilized very quickly after the accusations, but not always equally effectively. Nevertheless, the battle lines were soon drawn.

On Sunday, September 26, Long called for a press conference immediately before which he gave a sermon at New Birth entitled "The Reality of a Painful Situation." A rambling paean to self-pity, Long compared the scandals to the struggle between David and Goliath, with himself as David. During the sermon, filmed by CNN, MSNBC, and local television news outlets, Long proclaimed, "I am not a perfect man, but this thing I'm gon' fight." [Sic] However, his subsequent press conference essentially (and briefly) reiterated his claim of innocence and defiance and lasted barely two minutes. A few days before, on September 23, Long had arranged for an interview on the Tom Joyner Morning Show as well as a news conference but abruptly pulled out of both, sending an attorney to denounce unreservedly the "false charges" that purportedly smeared both Long and his 25,000 congregants at New Birth (Butler 2010). All the while Long persistently announced: "We continue to categorically deny each and every one of these ugly charges" (Chivvis 2010). Those who continued to support Long read revenge or some other reason into the negative publicity. Said one supportive New Birth member of media exposure and criticism to a reporter "It's propaganda, man . . . It's retribution for the 2004 march, the anti-gay-marriage march" (McKinley and Brown 2010).

Alternately, about seventy-four persons attended a rally in late October, led by Bishop "Prophet" H. Walker of True Light Pentecost Church in Spartanburg, South Carolina. Walker claimed that Long "had no right to continue as a leader of the Christian clergy" and urged Long's church members to demand his resignation. Walker said Long was a bad influence on Christianity generally (Jabali-Nash 2010). Meanwhile, news outlets such as Fox News tracked down and interviewed several of Long's alleged victims, who for their parts also took their cases through recorded interviews to the internet. Armchair psychologists in the media and within the internet asked, as the title of one article suggests, "Is Anti-Gay Pastor's Homophobia a

Smoke Screen?" They compared Long to the Reverend Ted Haggard, the outspoken antigay Colorado megachurch pastor (once president of the National Association of Evangelicals) who was caught in 2006 in his own homosexual–drug tryst (see for a synopsis, Shupe 2008, 25).

Long's supporters *and* critics earnestly desired confirmation of the accusations, if only to bring closure. For example, as media coverage escalated, two reporters wrote: "Some members of the church believe he is the victim of a smear campaign by people in favor of gay rights though they offer no proof" (McKinley and Brown 2010), while author Earl Olfari Hutchinson, on a Huffington Post.com blog wrote: "Did Long's long, open, and relentless crusade against homosexuals tag him and many other anti-gay prominent black church leaders as narrow, bigoted, and hypocritical in championing the very discrimination that King and the civil rights movement waged a titanic battle against?" (cited in Butler 2010).

These are only brief samples of the furor over Bishop Eddie Long within the black Christian community, the accusations of homosexual behavior, and sensationalist media coverage.

In civil cases like the Long scandals, civil or criminological responses would be represented by the prosecution of civil lawsuits and courtroom activities, if not the adjudication of criminal trials. In either case, social control responses (writ large as legal involvement) can alter the fate of the scandal.

In clergy scandal the social control mechanisms, if not action through the criminal justice system because felonies have been alleged, must occur in civil court arenas. And here is where the Reverend Eddie Long's scandals were headed. Long's legal denouement, however, offered no closure to the satisfaction of anyone.

Recall Bishop Long vowing in the midst of his denials of accusations that he had sexually abused the four plaintiffs that ". . . this thing I'm gon' fight." Well, that aggressive stance eventually fell victim to capitulation. Long, who provided cars and other amenities to the four core complainants and even put them on the New Birth payroll at one point, suddenly backed off his commitment to defend his name. A trial date for Long and the "New Birth Four" was originally set for July 11, 2011, but in November 2010 both sides abruptly agreed to mediation. This had a chilling effect on those who defended Long out of social identity and loyalty with the New Birth church and its larger minority community as well as personal loyalty to the pastor. It strongly resembled a mea culpa. Sums up blogger/reporter Anthena Butler (2011):

> That Long had decided he was not, after all, gon' fight, struck many as an admission of guilt. It was, blogged Morris O'Keefe on Huffington Post December 6, "an end run around the universally accepted moral and ethical responsibilities of any ecumenical leader."

Legal proceedings of the mediation were behind closed doors, not open to public scrutiny, and still not available at the time of this writing. The effects of the scandals on New Birth membership, church attendance, and giving are still not clear, though a few observers have foreseen the predictable outcomes of reductions in all three categories. One cynic foretold: "Most likely, his fate will be to resemble such other disgraced religious figures as Jim Bakker, Jimmy Swaggart, and Ted Haggard—faded televangelists relegated to the late-night time slots on down-market cable channels" (Butler 2011).

However, we would not wax so pessimistic. None of the above scandal-ridden (white majority) pastors held the advantage of membership fixed in the social–racial identity of a minority church. And that, we maintain, counts for something.

Thus, it would appear that there is a somewhat predictable progression of scandals in black minority churches. The same could be said for the numerous priest pedophile scandals which have racked the Roman Catholic Church in the United States since the mid-1980s. Prominent ordained priest-sociologist Andrew M. Greeley has claimed such Catholic congregations have played an ethnic or quasi-ethnic role in American Catholicism in precisely the same way black churches have done for African-Americans. Catholic churches provide for their adherents "the cultural means through which religionists gain from their churches their sense of self and what niche they occupy in a complex, diverse social order" (Shupe 2007, 12). Both Catholics and African-Americans hold "immigrant" faiths, whatever the dissimilarities as to how their members arrived in this country, and the issue of social identity is equivalent for members of both churches.

Thanks to such factors as the charisma of office (Wach 1967, 337) that attaches itself to clergy persons, pastors only with difficulty restrain themselves with identifying themselves with the majesty of their official (not personal) status. Otherwise, they may operate under the constant illusion of the law of clergy elitism (2007, 56–60), which can be summed up as follows:

> This can manifest itself, not just in the understandable elite reaction to scandal by protecting fellow elites and minimizing the damager to the organization's reputation, but also its attitudes regarding the church's ultimate mission and the clergy's role in this. These attitudes—again, unmonitored by modest self-reflection—can include *a sense of omniscience* ("We have the big, long range picture unlike those below/without access to our more complete understanding."); *conceit* ("We are not accountable for our actions and decisions to the same extent as are laity."), and *an exaggerated sense of confidence and righteousness* ("In the grand scheme of things it is for a greater good than our critics can imagine that we are justified in bypassing ordinary norms." . . . The result . . . is an inflated sense of importance, wisdom, and superior knowledge for religious elites. (Shupe 2008, 56)

Laity, for their parts, often seem to find that their side of the social exchange between pastor and lay persons for assurance versus obedience requires closing of the ranks with the accused pastor. Social identity grounded in racial identity makes this likely if not inevitable. A logic model of this evolution of a scandal often goes something like this:

- established respectability and public profile of the pastor
- high salience of identity with the church and pastor by parishioners
- accusations or revelations of malfeasance
- pastoral reaction of denial/congregational support of pastor
- further denial and counteraccusations
- criminal investigation/prosecution *or* legal entanglements, followed by capitulation to attorneys and discrediting of the pastor
- disillusion and confusion of the congregation.

These elements of pastoral scandal may give the impression of a chronological stepwise process. In reality, however, they can occur not necessarily the order presented but virtually simultaneously or often not in any linear progression.

Toward an Inductive Theory of Clergy Misconduct in Minority Churches

Our primary interest here lies in constructing inductive propositions leading toward a theory of pastoral misconduct in minority churches. Again, we are not concerned with individual motives or profiles of perpetrators, for that focus represents more than purview of psychologists, but rather *in the responses of specific audiences to pastoral scandals.* In the various audiences' responses should be found the predictability of such scandals in minority churches. These audiences would minimally include:

1. the perpetrators themselves (as well as their immediate subordinates);
2. the direct or primary victims of the perpetrator's actions;
3. the fellow congregants, or congregation, to which the victims belong; and
4. the larger community of nonmember observers.

Previously one of us developed a general theory of clergy malfeasance concerning reactions to such deviance in terms of different church polities, or political structures (Shupe 1995). In the case of minority churches, the lynchpin concept is *social identity*. Social identity, as reviewed in Chapter 2, should social psychologically provide a personal sense of self joined to the group through common membership and/or minority affinity. Social identity should include expressions of the value and sanctity of the group and its leadership as well as a sense of personal security for the members within the group's social reality. Social identity should therefore serve as primary filter for how the first three of the four audiences noted above "experience" or interpret the pastoral scandal.

The following set of propositions take into account data we have presented on black pastoral scandals in light of the black clergy's role in both the black church (i.e., in the lives of its congregants) and the black community but should, we maintain, apply equally to minority churches and their leaders within any majority culture. We offer the caveat that these propositions are preliminary but testable and invite further scrutiny. Our theoretical scheme is driven by two overarching considerations: *responses of the four audiences* involved in pastoral scandals and their *respective social identities* with religious congregations.

We offer six propositions, based on the data in this volume, for a preliminary understanding of the trajectory of pastoral scandal in a minority church. They do not all deal with each of the four audiences listed above. Before presenting each, however, we need to define several terms familiar at first glance to sociologists but used here in a somewhat unique sense.

By *normalization* and *neutralization* we do not mean that deviance is touted as noncontroversial, excused, or countered at the social psychological level by individual malfeasants. Rather, these are organizational strategies employed by elites (most often pastors) to create a view of "normality" sustained by most lay members about the formers' behaviors as fiduciaries. *Normalization* is to transform the interpretation of an otherwise deviant, abusive practice (beatings of parishioners or their children, excessive authoritarian control of members' lives, excessive or exorbitant financial remuneration for the pastor, even pastoral sex with congregants) into something acceptable and appropriate. *Neutralization* is to socially construct an acceptable (i.e., congregationally accepted) rationalization or narrative for behavior that is otherwise rather obviously untoward and pastorally inappropriate. To be clear, while the pastor plays a role in spreading interpretations of his/her deviant behavior to both victims and congregational members, it is the general viewpoint of the church members that determines if an interpretation of deviant pastoral behavior is normalized or neutralized.

Now we turn to our theorizing. What follows are six propositions accompanied by discussion grounded in the various examples presented throughout this volume.

These six propositions are:

I. Social identity with a minority church is intensified if the minority has been or is the recipient of servitude, racial, or ethnic discrimination, or oppression by the majority society.

This first proposition concurs with the general notion of structural conduciveness, or past-to-current cultural conditions as social facts of the minority–majority nexus. Thus, in the case of the specific minority religion considered here, the modern situation of the black church and its clergy cannot be understood without reference to the history of both: the imposition of (largely) Protestant Christianity on black slaves in the hopes of furthering their social control by white owners; the emergence of a semi-independent leadership corps within the black community focused on the solidarity and covenants of their churches in whatever if any denominations, both of which only grew in importance to the larger black community over time; the continued discrimination and repression of blacks in both the South and North after the Civil War and Reconstruction, with the latter's Jim Crow laws; and the solidarity built within the black sacred community as its religious leaders emerged as the focal spokespersons and ram-rods of the civil rights movement. It is a sociological truism that conflict creates solidarity within groups and creates an ideology of we-versus-them. The facts of the black media's treatment of black second-class American citizenship before and after World Wars I and II, discussed in Chapter 5, illustrate this point.

Propositions II through VI deal with the victims, congregational members, and the outside observers as audiences.

II. Accountability of leadership in a minority church declines as the pastor assumes a greater prophetic, rather than priestly, role.

A little observed but excellent work by Southern Baptist clergyman Edwin R. Bratcher entitled *The Walk-on-Water Syndrome* (1984) notes that it is the natural tendency of parishioners of most churches, sects, and cults to revere and even unrealistically elevate their pastor as an exemplar of virtue. Sinners and/or disciples want to believe that their religious leader does not partake of their own limitations and mortal foibles or lack of enlightenment. For their parts, religious institutions, which most often are interested in conformity rather than dissent, end up not discouraging this perception (which can lead to what Bratcher termed "pastorology"). Bratcher writes (25):

> When the laity place the clergy on a pedestal, the clergy give a helping hand, enjoy the intoxication of the higher elevation, and strive to stay on the pedestal. . . . The paradox is that although the Bible teaches that pride and the desire to be like God are the sources of man's tragic fall, it is precisely at this point that we as ministers most often succumb.

Likewise, Shupe (2007) refers to this as "the conceit of calling," similar to the law of clergy elitism described above.

Thus, the priestly role of a pastor finds itself concerned with the more mundane aspects of congregational life: budgets, committees, counseling, micromanaging sermons and coordinating such details as prayer and hymns during church services, monitoring the parking situation, and so forth. The prophetic role, as Weber emphasized, is unquestionably elevated above such concerns: it is to lead, inspire, exhort, even deliver what may be genuinely believed as divinely provided messages. The more a leader leans toward the prophetic rather than the priestly role, the more removed he or she is from the this-worldly trivia of managing an organization (in this case, a congregation, however small or large), the less likely either the pastor or members of the congregation are to question the former's actions. Increasingly prophetic, with a regular message that becomes something more like a grand mission, the less the members of the congregation are to question the actions and statements of the former. The prophetic role, in other words, elevates the pastor's perceived status to a greater extent than the priestly does, with consequences for facilitating the context of deviance.

III. Opportunity structures for pastoral misconduct increase with the decline of the pastor's public accountability.

The decline of the pastor's public accountability can be operationalized in such features as a lack of personal accessibility of the pastor to rank-and-file members of the congregation or outside observers (say, in the media). This lack of public accountability becomes even greater with the insulation lent by an intermediary cadre of caretaking lieutenants, secretaries, even bodyguards, and creates, practically speaking, a virtual invisibility for many of his/her daily affairs and decisions, whether these are on behalf of the church or for the benefit of himself/herself. Those of any inner cadre in a position to know and evaluate are in a sense compromised by their very proximity to the prophetic leader and/or dependence on the pastor for such mundane things as a job and/or unwillingness to "blow the whistle" because of faith in his/her "greater importance." Indeed, they may be legally accomplices before the fact or complicit themselves in abusive networks of activities.

Such persons are also able to rationalize pastoral foibles of which they learn in light of the larger mission. Many American Buddhists, for example, have known some of their enlightened leaders had feet of considerable clay, yet kept silent for the sake of respecting the role of the leader in the larger Asian tradition of vertical teacher (*roshi*)–disciple (*deshi*) relationships (Downing 2001; Shupe 2008, 94–95, 182).

IV. The extent to which a pastor's deviant actions have been previously normalized predicts the extent of victim and congregational acceptance of that deviance's neutralization.

This proposition is not circular, since normalizing means creating an atmosphere of an action's total acceptability versus neutralization, which is to explain or rationalize an action that is not successfully normalized. For example, a pastor who has encouraged his congregation to use severe corporal punishment (which would classify as physical abuse or assault in the noncongregational society) on children or even adults, or to make members so dependent on him or her that they must consult the latter for "permission" to read or view certain items or even change aspects of their personal lives, or to inure them to a pastoral fiscal lifestyle on the level of a multimillionaire, or to encourage them to view something like adultery as appropriate, has normalized deviance. When more egregious events are discovered, pastoral neutralization then becomes more believable, at least for a time. A minority pastor has the edge, initially at least, in claiming "those" critics in the outside world either do not understand or do not wish to understand or are hostile anyway to the "we" group. In the case of pastors such as Florida's Henry Lyons, "playing the race card" in accusing media investigators and other critics of his hypocritical and illegal behavior as racists, or Eddie Long claiming his critics were in part motivated by a progay agenda, represent examples of this neutralization strategy.

V. *The credibility of victims' claims to have been exploited by the pastor is exponentially related to the number of separate victims.*

Victim credibility is heightened by not just the seriousness of any single victim's claim or claims, no matter how outrageous, but by the sheer number of persons coming forward to make similar claims. However, it does not appear to be simply an additive function of the number of victims. Rather, each new victim enhances the credibility of the previous victim(s) and *each succeeding victim* as well. Since many acts of malfeasance do not have ready witnesses, the weight of additional victim claims tend to enhance *all* victim claims, past and future. And if the pastor has been a serial abuser, the eventual willingness of one victim to come forward and charge harm, emboldening then a second or perhaps more victims, then a snowball effect takes place. This snowballing of spreading revelations of victimization is what has happened in numerous instances of priestly pedophile scandal in the Roman Catholic Church (as occurred in 2002 in the Boston Archciocese, for example—*Boston Globe* 2002) and in Protestant cases cited (for example, Fortune 1989; Stockton 2000a).

VI. *The credibility of denials of misconduct by minority clergy is curvilinear.*

Relatively charismatic pastors, buttressed by the weight of their supporters' faith and wishes for scandal claims to be eventually disproved, and their savvy in neutralizing accusations (through discrediting victim claims, exuding confidence in their own rectitude, making emotional appeals to the minority faith tradition, and so forth), can stall the credibility or acceptance of victims' claims for a time but not indefinitely. If their charisma and appearance of rectitude were purely linear in the face of scandal, there would ultimately be no bona fide scandal but only rumors or discredited claims. However, at a point, as allegations of misconduct mount, pressing calls for investigation and substantiation one way or another also increase. Then inspection does occur and revelations of actually harm-doing, if discovered, takes over and "tips" the until-then linear progression of scandal and increasing denials over into a downward sloping mode. That is to say, pastoral denials begin to lose their credibility.

This inspection can be due to outside observers (outside to the pastor and his/her congregation, that is), such as fellow pastors in other churches, denominational officials (if there are any), suspicious or angry ex-congregational members, and noncongregational observers, particularly the media but also police and attorneys. Internal Revenue Service officials largely brought down the ministry of Florida's free-spending Rev. Henry Lyons; child welfare inspectors literally rounded up parents and children in the Atlanta church of the Reverend Arthur Allen, Jr. after reports of abuse; the Reverend Eddie Long suddenly abandoned his pious earlier denials of having had sex with several young men in congregation in 2011 and was willing to seek legal mediation, which was a blow to his ministry (though the final effects are still yet to be finally assessed). Thus, neutralization may work for an indefinite time within the congregation, especially when pastoral deviance has been previously normalized for members, but it carries less assurance with outside observers. Meanwhile, the exponential effect of multiple claims of abuse by a succession of multiple victims continues.

Of course, the "tipping point" that makes clergy denials and maintenance of credibility futile is not inevitable. Even in the face of exposes and negative investigative reports, if the evidence is only circumstantial and not about outrageously personal injuries to specific victims (and additional victims are not forthcoming), personal charisma and cultivated media skills can prevent or at least militate the curve toward discredibility. There are also the media and public needs for spokespersons of apparent stature who can outlast the accusations and reaffirm the image of the pastorate. And the investigative mainstream media have notoriously short-term memories.

Thus, a Jesse Jackson continues as a practiced surviving spokesperson for a generation of black interests and a "grand old man" of the remaining black civil rights movement, despite his documented coercive (high-pressure) "shakedown" techniques on white businesses while championing a black "Protestant Ethic" foreign to his own sources of income. Or he can weather public knowledge of his adulterous affair with a staffer producing a child when meanwhile extolling sexual responsibility among young African-Americans. Similarly a much less abrasive and more mellowed Al Sharpton, compared to his early years of Jackson-like shakedowns on businesses with his overt anti-Semitism and deadbeat behavior in his personal financial affairs, can assume the calmer role as a news talk show host on a cable station such as MSNBC.

Not every pastor is doomed to the curvilinear descent.

Final Remarks

Religion is about ultimate truth, ideally unconditioned by human desires or conceits, and yet there is no objective way to establish its validity in the sense known to scientific measures. There is only subjectively known validity. Yet, religion in the here-and-now world can display statistical reliability by one person believing and finding others who believe the same thing and then discovering still others who agree. Thus, as in statistics, spiritual reliability can be apprehended by sheer numbers of like-minded persons. However, the irony in religion, as with any other set of beliefs about the world or reality, is that reliability does not insure validity.

So it is with putting faith in a pastor, which can eventually be a frail thing.

These then are our conclusions and propositions deserving far more sophistication in methodologies and a far greater range of minority religions than we could possibly present in one book by two researchers. We have attempted an examination of one minority "church," albeit the largest minority religion in North America, and we have only offered a preliminary glance at it. We do not pretend that we have adequately or representatively surveyed all cases of malfeasance in the black pastorate. Indeed, mindful of the disparity in size among black churches and even the availability of learning of deviance in many smaller congregations, plus a dependence on at least one's recognition of acts of pastoral malfeasance as such to even discover the ones known about, we aware of our study's limitations.

What the entire field of clergy malfeasance needs, when its investigators turn to minority religions, is something of a catalogue approaching Lanternari's earlier *The Religions of the Oppressed* (1963) that examined cults, religious movements, and their charismatic leaders in such disparate regions as North America, Melanesia, Africa, and the Far East. However, unlike Lanternari, future researchers will need more than simply a descriptive eye to viewing such phenomena as exotic expressions of the downtrodden but rather to perceive them as specific examples of something more general and theoretical. For all churches, movements, and causes require leadership, and, to pose a maxim in this arena (with apologies to elitist theorist Robert Michels), who says religious leadership also says opportunity structures for abuse.

References

Agee, Mark. "Trial to Lift Silence in Hornbuckle Case." *Fort Worth Star-Telegram*, August 1, 2006.
Anderson, Lavina Fielding, and Janice Merrill Allred, eds., 1996–1998. *Case Reports of the Mormon Alliance*. Vols. 1–3. Salt Lake City, UT: The Mormon Alliance.
Ashmore, Harry S. 1994. *Civil Rights and Wrongs*. New York: Pantheon.
Associated Press. "Baptist Leader, a Tyson Ally, Is Indicted on Charge of Lying." *The New York Times*, July 25, 1992.
―――. "Al Sharpton vs. the Boondocks." *New York Daily News*, January 25, 2006.
―――. "Clergyman Accused of Identity Theft." *Mobile Register*. Mobile, AL, January 9, 2008.
Baclh, Robert W. 1995. "Charisma and Corruption in the Love Family": Toward a Theory of Corruption in Charismatic Cults." In *Sex, Lies, and Sanctity: Religion and Deviance in Contemporary North America*, eds. Mary Jo Neitz and Marion S. Goldman, 155–79. Greenwich, CT: JAI Press.
―――, 1998. "Money and Power in Utopia: An Economic History of the Love Family." In *Money and Power in the New Religions*, ed. James T. Richardson, 185–221. Lewiston, NY: Edwin Mellen Press.
Beito, David T., and Linda Royster Beito. 2009. *Black Maverick: T. R. M. Howard's Fight for Civil Rights and Economic Power*. Urbana, IL: University of Illinois Press.
Bennett, Chuck. "Subpoena Blitz Puts Heat on Al." *New York Post*, June 19, 2008.
Barrett, Leonard E. 1974. *Soul-Force: African Heritage in Afro-American Religion*. Garden City, NY: Anchor/Doubleday.
Berry, Jason. 1992. *Lead Us Not into Temptation: Catholic Priests and the Sexual Abuse of Children*. New York: Doubleday.
Berry, Jason, and Gerald Renner. 2004. *Vows of Silence: Abuse of Power in the Papacy of John Paul II*. New York: The Free Press.
Bertelson, Arthur B. 1967. "Keeper of a Monster." In *Race and the News Media*, ed. Paul L. fisher and Ralph L. Lowenstein, 61–62. New York: Praeger.
Black, Hugo. 1947. *Everson v. Board of Education*. 330 U.S. 1: 15–16.
Blake, John. "The Soul Patrol Demanding Conformity. It Scorns Blacks Who Don't Act 'Black Enough.'" *Atlanta Journal-Constitution*, March 15, 1992, 16.
Blood, Linda. "Shepherding/Discipleship Theology and Practice of Absolute Obedience." *Cultic Studies Journal* 2, no. 2 (1986): 23–45.

Blue, Ken. 1993. *Healing Spiritual Abuse*. Downers Grove, IL: InterVarsity.

Borg, Meerten B. Ter. 2009. "Religion and Power." In *The Oxford Handbook of the Sociology of Religion*, ed. Peter B. Clarke, 194–209. Oxford, UK: Oxford University Press.

Boston Globe. 2002. *Betrayal: The Crisis in the Roman Catholic Church*. Boston, MA: Little Brown.

Bratcher, Edwin B. 1984. *The Walk-On Water Syndrome*. Waco, TX: Word Books.

Brewer, Marlyn B. "The Many Faces of Social Identity: Implications for Political Psychology." *Political Psychology* 22, no. 1 (2001): 115–25.

Bromley, David G., and Anson D. Shupe, Jr., 1979. *"Moonies" in America: Cult, Church, and Crusade*. Beverly Hills, CA: Sage.

———. 1981. *Strange Gods: The Great American Cult Scare*. Boston, MA: Beacon Press.

Bromley, David G., and J. Gordon Melton, eds. 2002. *Cults, Religion and Violence*. Cambridge, UK: Cambridge University Press.

Bortz, Howard M. 1970. *The Black Jews of Harlem*. New York: Shocken Books.

Bosworth, Jr., Charles. "7 Federal Prosecutors Honored for Work in Metro East." *St. Louis Post-Dispatch*, St. Louis, MO, May 21, 1994.

Brodie, Fawn M. 1995. *No Man Knows My History: The Life of Joseph Smith the Mormon Prophet*, 2nd ed. New York: Alfred A. Knopf.

Brown, Tony N., James S. Jackson, Kendrick T. Brown, Robert M. Sellers, Shelley Keiper, and Wade J. Manuel. "There's No Race on the Playing Field." *Journal of Sport and Social Issues* 27, no. 2 (2003): 162–83.

Burgess, Stanley M., Gary B. McGee, and Patrick H. Alexander, eds. 1988. *Dictionary of Pentecostal and Charismatic Movements*. Grand Rapids, MI: Zondervan.

Burke, Peter J. "Identity Processes and Social Stress." *American Sociological Review* 56 (1991): 836–49.

Burkett, Elinor, and Frank Bruni. 1993. *A Gospel of Shame: Children, Sexual Abuse, and the Catholic Church*. New York: Viking Press.

Burkholder, John Richard, 1974. "The Law Knows No Heresy: Marginal Religious Movements and the Courts." In *Religious Movements in Contemporary America*, ed. Irving I. Zaretsky and Mark P. Leone, 27–50. Princeton, NJ: Princeton University Press.

Burnham, Kenneth E. 1979. *God Comes to America: Father Divine and the Peace Mission Movement*. Boston, MA: Lambeth Press.

Butler, Anthena. "The Fall of Eddie Long." *Religion in the News* 13, no. 2 (2011): 13–15.

Butler, Jon. 1984. "Enlarging the Bonds of Christ: Slavery, Evangelicalism, and the Christianization of the White South, 1690–1790." In *The Evangelical Tradition in America*, ed. Leonard I. Sweet, 87–112. Macon, GA: Mercer University Press.

Callahan, Daniel. 1965. *Honesty in the Church*. New York: Charles Scribner's Sons.

Callero, P. "Role-Identity Salience." *Social Psychology Quarterly* 48 (1985): 203–14.

Chadwey, Annette. "Church Center of Controversy." *University of Southern California Daily Trojan*. Los Angeles, CA, December 3, 1990.

References

Chambers, Stanley B. "Man Held in Death of Woman Found on I-540." *The News and Observer.* Raleigh, NC, February 3, 2008.

Chattanooga Times Free Press. "Clergyman Pleads Guilty to Fraud." Chattanooga, TN, January 6, 2008.

Chicago Daily Law Bulletin. "Activist Loses Appeal in Arson Case." Chicago, IL, December 16, 1992.

Chicago Tribune. "PUSH/Excel Gets Low Grades." December 28, 1983.

Chivvis, Dana. "Fourth Man Sues Pastor in Growing Sex Scandal." September 24, 2010. http://aolnews.com.

Coleman, James William. 2007. *The Criminal Elite: Understanding White-Collar Crime.* New York: Worth Publishers.

Cloward, Richard A., and Lloyd E. Ohlin. 1960. *Delinquency and Opportunity: A Theory of Juvenile Gangs.* New York: The Free Press.

CNN.com. "Rainbow-PUSH Board Says Payment to Stanford Was Severance Pay." January 20, 2001.

Colton, Elizabeth O. 1989. *The Jackson Phenomenon: The Man, the Power, the Message.* New York: Doubleday.

Coser, Lewis. 1956. *The Functions of Social Conflict.* New York: The Free Press.

Cowan, Douglas E., and David G. Bromley. 2008. *Cults and New Religions.* Malden, MA: Blackwell Publishing.

CPI (Center for Public Integrity). 2004. "The Buying of the President 2004." Washington, DC. http://www.buyingofthepresident.org/index.

Curry, Thomas T. 1986. *The First Freedom: Church and State in America to the Passage of the First Amendment.* New York: Oxford University Press.

Dallam, Marie W. 2007. *Daddy Grace.* New York: New York University Press.

Davidson., E. Jane. 2005. *Evaluation Methodology Basics.* Thousand Oaks, CA: Sage.

DeLamater, John D., and Daniel J. Myers. 2011. *Social Psychology.* 7th ed. Belmont, CA: Wadsworth.

Delgado, Richard. "Limits to Proselytizating." *Society* 17 (March/April 1980): 25–33.

Djilas, Milovan. 1957. *The New Class: An Analysis of the Communist System.* New York: Praeger.

Dodd, D. Aileen. "Face of Domestic Violence; Bynum Files for Divorce." *The Atlanta Journal-Constitution*, September 7, 2007.

_____. "Reunion for Religious Couple?" *The Atlanta Journal-Constitution*, February 17, 2008.

Doyle, Thomas P., A. W. Richard Sipe, and Patrick J. Wall. 2006. *Sex, Priests, and Secret Codes: The Catholic Church's 2000-year Paper Trail of Sexual Abuse.* Los Angeles, CA: Volt Press.

Downing, Michael. 2001. *Shoes Outside the Door: Desire, Devotion, and Excess at San Francisco Zen Center.* Washington, DC: Counterpoint.

Du Bois, E. B. 1899. *The Philadelphia Negro.* Philadelphia, PA: University of Pennsylvania Press.

Durnell, Nannetta. 1998. "National News Magazines' Portrayal of the Reverend Jesse Jackson as a Mythical Hero during the 1988 U.S. Presidential Campaign." In *Black Religious Leadership from the Slave Community to the Million Man March*, ed. Fulton O. Best, 189–209. Lewiston, NY: The Edwin Mellen Press.

EchoStar. 2002. "EchoStar Offers Statement Concerning Rev. Al Sharpton and National Action Network." Internet document filed by EchoStart Communications, St. Louis, MO. February 21, 2002.

Elbow, Steve. "Mayo Pastor Held in Child Porno Case." *The Capital Times.* Madison, WI. November 15, 2005.

Emmons, R. A., E. Diener, and R. J. Larsen. "Choice and Avoidance of Everyday Situations and Affect Congruence: Two Models of Reciprocal Interactionism." *Journal of Personality and Social Psychology* 51 (1986): 815–26.

Ewing, Russ. "Jesse Jackson: Penthouse Interview." *Penthouse Magazine,* April 10, 1973, 107ff.

Fauset, Arthur H. 1970. *Black Gods of the Metropolis.* New York: Octagon Books. (Orig. pub. 1944.)

Faw, Bob, and Nancy Skelton. 1986. *Thunder in America: The Improbable Presidential Campaign of Jesse Jackson.* Austin: Texas Monthly Press.

Finke, Roger. "Religious Regulation: Origins and Consequences." *Journal of Church and State* 23 (1990): 609–25.

Finke, Roger, and Rodney Stark. 1992. *The Churches of America 1776–1990.* New Brunswick, NJ: Rutgers University Press.

Finke, Roger, and Lawrence K. Iannaccone. "The Illusion of Shifting Demand: Supply-Side Explanations for Religious Change in America." *Annals of the American Academy of Political and Social Science* 527 (1993): 27–39.

Firestone, David. "Child Abuse at a Church Creates a Stir in Atlanta." *New York Times,* March 30, 2001.

Fisher, Paul L., and Ralph L. Lowenstein. 1967. "Introduction and Guidelines." In *Race and the News Media,* ed. Paul L. Fisher and Ralph L. Lowenstein, 3–10. New York: Praeger.

Fitts, Leroy. 1985. *A History of Black Baptists.* Nashville, TN: Broadman Press.

Floyd, Jacquielynn. "The Dallas Morning News Jacquielynn Floyd Column: Pastor Aimed Low; Victims Rise Above." *Dallas Morning News,* September 1, 2002.

Flynt, Wayne. 1981. "One in the Spirit, Many in the Flesh: Southern Evangelicals." In *Varieties of Southern Evangelicalism,* ed. David E. Harrell, Jr., 23–44. Macon, GA: Mercer University Press.

Fogel, Robert William, and Stanley L. Engerman. 1974. *Time on the Cross: The Economics of American Negro Slavery.* Boston, MA: Little, Brown.

Fortune, Marie M. 1989. *Is Nothing Sacred?* San Francisco, CA: Harper San Francisco.

Frady, Marshall. 1996. *Jesse: The Life and Pilgrimage of Jesse Jackson.* New York: Random House.

Frame, Randy. "An Idea Whose Time Has Gone?" *Christianity Today,* March 19, 1990, 40–42.

Frazier, E. Franklin. 1957. *Black Bourgeoisie.* New York: Collier Books.

———. 1974. *The Negro Church in America.* New York: Shocken Books.

Gabbidon, Shawn L., and Helen Taylor Greene. 2008. *Race and Crime.* 2nd ed. Walnut Creek, CA: Sage.

Gardell, Mattias. 1996. *In the Name of Elijah Muhammad: Louis Farrakhan and the Nation of Islam.* Durham, NC: Duke University Press.

Garrow, David J. 1981. *The FBI and Martin Luther King, Jr.* New York, NY: Penguin Books.

References

Gaustad, Edwin Scott. 1985. "The Emergence of Religious Freedom in the Early Republic." In *Religion and the State*, ed. James E. Wood, Jr., 25–42. Waco, TX: Baylor University Press.

Gayrand, Wilmore S. 1973. *Black Religion and Black Radicalism.* Garden City, NY: Anchor Press.

Gecas, V., and Peter J. Burke. 1995. "Self and Identity." In *Sociological Perspectives on Social Psychology*, ed. K. S. Cook, G. A. Etree, and J. S. House, 41–67. Needham Heights, MA: Allyn & Bacon.

Gibson, D. Parke. 1969. *The $30 Million Negro.* New York: Macmillan.

Goffman, Erving. 1963. *Stigma: Notes on the Management of Spoiled Identity.* New York: Simon & Schuster.

Greeley, Andrew M. 1972. *The Denominational Society.* Glenview, IL: Scott, Foreman.

———. "Clerical Culture and Pedophilia." Taped Address to the First Annual Conference of VOCAL (Victims of Clergy Abuse Linkup). Chicago, IL: October 16, 1992.

Green, Rebecca S. 2009. "Pastor Pleads in Cocaine Case." *Fort Wayne Journal Gazette.* Fort Wayne, IN, October 10, 2009.

Hacker, Andrew. 1992. *Two Nations.* New York: Ballantine Books.

Hadden, Jeffrey K., and Anson Shupe. 1988. *Televangelism: Power and Politics on God's Frontier.* New York: Henry Holt.

Hadden, Jeffrey K., and Charles E. Swann. 1981. *Prime Time Preachers.* Reading, MA: Addison-Wesley.

Hall, John R. 1989. *Gone from the Promised Land: Jonestown in American Cultural History.* New Brunswick, NJ: Transaction.

Hall, John R., Philip D. Schuyler, and Sylvaine Trinh, 2000. *Apocalypse Observed.* New York: Routledge.

Holloway, Joseph E., ed. 1990. *Africanisms in American Culture.* Bloomington, IN: Indiana University Press.

Hamilton, Charles V. 1972. *The Black Preacher in America.* New York: William Morrow.

Harris, Sara. 1971. *Father Divine.* Rev. ed. New York: Macmillan.

Hayden, Martin S. 1967. "Reporting the Racial Story in Detroit." In *Race and the News Media*, ed. Paul L. Fisher and Ralph L. Lowenstein, 23–36. New York: Praeger.

Helgeson, Baird, and Michelle Bearden. "In God's Hands or the Pastor's?" *Tampa Tribune.* Tampa, FL, July 1, 2007.

Henry, Mitchell. 1974. "Black Preaching." In *The Black Experience in Religion*, ed. C. Eric Lincoln, 70–75. Garden City, NY: Anchor Press.

Herrnstein, Richard, and Charles A. Murray. 1994. *The Bell Curve: Intelligence and Class Structure in American Life.* New York: Dorsey.

Herskovitz, Melville J. 1941. *The Myth of the Negro Past.* Boston, MA: Beacon Press.

Hoffman, Lisa. "Beatings, Sex Inflicted on Faithful, 6 Charge." *Miami Herald*, February 27, 1983.

Hogg, M. A., D. J. Terry, and K. M. White. "A Tale of Two Theories: A Critical Comparison of Identity Theory with Social Identity Theory." *Social Psychology Quarterly* 58 (1995): 255–69.

Hopkins, Nancy Myer. 1998. *The Congregational Response to Clergy Betrayals of Trust*. Collegeville, MN: Liturgical Press.

Hopkins, Nancy Myer, and Mark Lasser, eds. 1995. *Restoring the Soul of a Church*. Collegeville, MN: Liturgical Press.

Horowitz, Irving Louis. 2012. *Daydreams and Nightmares*. 2nd ed. New Brunswick, NJ: Transaction Publishers.

Horst, Elizabeth A. 1998. *Recovering the Lost Self: Shame-Healing for Victims of Clergy Sexual Abuse*. Collegeville, MN: Liturgical Press.

House, Ernest, 1988. *Jesse Jackson and the Politics of Charisma: The Rise and Fall of the PUSH/Excel Program*. Boulder, CO: Westview Press.

Hunt, Al. "The Phony Protest—and Leaders." *Wall Street Journal*, January 12, 2002.

Hunt, George P. 1967. "The Racial Crisis and the News Media: An Overview." In *Race and the News Media*, ed. Paul L. and Ralph L. Lowenstein, 10–20. New York: Praeger.

Illescas, Carlos. "Hearing Slated in Preacher's Fraud Case." *The Denver Post*, Denver, CO, October 17, 2007.

_____. "Contrite Pastor Spared Jail in Fraud Plea Deal." *The Denver Post*, Denver, CO, June 6, 2008.

Jabali-Nash, Naimah. "Bishop Eddie Long Scandal: Rally Calls for Embattled Pastor to Resign." March 1, 2010, http://cbsnews.com

Jackson, Sr., Jesse L., and Jesse L. Jackson, Jr. 1999. *It's About the Money!* New York: Random House.

Jacoby, Jeff. "The Sharpton Hypocrisy." *Boston Globe*, January 16, 2003.

James, William. 1989 [1892]. *Psychology: The Briefer Course*. Notre Dame, IN: University of Notre Dame Press.

Jenkins, Holman. "Business World: Jesse Jackson, Rainmaker." *Wall Street Journal*, January 7, 1998.

Jenkins, Philip. 2000. *Mystics and Messiahs*. New York: Oxford University Press.

Johnstone, Ronald J. 2004. *Religion in Society*. 7th ed. Upper Saddle River, NJ: Pearson/Prentice Hall.

Jones, William. 1974. "A Question for Black Theology: Is God a White Racist?" In *The Black Experience in Religion*, ed. C. Eric Lincoln, 139–53. Garden City, NY: Anchor Press.

Judd, Alan. "Church Faces Abuse Probes over Whipping of Children." *The Atlanta Journal*, March 20, 2001.

Kass, John. "Jackson's Role as King of Beers. Whassup?" *Chicago Tribune*, February 6, 2001.

Kennedy, Eugene. 2001. *The Unhealed Wound*. New York: St. Martin's Griffin.

Kennedy, Randall. 2008. *Sellout: The Politics of Race Betrayal*. New York: Pantheon Books.

Klein, Woody. 1967. "The New Revolution: A Postscript." In *Race and the News Media*, ed. Paul L. Fisher and Ralph L. Lowenstein, 141–58. New York: Praeger.

Konvitz, Milton R. 1985. "The Problem of a Constitutional Definition of Religion." In *Religion and the State*, ed. James E. Wood, Jr., 1247–65. Waco, TX: Baylor University Press.

References

Lanternari, Vittorio. 1963. *The Religions of the Oppressed.* Trans. Lisa Sergio. New York: New American Library.

Larkey, Linda Kathryn, and Michael Ll. Hecht. "A Comparative Study of African American and European American Ethnic Identity." *International Journal of Intercultural Relations* 19, no. 4 (1995): 483–504.

Lawrence, James A. 1974. "They Sought a City." In *The Black Experience in Religion,* ed. C. Eric Lincoln, 7–23. Garden city, NY: Anchor Books.

Lazenby, Brian, and Lauren Gregory. 2008. "Federal Witness Unveiled." *Chattanooga Times Free Press.* Chattanooga, TN, February 9, 2008.

Levinsohn, Florence Hamlish. 1997. *Looking for Farrakhan.* Chicago, IL: Ivan R. Dee.

Levy, Leonard W. 1985. "The Original Meaning of the Establishment Clause of the First Amendment." In *Religion and the State,* ed. James E. Wood, Jr., 43–83. Waco, TX: Baylor University Press.

Lewis, James R., ed. 2004. *The Oxford Handbook of New Religious Movements.* New York: Oxford University Press.

Lincoln, C. Eric. 1967. *Sounds of the Struggle: Persons and Perspectives in Civil Rights.* New York: William Morrow.

———. 1974a. *The Black Church Since Frazier.* (Includes *The Negro Church in America* by E. Franklin Frazier). New York: Shocken Books.

———. 1974b. "Black Preachers, Black Preaching, and Black Theology: The Genius of Black Spiritual Leadership." In *The Black Experience in Religion,* ed. C. Eric Lincoln, 65–69. Garden City, NY: Anchor Press.

———. 1994. *The Black Muslims in America.* 3rd ed. Grand Rapids, MI: William B. Eerdmans.

Lincoln, C. Eric, and Lawrence H. Mamiya. 1990. *The Black Church in the African-Experience.* Durham, NC: Duke University Press.

Lipset, Seymour Martin. 1967. *The First New Nation.* New York: Doubleday Anchor.

Lomax, Louis E. 1963. *When the Word Is Given . . . .* New York: New American Library.

Loury, Glenn C. 1995. *One by One from the Inside Out: Essays and Reviews on Race and Responsibility in America.* 1st ed. New York: Free Press.

Lowry, Rich. "Al Sharpton's Victory." December 3, 2003, http://Nationalreviewonline.

Lucadamo, Kathleen, John Marzulli, and Thomas Zambito. "Robbing the cradle. Feds Nab AGS Staffers in 1.5M Subsidy Scam." *Daily News,* New York, NY, July 17, 2008.

Magida, Arthur J. 1996. *Prophet of Rage.* New York: Basic Books.

Mahone, Derrick. "Preacher Charged in Theft of $70,000." *The Atlanta Journal-Constitution.* Atlanta, GA, December 9, 2008.

Marty, Martin E. 1970. *Righteous Empire: The Protestant Experience in America.* San Francisco, CA: Harper & Row.

Martz, Ron. "DFCS to Take 10 More Kids from Members of Atlanta Church in Wake of Abuse Probe." *The Atlanta Journal,* March 20, 2001.

Mathison, Richard R. 1960. *Faiths, Cults and Sects in America.* Indianapolis: Bobbs-Merrill.

Maxa, Rudy. "The Boys from Brazil." *Penthouse Magazine,* December, 1996, 38–43, 74, 164ff.

McCall, G. J., and J. L. Simmons, 1978. *Identities and Interaction*. New York: The Free Press.

McCarty, James F., and Daniel Briggs. "Free Minister Charged in Thefts." *Plain Dealer*, Cleveland, OH, January 8, 2008.

McClelland-Copeland, April. "Pastor Backed Baptist Leader." *Plain Dealer*, Cleveland, OH, September 11, 1997.

McCray, Walter Arthur. 1990. *The Black Presence in the Bible*. Chicago, IL: Black Light Fellowship.

Mcdonald, Meolody. "Trial of Minister Getting Started." *Fort Worth Star-Telegram*, July 28, 2006a.

———. "Hornbuckle Used Position to Start Affair, Woman Says." *Fort Worth Star-Telegram*, August 10, 2006b.

———. "3rd Woman Testifies against Hornbuckle." *Fort Worth Star-Telegram*, August 11, 2006c.

———. "Minister Demanded Loyalty, Aide Says." *Fort Worth Star-Telegram*, August 12, 2006d.

———. "Hornbuckle Tells Court He Can't Afford Lawyer." *Fort Worth Star-Telegram*, September 15, 2006e.

Mcdonald, Meolody, and Traci Shurley. "Pastor Called 'Evil' in Every Way." *Fort Worth Star-Telegram*, August 29, 2006.

McDonald, Thomas. "Suspect in Woman's Death is Bishop." *The News and Observer*. Raleigh, NC, February 8, 2008a.

———. "Woman Found Off I-540 May Have Been Raped." *The News and Observer*. Raleigh, NC, May 24, 2008b.

———. "Slaying Called a Case of Envy." *The News and Observer*. Raleigh, NC, December 1, 2008c.

McIntyre, Michael K. "Pastor's New Found Addictions Aiding Addicted Souls." *Plain Dealer*. Cleveland, OH, May 31, 1996.

McKay, Claude. "'There Goes God!': The Story of Father Divine and His Angels." *The Nation*, February 6, 1935, 151–53.

McKinley, James C., and Robbie Brown. "Sex Scandal Threatens a Georgia Pastor's Empire." *New York Times*, September 25, 2010.

McKinney, P. C. "Judge Blasts Jemison in Ruling on Church Vote." *The Advocate*. Baton Rouge, LA, July 8, 1995.

McLoughlin, William G. 1978. *Revivals, Awakenings and Reform*. Chicago, IL: University of Chicago Press.

McWirter, Cameron. "Church Ousts Ex-rep Sailor." *The Atlanta Journal-Constitution*. Atlanta, GA, April 1, 2008.

McWirter, Cameron, and John Perry. "Legislator Didn't Disclose Most Donations." *The Atlanta Journal-Constitution*. Atlanta, GA, March 21, 2008.

Mellov, Kiljiank. 2010. "Is Anti-Gay Pastor's Homophobia a Smokescreen?" http://www.edgeboston.com (accessed September 29, 2010).

Mercer, Monica. "Long's Defense Still Seeks Hearing." *Chattanooga Times Free Press*. Chattanooga, TN, August 14, 2008.

Metro. "Televangelist Pays Back Property Taxes." *The Augusta Chronicle*. October 20, 2007.

Metro, CT. "Minister Gets Probation for Child Porn." *The Capital Times*. Madison, WI, August 18, 2006.

References

Metro, State Journal Staff. "Pastor Is Arrested on Tentative Child Porn Charge." *Wisconsin State Journal.* Madison, WI, November 15, 2005.

Michels, Robert. 1959. *Political Parties.* New York: Dover Books. (Orig. pub. 1959.)

Miller, Steve, and Jerry Seper. "Jackson's Income Triggers Questions: Minister Says Money Not His Objective." *Washington Times*, February 26, 2001.

Miktchell, Henry. 1974. "Black Preaching." In *The Black Experience in Religion*, ed. C. Eric Lincoln, 70–75. Garden City, NY: Anchor Press.

Monroe, Jr., William B. 1967. "Television: The Chosen Instrument of the Revolution." In *Race and the News Media*, ed. Paul L. Fisher and Ralph L. Lowenstein, 83–97. New York: Praeger.

Moon, Henry Lee. 1967. "Beyond Objectivity: The "Fighting" Press." In *Race and the News Media*, ed. Paul L. Fisher and Ralph L. Lowenstein, 133–40. New York: Praeger.

Moore, Waveney Ann. "Bethel Renders Praise Choice for New Minister." *St. Petersburg Times.* St. Petersburg, FL, December 3, 2000.

———. "New Pastor Sees Rift at Scandalized Church." *St. Peterburg Times*, October 3, 2002.

———. "Rift between Church, Pastor Widens, Worsens." *St. Petersburg Times.* St. Petersburg, FL, February 12, 2003a.

———. "Church Terminates Rev. Lyons' Successor." *St. Petersburg Times.* St. Petersburg, FL, March 12, 2003b.

———. "New Pastor Eager to See Harmony at Bethel." *St. Petersburg Times.* St. Petersburg, FL, July 7, 2004.

Morgan, Richard E. 1968. *The Politics of Religious Conflict.* New York: Pegasus.

Mosca, Gaetano. 1939. *The Ruling Class.* Trans. Hannah D. Kohn, ed. and rev. Arthur Livingston. New York: McGraw-Hill.

Mosier, Jeff. "Minister's Sexual Assault Trial Set to Begin this Week." *Dallas Morning News*, July 30, 2006a.

———. "Lawyer: Pastor Is Being Framed." *Dallas Morning News*, August 4, 2006b.

———. "In Court, Arlington Pastor Cast as Playboy, Predator." *Dallas Morning News*, August 3, 2006c.

———. "Woman: Deion Sanders Discouraged Rape Report." *Dallas Morning News*, August 9, 2006d.

———. "Accuser Describes Pastor's Meth Use Before Alleged Rape." *Dallas Morning News*, August 11, 2006e.

———. "Pastor Guilty of Sex Assault." *Dallas Morning News*, August 23, 2006e.

———. "Hornbuckle Handed 15 Years." *Dallas Morning News*, August 29, 2006g.

———. "Hornbuckle's Church Fires Him, Says He Can't Return." *Dallas Morning News*, September 8, 2006h.

Murray, Charles A. 1984. *Losing Ground.* New York: Basic Books.

Myrdal, Gunnar. 1944. *An American Dilemma.* New York: Harper and Brothers.

Nelson, Jr., William E. 1998. "Black Church Politics and the Million Man March." In *Black Religious Leadership from the Slave Community to the Million Man March*, ed. Felton O. Best, 243–57. Lewiston, NY: The Edwin Mellen Press.

Newkirk, Pamela. 2000. *Within the Veil: Black Journalists, White Media.* New York: New York University Press.
Ofari, Earl [Hutchinson]. 1970. *The Myth of Black Capitalism.* New York: Monthly Review Press.
Olmstead, Rob. "Scandal against Cook Office." *Chicago Daily Herald.* Chicago, IL, January 26, 2008.
Ostling, Richard N. "U.S. Protestants Face Sex Abuse Scandals, too, but with Less Publicity." *Fort Wayne Journal Gazette,* April 6, 2000.
Ostling, Richard N., and Jan K. Ostling. 2002. *Mormon America: The Power and the Promise.* San Francisco, CA: Harper San Francisco.
Padover, Saul K., ed. and trans. 1974. *Karl Marx on Religion.* New York: McGraw-Hill.
Page, Clarence. "Rev. Jackson: Does Reach Exceed his Grasp?" *Chicago Tribune,* September 9, 1979.
Penthouse News Release. "Headline: Penthouse Retracts Article." June 24, 1998.
Peters, William. 1967. "The Visible and Invisible Images." In *Race and the News Media,* ed. Paul L. Fisher and Ralph L. Lowenstein, 81–82. New York: Praeger.
Peterson, Jesse Lee. 2003. *SCAM.* Nashville, TN: WIND Books.
Pfeffer, Leo. 1974. "The Legitimation of Marginal Religions in the United States." In *Religious Movements in Contemporary America,* ed. Irving I. Zaretsky and Mark P. Leone, 9–26. Princeton, NJ: Princeton University Press.
Philadelphia News. "Disgraced Pastor Gets Deal to Stay Out of Jail." Philadelphia, PA, February 17, 2007.
Phillips, J. B. 1972. *The New Testament in Modern English.* Rev. ed. Trans. J. B. Phillips. New York: Macmillan.
Poston, Ted. 1967. "The American Negro and Newspaper Myths." In *Race and the News Media,* ed. Paul L. Fisher and Ralph L. Lowenstein, 63–72. New York: Praeger.
Raboteau, Albert F. 1984. "The Black Experience in American Evangelicalism: The Meaning of Slavery." In *The Evangelical Tradition in America,* ed. Leonard I. Sweet, 168–95. Macon, GA: Mercer University Press.
Rankin, Bill. "Ex-legislator Gets 5 Years." *The Atlanta Journal-Constitution.* Atlanta, GA, September 17, 2008.
Reynolds, Barbara. 1975. *Jesse Jackson: The Man, the Movement, the Myth.* Chicago, IL: Nelson-Hall.
Richardson, James T. 1982. "A Comparison between Jonestown and Other Cults." In *Violence and Religious Commitment: Implications of Jim Jones' Peoples' Temple Movement,* ed. Ken Levi, 21–34. University Park, PA: The Pennsylvania State University Press.
———. 2004. "Regulating Religion: A Sociological and Historical Introduction." In *Regulating Religion: Case Studies from Around the Globe,* ed. James T. Richardson, 1–22. New York: Kluwer Academic/Plenum Publishers.
Roberts, Gene, and Hank Klibanoff. 2006. *The Race Beat.* New York: Alfred A. Knopf.
Robinson, John W. 1974. "A Song, a Shout, and a Prayer." In *The Black Experience in Religion,* ed. C. Eric Lincoln, 213–35. Garden City, NY: Doubleday/Anchor.
Rossetti, Stephen J. 1996. *A Tragic Grace: The Catholic Church and Child Sexual Abuse.* Collegeville, MN: The Liturgical Press.

References

Rutter, Peter. 1989. *Sex in the Forbidden Zone.* Los Angeles, CA: Jeremy P. Tarcher.

Sanders, Rob Ray. "A Bad Pastor Gets an Exemplary Trial." *Fort Worth Star-Telegram*, August 23, 2006.

Sanders, Vetta L. Thompson. "Variables Affecting Racial-Identity Salience among African Americans." *The Journal of Social Psychology* 139, no. 6 (1999): 748–61.

Schwab, Charlotte Rolnick. 2002. *Sex, Lies, and Rabbis: Breaking a Sacred Trust.* Bloomington, IN: 1st Books Library.

Sellers, Robert M., Mia A. Smith, J. Nicole Shelton, Stephanie A. J. Rowley, and Tabby M. Chavous. "Multidimensional Model of Racial Identity: A Reconceptualization of African American Racial Identity." *Personality and Social Psychology Review* 2, no. 1 (1998): 18–39.

Shah, Nirvi. "Dismissal Leads to New Church; Cathedral Church's Founder Is the Fourth Pastor in Five Years Removed." *Atlanta Journal and Constitution*, August 22, 1998.

Sharpton, Al, and Anthony Walton. 1996. *Go and Tell Pharaoh.* New York, NY: Doubleday.

Shover, Neal, and John Paul Wright, eds. 2001. *Crimes of Privilege.* New York: Oxford University Press.

Shelton, J. Nicole, and Robert M. Sellers. "Situational Stability and Variability in African American Racial Identity." *Journal of Black Psychology* 26, no. 1 (2000): 27–50.

Shupe, Anson. 1995. *In the Name of All that's Holy: A Theory of Clergy Malfeasance.* Westport, CT: Praeger.

———, ed. 1998. *Wolves within the Fold: Religious Leadership and Abuses of Power.* New Brunswick, NJ: Rutgers University Press.

———. 2007. *Spoils of the Kingdom: Clergy Misconduct and Religious Community.* Urbana and Chicago, IL: University of Illinois Press.

———. 2008. *Rogue Clerics: The Social Problem of Clergy Deviance.* New Brunswick, NJ: Transaction Publishers.

Shupe, Jr., Anson D., and David G. Bromley. 1980. *The New Vigilantes: Deprogrammers, Anti-Cultists, and the New Religions.* Beverly Hills, CA: Sage.

Shupe, Anson, and Susan E. Darnell. 2006. *Agents of Discord: Deprogramming, Pseudo-Science, and the American Anticult Movement.* New Brunswick, NJ: Transaction Publishers.

Shupe, Anson, and Christopher S. Bradley. 2010. *Self, Attitudes and Emotion Work: Western Social Psychology and Eastern Zen Buddhism Confront Each Other.* New Brunswick, NJ: Transaction Publishers.

Shupe, Anson, William A. Stacey, and Susan E. Darnell, ed. 2000. *Bad Pastors: Clergy Misconduct in Modern America.* New York: New York University Press.

Shurley, Traci. "I was Leaving . . . to Get a Gun and Kill Him!" *Fort Worth Star-Telegram*, August 4, 2006a.

———. "Pastor Told Aide Accusers Were Plotting against Him." *Fort Worth Star-Telegram*, August 11, 2006b.

———. "Trial Mailbox." *Fort Worth Star-Telegram*, August 12, 2006c.

Shurley, Traci, and Melody Mcdonald. "Jail Inmate Says Hornbuckle Traded Coffee for Drugs." *Fort Worth Star-Telegram*, August 23, 2006.

Singh, Robert. 1997. *The Farrakhan Phenomenon*. Washington, DC: Georgetown University Press.

Simon, David. 2006. *Elite Deviance*. 8th ed. Boston, MA: Pearson Education.

Sipe, A. W. Richard. 1990. *A Secret World: Sexuality and the Search for Celibacy*. New York: Brunner/Mazel.

_____. 1995. *Sex, Priests and Power: Anatomy of a Crisis*. New York: Brunner-Mazel.

_____. 1998. "Clergy Abuse in Ireland." In *Wolves within the Fold: Religious Leadership and Abuses of Power*, ed. Anson Shupe, 133–51. New Brunswick, NJ: Rutgers University Press.

_____. 2003. *Celibacy in Crisis: A Secret World Revisited*. New York: Brunner-Routledge. Sitten, Claude. 1967. "Racial Cover Up: Planning and Logistics." In *Race and the News Media*, ed. Paul L. Fisher and Ralph L. Lowenstein, 75–78. New York: Praeger, 75–78.

Smelser, Neil J. 1962. *Theory of Collective Behavior*. New York: Free Press.

Smith, Ben. 2008. "Sailor Enters Guilty Plea." *The Atlanta Journal-Constitution*. Atlanta, GA, June 18, 2008.

Smith, Ben, and George Chidi. "Representative Arrested, Charged with Felony Fraud." *The Atlanta Journal-Constitution*. Atlanta, GA, August 14, 2007.

Sorkin, Michael D. "Activist Is Charged with Theft, Fraud." *St. Louis Post Dispatch*. St. Louis, MO, August 5, 1989.

Sperry, Willard L. 1946. *Religion in America*. New York: The Macmillan.

Spong, Rt. Rev. John S. "A Statement from the Bishop of Newark." *Office of the Diocese of Newark*, NJ, November 9, 1996.

Stampp, Kenneth. 1956. *The Peculiar Institution*. New York: Knopf.

Stark, Rodney. 1987. "How New Religions Succeed: A Theoretical Model." In *The Future of New Religious Movements*, ed. David G. Bromley and Phillip E. Hammond, 11–29. Macon, GA: Mercer University Press.

Stark, Rodney, and William Sims Bainbridge. "Towards a Theory of Religion: Religious Commitment." *Journal for the Scientific Study of Religion* 19 (June 1980): 114–28.

_____. 1985. *The Future of Religion*. Berkeley, CA: University of California Press.

Steele, Shelby. 2006. *White Guilt*. New York: Harper Perennial.

Stets, J. E., and Peter J. Burke. "Identity Theory and Social Identity Theory." *Social Psychology Quarterly* 63 (2000): 224–37.

Stiles, Hilary. 1987. *Assault on Innocence*. Albuquerque, NM: B + K Publishers.

Stockton, Ronald R. 2000a. *Decent and Order: Conflict, Christianity and Polity in a Presbyterian Congregation*. Westport, CT: Praeger.

_____. 2000b. "The Politics of a Sexual Harassment Case." In *Bad Pastors: Clergy Misconduct in Modern America*, ed. Anson Shupe, William A. Stacey, and Susan E. Darnell, 131–54. New York: New York University Press.

Stone, Eddie. 1984. *Jesse Jackson*. Los Angeles, CA: Halloway House.

Streck, Laura West, Druann Maria Heckert, and D. Alex Heckert. "The Salience of Racial Identity among African American and White Students." *Race and Society: Official Journal of the Association of Black Sociologists* 6, no. 1 (2003): 57–73.

Stryker, Sheldon. 2002. *Symbolic Interactionism: A Social Structural Version*. Caldwell, NY: Blackburn Press.

References

———. "Integrating Emotion into Identity Theory." *Theory and Research on Human Emotions* 21 (2004): 1–23.
Stryker, Sheldon, and A. Statham. 1985. "Symbolic Interaction and Role Theory." In *Handbook of Social Psychology*, ed. Gardner Lindzey and Elliot Aronson, 3rd ed., vol. I, 311–78. New York: Random House.
Stryker, Sheldon, and Richard T. Serpe. "Identity Salience and Psychological Centrality: Equivalent, Overlapping or Complementary Concepts?" *Social Psychological Quarterly* 57, no. 1 (1994): 16–35.
Stryker, Sheldon, and Peter J. Burke "The Past, Present, and Future of an Identity Theory." *Social Psychology Quarterly* 63 (2000): 284–97.
Swanson, Guy. 1960. *The Birth of the Gods.* Ann Arbor, MI: University of Michigan Press.
———. 1967. *Religion and Regime: A Sociological Account of the Reformation.* Ann Arbor, MI: University of Michigan Press.
Sweet, William Warren. 1950. *The Story of Religion in America.* New York: Harper and Row.
Taylor, Clarence. 1998a. "How Should Black Leadership Respond to Farrakhan's Attempt to Legitimate His Leadership in Black America?" In *Black Religious Leadership from the Slave Community to the Million Man March*, ed. Felton O. Best, 211–22. Lewiston, NY: The Edwin Mellen Press.
———. 1998b. "The Political Dilemma for the Reverend Al Sharpton." In *Black Religious Leadership from the Slave Community to the Million Man March*, ed. Felton O. Best, 223–41. Lewiston, NY: The Edwin Mellen Press.
Thompson, Vetta L. Sanders, and Maysa Akbar. "The Understanding of Race and the Construction of African American Identity." *The Western Journal of Black Studies* 27, no. 2 (2003): 80–88.
Timmerman, Kenneth R. 2002. *Shakedown: Exposing the Real Jesse Jackson.* Washington, DC: Regnery Publishing.
Tocqueville, Alexis de. 1954. *Democracy in America.* Vols. I + II. New York: Vintage Books.
Vaillancourt, Jean-Guy. 1980. *Papal Power: A Study of Vatican Control over Lay Catholic Elites.* Berkeley, CA: University of California Press.
Vogell, Heather. "Ex-rep. Fell Flat in Real Estate." *The Atlanta Journal-Constitution.* Atlanta, GA, May 4, 2008.
Wach, Joachim. 1967. *Sociology of Religion.* Chicago, IL: University of Chicago Press.
Walker, Jr. Orris G. "Response by the Bishop of Long Island." *Open Letter to Clergy and Laity of the Diocese of Long Island et al.*, June 30, 1997.
Walton, Jonathan L. 2009. *Watch This! The Ethics and Aesthetics of Black Televangelism.* New York: New York University Press.
Washington, Jr., Joseph R. 1973. *Black Sects and Cults.* Garden City, NY: Doubleday/Anchor.
———. 1981. "The Peculiar Peril and Promise of Black Folk Religion." In *Varieties of Southern Evangelicalism*, ed. David E. Harrell, Jr., 59–69. Macon, GA: Mercer University Press.
Weber, Max, 1964a. *The Sociology of Religion.* Trans. Ephraim Fischoff. Boston, MA: Beacon.
———. 1964b. *The Theory of Social and Economic Organization.* Trans. A. M. Henderson and Talcott Parsons. Glencoe, IL: The Free Press.

Weisbrot, Robert. 1983. *Father Divine.* Boston, MA: Beacon Press.
Weiser, Benjamin. "Ex-Official Pleads Guilty in Fraud at Welfare Agency." *New York Times,* August 1, 2008.
Williams, Juan. 2006. *Enough: The Phony Leaders, Dead-End Movements, and Culture of Failure that Are Undermining Black America—And What We Can Do About It.* New York: Crown Publishers.
Williams, Patricia J. 1991. *The Alchemy of Race and Rights.* Cambridge, MA: Harvard University Press.
Winkelman, Cheryl. "Disgraced Pastor Gets Deal to Stay Out of Jail." *Contra Costa Times,* February 17, 2007.
Wood, Forrest G. 1990. *The Arrogance of Faith: Christianity and Race in America from the Colonial Era to the Twentieth Century.* New York: Alfred A. Knopf.
Work, John Wesley. 1974. "What the Negro's Music Means to Him." In *The Black Experience in Religion,* ed. C. Eric Lincoln, 45–61. Garden City, NY.
Wyatt, Kristen. "Kids in Foster Home after Abuse." *Associated Press,* March 28, 2001.
Young, Thomas. 1967. "Voice of Protest, Prophet of Change." In *Race and the News Media,* ed. Paul L. Fisher and Ralph L. Lowenstein, 125–32. New York: Praeger.
York, Anthony. "Jackson Retreats." January 19, 2001, http://Archives.salon.com

Index

Abernathy, Ralph, 89, 107, 117
Adell Broadcasting Corporation, 93–4
Affinity crimes defined, x–xi. *See Also Opportunity Structures*
Africanisms in American black Christianity, 35–38
African Methodist Episcopal Church (A.M.E.), 53–54, 63
Agape Christian Fellowship Church. *See Hornbuckle, Terry Lee*
AIG Life Insurance Company, 58
Ali, Muhammad, 117
Allen, Jr., Arthur, 63, 72–73, 77
Andries, William Lloyd, 68–70
Arafat, Yasir, 125
Ashmore, Harry S., 147–48
Audiences to pastoral abuse, 168–69
AUM Shinrikyo, 2
Authoritative abuse defined and illustrated, 70–78
Awakenings (religious) in U.S. history, 10, 34–35

Bakker, Jim, 7, 11, 80, 167
Bakker, Tammy Faye, 7, 11
Baker, George. *See Father Divine*
Barnett, Donald, 77–78
Berg, David "Moses," 12
Bernardin, Cardinal Joseph, 67
Black cults and sects, 14–28
Black, Hugo, 5
Black Jews, 16–17
Black Jews of Harlem, 17
Black media, 134–47
Black megachurches, 140
Black pastor drug involvement, ix, 54–55
Black pastoral charisma, 38–39, 49–52

Black, pastoral status, 28–30, 32–39
    emergence in the black church and black community, 38–39, 49–52
    with oligarchic parallels, 151
    with whites, 39
Black United Fund, 94
Blair, Tony, 161
Bond, Julian, 107
Bradley, Christopher S., 47
Branch Davidians, 2, 7
Bratcher, Edwin R., *See Walk-on-Water Syndrome*
Brawley, Tawana, 91, 96
Brotherhood Organization of A New Destiny. *See Patterson, Jesse Lee*
Burnham, Kenneth, 18–19
Bush, U.S. President George W., 160
Bynum, Juanita, 65–67

Castro, Fidel, 125
Campbell, Earl, 90
Cambellites, 13
Carter, Quincey, 83
Cathedral Church (Decatur, GA), 59
Center for Public Integrity, The, 95, 97
Charisma, 131–34, 137–42, 146–47
Cherry, Prophet F. S., 16–17
Chicago Defender, 136
Children of god, 12
Christian Science, 13
Christian Hope Church, 57
Christian Right, 7
Church of God. *See Black Jews*
Church of God and Saints of Christ, 16
Church of Jesus Christ of Latter-day Saints, 13
Church of Scientology, 12

191

Clergy malfeasance, study of, ix–xi, 155–57
Cleveland Foundation, 56
Coleman, Milton, 145–46
Colton, Elizabeth O., 150–52
Commandment Keepers of the Living God, The. *See Black Jews of Harlem*
Communication Act of 1934, 10
Community Chapel (Seattle, WA), 77–78
Cornish, Samuel, 134–35, 137
Craig, U.S. Senator Larry, 79
Crowdy, Prophet William S., 16–17
Crown heights (NY), 91, 96
Cult-sect hysteria following World War Two, 12–14
Cuomo, Governor Mario, 90

Dallam, Marie W., 15–16, 18, 20, 22, 24, 26
Dallas Cowboys, 83, 85–86
Dearth of previous research on black pastoral malfeasance, ix–xi, 2–3
Delany, Martin R., 143
Delgado, Richard, 6
Discipling, 72–73
Divine Faith Baptist Church, ix
Divine, Father, 2, 17–28, 95, 123, 137, 143, 152–53
Divine Light Mission, 12
Douglass, Frederick, 137
Durnell, Nanetta, 145
Duvall, Mike, 79
DuBois, W. E. B., 143

EchoStar Communications Corporation, 91
Economic abuse defined and illustrated, 52–60
Edward Waters College, 53
Edwards, John, 79
Ekert, Robert, 63
Electronic church, 10–12
est, 12
Establishment Clause (U.S. Bill of Rights), 3–6
Evangelical Lutheran Church in America, 63–64

Family, The, 12
Farrakhan, Louis, 98, 125, 140–41

Fauset, Arthur H., 15, 18, 24–25, 152
First Amendment (U.S. Bill of Rights), 3–8
Foley, (U.S. Representative) Mark, 79
Freedom's Journal, 135
Freud, Sigmund, 62
Fox, Red, 117

Garca, Manueal de. *See Grace, Bishop "Daddy"*
Garrison, William Lloyd, 135
Garvey, Marcus, 137
Gates, Henry Louis, 101
Gaustad, Edwin Scott, 4
Gaye, Marvin, 90
Gibson, D. Parke, 110
Global Destiny Ministries, 65–67
Gospel of prosperity, 121–22
Gospel Train Unity Inspirational Hour, ix
Grace, Bishop "Daddy," 2, 15–28, 95, 152, 160
Greater New Light Missionary Baptist Church, 54–55
Greeley, Andrew M., 167

Hacker, Andrew, 149–50
Hadden, Jeffrey K., 2, 10
Haggard, Ted, 80, 167
Hamilton, Charles V., 49, 52–54
Hare Krishnas, 12
Harris, Sara, 23–24
Hart, (U.S. Senator) Gary, 79
Heaven's Gate UFO cult, 2
Henry, Patrick, 5
Herskovitz, Melville J., 36
Hornbuckle, Terry Lee, 83–88, 107, 129, 141, 163
House of Prayer for All People. *See Grace, Bishop "Daddy"*
Howard, T. R. M., 111
Hunt, Al, 100–1, 152
Hunt, George P., 138
Hutchenson, Earl Ofari, 151–52

Identity salience: hierarchies of, 42–43
  related to charisma, 131–34
  with regard to black parishioners, 42–47

Index

Idiosyncrasy credits awarded to black pastors by congregants, 81
Inductive theory of clergy misconduct in minority religions, 168–75
Iron law of clergy elitism, 51, 134
Irvin, Michael, 83

Jackson, Jesse: 88–89, 99, 101–29, 132–34, 141, 144–5, 150–52, 174
   anti-Semitism and sexual hypocrisy, 125–27
   dependence on government grants, 123–5
   early years, 102–07
   Operation PUSH, PUSH-EXCEL, 119–25
   presidential campaigns, 125–27
   relationship to Martin Luther King, Jr. and Southern Christian Leadership Conference, 107–110, 117–18
   shake-down tactics against corporations, 110–25
   violent gang relationships, 116, 120
Jackson, Jr., (U.S. Representative) Jesse L., 151
Jackson, Mahalia, 89
Jackson, Michael (and family), 90, 117
Jakes. T. D., 86, 160, 163
Jamison, T. J., 76
Jefferson, Thomas, 5
Jehovah's Witnesses, 13
Jenkins, Philip E., 13
Jerry Lewis Labor Day Telethon fund-raising model, 11
Jews for Jesus, 12
Jones, Tim, 71–72
Jordan, Vernon, 143
Joyner, Tom, 165

Kennedy, Randall, 142–43
King, Bernice, 162
King, Coretta, 162
King, Don, 90, 95
King, Jr., Martin Luther, 98, 106, 110–12, 115, 144, 137, 162
Koen, Charles, 57

Lane Metropolitan Christian Methodist Episcopal church, 56
Lanternari, Vittorio, 32, 175
Lea, Larry, 11

LeGrande, Spencer, 162
Lincoln, Joseph C., and Lawrence Mamiya, 49–52
Lipset, Seymour Martin, 8–9
Living in Favor with God Network Ministries, 64–65
Logic model approach to theorizing about minority clergy abuse, 157–58
Long, Eddie, 158–68, 174
Longfellows Youth Academy, 162
Luminaries as pastoral brokers, 82–83
   as spokespersons, 80
Lyons, Henry, 58–59, 61–62, 74–76, 140–142

Madison, James, 5
Malcolm X, 140
Marketplace model of North American religion, 9–14
Marshall, U.S. Justice Thurgood, 137
Matthew, Wentworth A., 17
Marty, Martin E., 37
Marvin, Joaquin, 75–77
Maxa, Rudy, 69
Michaels, Robert, 176
Millerites, 12
Minority religion defined, 7
Moon, Henry Lee, 134, 137
Moon, Sun Myung, 12, 48, 122
Moral Majority, 7
Mount Gilead Baptist Church and New Birth Temple of Praise, 58
Murray, Charles A., 124

Nation of Islam, 14, 141
National Action Network, 91–92, 94–96
National Association for the Advancement of Colored People, 94, 134
National Association of Evangelicals, 80
National Baptist Church USA, 1–2, 58, 75–76, 140–1
New Birth Baptist Church, 158–67
Newkirk, Pamela, 146
Nicholas, Bishop D. Ward, 53–54
Normalization vs. neutralization of pastoral scandals defined, 170, 172–73

Opportunity structures, x, 6, 51, 172–73

193

Operation Breadbasket, 89, 108, 110, 112–17
Order of the Solar Temple, 12
Osarenkhoe, Nigel, 60
Overstreet, L. Eugene, 59

Parishioner loyalty in relation to social identity and identity salience, 44–46
Packer, Angela, 152
Pagones, Steve, 96
Pataki, (NY governor) George, 90
Patterson, Jesse Lee, 90, 142, 144
Pastoral fraud. *See Economic Exploitation*
Penthouse magazine "expose" of alleged black priest abuse, 68–70
Peace Movement. *See Divine, Father*
Peoples Temple, 2, 12, 71–72
Pfeffer, Leo, 6, 8
Phillips, Acen, 58
Pittsburgh Courier, The, 136
Physical abuse of children, 63
Physical abuse of adult congregants, 63, 72–73
Poston, Ted, 138
Powell, (U.S. Representative) Adam Clayton, 90
Powell, (U.S. General) Colin, 143
Prophetic vs. priestly leadership, 49–52, 171–72
PUSH, PUSH-EXCEL. *See Jackson, Jesse*
PTL Network, 11
Public compliance of Jackson-PUSH donors, 115–17

Qaddafi, Colonel Muammar, 125
Quakers, 13

Racial affinity leadership deviance, 2–3, 29–30, 45–47, 51–52
Radic, Randall, 55–56
Reeves, Robert, 64–65
Reverse identity salience, 147–52
Reynolds, Barbara, 152
Rice, Candoleezza, 143
Richardson, Donna, 161
Richardson, James T., 72
Richardson, W. Franklyn, 76
Roberts, Oral, 11
Robertson, Pat, 11
Robinson, Donald Ray, 56

Robinson, Jr., Noah, 120–21
Rosenblaum, Yankel, 91
Roundtree, Richard, 117
Royal Order of Ethiopian Jews. *See Black Jews of Harlem*

Sanctuary Church of the Living God, 59
Sailor, Jr., Ron, 54–55
Saint Gabriel's Episcopal Church, 68
San Francisco Zen Center scandal, 155
Sanders, Deion, 83, 86
Sanford, South Carolina Governor Mark, 80
Schara, Jerald, 63
Selective Patronage System, 111–12
"Sellouts" of the black community, 107, 127–28, 140–41
Sexual abuse defined and illustrated, 60–70, 77
Sharpton, Al: 88–101, 127–29, 107, 128–28, 140–41
  anti-Semitic remarks, 91–92
  as celebrity agent-promoter, 89–90
  as imitator of Jesse Jackson, 88–89
  demagoguery, 90–92, 101
  financial irresponsibility, 92–99
  run for U.S. presidency, 98–100
  run for U.S. Senate, 98–99
  shake-down tactics, 89, 93–95
Shepherding. *See Discipling*
Smelser, Neil, 157
Smith, Emmett, 86
Social identity defined, 39–44, 170–71
Southern Christian Leadership conference, 89, 107–10, 117–18, 136
Sowell, Thomas, 143
Spiritualists, 13
Stampp, Kenneth, 33
Statute of Virginia for Religious Freedom, 5
Steele, Shelby, 148–50
Stryker, Sheldon, 41–42
Sullivan boycott strategy, 110–12, 127
Summers, Larry, 100–01
Swaggart, Jimmy, 167
Spong, John S., 70
Stone, Roger, 99

Televangelism, 10–12
Theology and social structure, 31–32
Theosophists, 13

Index

Thomas, U.S. Justice Clarence, 143
Thomas, Wilbert, 1, 72, 77
Tilton, Robert, 11
Tocqueville, Alexis de, 8
Transcendental meditation, 12
Transcendentalists, 13
Tyson, Mike, 76

Unification Church, 12
Urban League, 94

Validity vs. reliability in religion, 175
Vesey, Denmark, 137
Virginia Assembly. *See Statute of Virginia for Religious Freedom*
Volunteerism, American tradition of, 8

Walk-on-Water Syndrome, 171
Walker, Jr., Orris G., 68
Washington, booker T., 137, 142
Weber, Max, 31–32, 50, 81, 131–32
Weeks, III, Thomas, 65–67
Weisbrot, Robert, 25, 27
West, Cornell, 100–1
White, III, Curtis, ix
White guilt, 147–52
Williams, Juan, 93–94, 141
Will, George P., 152

Young, Andrew, 107
Young, Thomas W., 139